TRADING LIFE

TRADING LIFE

Organ Trafficking, Illicit Networks, and Exploitation

SEÁN COLUMB

STANFORD UNIVERSITY PRESS
Stanford, California

Stanford University Press
Stanford, California

© 2020 by the Board of Trustees of the Leland Stanford Junior University. All rights reserved.

No part of this book may be reproduced or transmitted in any form or by any means, electronic or mechanical, including photocopying and recording, or in any information storage or retrieval system without the prior written permission of Stanford University Press.

Printed in the United States of America on acid-free, archival-quality paper

Library of Congress Cataloging-in-Publication Data is available upon request.

ISBN 978-1-5036-0807-8 (cloth)
ISBN 978-1-5036-1255-6 (paper)
ISBN 978-1-5036-1256-3 (electronic)

Cover design: Angela Moody
Cover Image: GVS | Adobe Stock
Typeset by Motto Publishing Services in 10/14 Minion Pro

To the lives we share

CONTENTS

	Preface	ix
	Acknowledgments	xix
1	Excavating the Organ Trade	1
2	The Illegal Trade in Organs	17
3	Organ Trading Networks	37
4	Disqualified Bodies	62
5	Exodus	86
6	Organ(ized) Crime	110
7	Regulating the Organ Trade	133
	Notes	157
	References	163
	Index	185

PREFACE

June 16, 2018, Cairo
Present: Seán Columb (S), Solomon (X), Petros (P), and Dawitt (Q)

S: This is it [points to recording device]. It's just recording our conversation. I'll delete the file afterwards. After we talk, I'll write up your story and then I'll delete the audio file. No name [will be recorded]; look no name on the recording, nothing. I will leave it [recorder] here; it's easier. I can speak more naturally, and we can leave this to record without having to write everything down.
P: Yes, you can record.
S: Thanks. So, as you know, I spoke to Dawitt [his friend who sold a kidney] about the organ trade. I was hoping to hear about your experience, so I can understand better what's involved. Also, I think it's important that people outside of Egypt have an understanding, not just about the organ trade but the circumstances behind it. I'm trying to talk to as many people as possible to represent this accurately. If I'm not making sense, let me know. And, please don't feel like you need to answer all my questions. We can stop anytime, OK?
P: OK.
S: Can you tell me about Eritrea?
P: I was living in Tessenei in Eritrea. It's a small village near the Sudanese border. People are facing injustice from the regime, everyone. When I turned 14 years old, they took me to Sawa. This was not correct. I was too young and still at school. But they came in cars and took us away from our families.
S: Sawa . . . what is that?
P: It's a military camp near the Sudanese border. They beat people and

force you into military service. They separate you from your parents and you never see them again. Your life is no longer yours. My brother was with me at Sawa. They tried to brainwash us. They don't want people to have political ideas, thoughts.

S: How did they try to brainwash you?

P: The government take girls as servants for the police to make them food, serve drinks, and to have sex with them. They do this to everybody. They take the girls and put them to work as sex servants on [military] camps, and they take the boys for the camps like Sawa to serve and kill. We have no media or journalists in Eritrea. This is forbidden. I was arrested along with my father and brother for using social media.

S: OK, let's back up a bit. You were in Sawa and then after this you were arrested for using social media?

P: We have groups, and these groups were in opposition to the regime. The regime assumed that me and my father belonged to this opposition group, my brother also. They took us out of training and put us in prison for a few months and then released us back into Sawa to continue our service.

S: How long were you in Sawa?

P: It never ends. We stay at Sawa and then we serve in the military until we die. This is why we had to escape and leave this country. Our uncles helped us [Petros and his brother] to get from Eritrea to Sudan. We went at night by car until we arrived at a town called Kassala [in Sudan]. It's the closest town to the Eritrean border. We were a lot of people, about 25 people, all in a car. We had to go without our parents because the [Eritrean] government was watching them. When we got to Kassala, the police took us to a place, like a camp. I think it was called El Sawra [displaced persons camp] but I'm not sure. We stayed in Kassala for about a year. We had relatives there who helped us to get Sudanese nationality. We changed our names to something Sudanese, so we could get passports. After they changed our names, they took us to Khartoum. There were elder people with us, who were taking charge of the situation. They are the ones who made us the [Sudanese] nationality and passport.

S: Was your plan to come to Egypt?

P: No, it wasn't. My plan was to stay in Sudan, in safe places.

S: Why did you come to Egypt?

P: People who were with us on the journey from Eritrea to Sudan were now in Egypt. There were five of them who had been traveling with us. They were in contact with the guys who made us the passports and they recommended that we go there [Cairo]. They told us, "Come to Egypt. Here is good and you can come register at the UN and it is good."

S: So, you came to register with the UN?

P: I worked in Sudan to collect some money, and this [money] I used to come to Egypt.

S: How did you get here [Egypt]? Did you take a bus?

P: I came by bus, and after that we crossed through Shalatin [a disputed territory between Sudan and Egypt] by smuggling.

S: I want to make sure I have this right: You took a bus from Khartoum to the Egyptian border at Shalatin, and then you paid a smuggler to take you as far as Cairo? What was that like?

P: From Sudan to Egypt wasn't that bad. The car was secure because we gave a lot of money, and the *samsar* [smuggler] will not receive his money until after when we arrived. We know we cannot trust this guy, so we arranged it that way with our friends in Cairo. They would only pay him if we arrived safely.

S: It is expensive?

P: It was expensive. We gave him about 500 per person.

S: U.S. dollars?

P: Yes.

S: And what happened when you came to Egypt?

P: When we arrived here, we registered ourselves with the UN at 6th of October [a district in Cairo]. We were staying at an apartment with some of our relatives and those who first came to Egypt.

S: Sorry, I forgot to ask, who did you travel with? Were you traveling with your brother?

P: I came to Egypt with my brother and also some guys who escaped. They came with us until Egypt, and some other people.

S: When you got to Cairo, did someone approach you about your kidney?

P: That wasn't directly after we came to Egypt. The approach about the kidney happened after a year in Cairo. At the time we were living in an apartment in 6th of October. We were kicked out from the apartment because we didn't have money, and we don't have work. We stayed with some Sudanese. When they noticed we were broke, they suggested that we sell a kidney. Someone who came with us, by smuggling from Sudan, first he sold his kidney secretly without the knowledge of any one of us. He told us, "It's an easy way you can have money. It's not dangerous to sell your kidney. You will get about $5,000 [USD] for a kidney." Five people who came before us, all of them have sold their kidney. And we all were about thirteen people who came after them. There were about seven Sudanese people with us, and we were about eight Eritrean people.

S: Who approached you?

P: The one who approached me is that one who sold [his kidney] first. He told us, "When you sell, you will get big money. You can send some money to your family, and you and your family can live in a good life when you have the money."

S: What year was this?

P: This was about two years ago [2016].

S: How old were you then?

P: I was 17 years old. I was just 17 years old. That person who approached us [Petros, his brother, and six others from Eritrea], he told us they [brokers] would give about $5,000 for a kidney at that time. We needed money because when we [Petros and his brother] called our family, we realized that they really needed help to survive.

S: You wanted to send money to your parents?

P: Yes, I want to send money to my family. I have sisters. I wanted to send them money because they were in need.

[Petros was visibly upset. He needed time to compose himself.]

S: Do you want a coffee?

P: No. Do you want a cigarette? [laughing]

S: No thanks. I'm going to turn this off [the recorder]. Let's talk about something else for a while. I know this is difficult.

[Recording starts again.]

S: You mentioned that you were approached by someone about selling your kidney.

P: This guy, he was from Sudan and he told us about someone [a broker] who arrange everything for us. In the beginning I told him I want to see the place [hospital] and this person [broker] or I won't agree. He told me, "You can't see the place unless you agree. When you say yes, Hasim [the broker] will come to see you." The next time I spoke to him, he was with an Egyptian guy [Hasim]. He came and explained to us about the kidney procedure. At that time, we were badly in need of money, and the broker offered the money that we needed. After we talked, we agreed.

S: What did he say to you?

P: The Egyptian told us it's a very easy operation. It won't take more than 3 hours and after the operation I will give you the money directly.

S: What happened then?

P: In the beginning we all agreed we won't go to the operation all at the same time, but we will do the operation one by one. If they give the money, the other one will go to the operation.

S: All thirteen?

P: No. There was seven of us.

S: How old were you?

P: We were about 18, 17, 16, and youngest one was 15 years old.

S: Did you have to have any medical tests?

P: They made a check for us. They came and took us by a black car to some place to do checks. They made blood tests and scanning.

S: Can you remember where it was?

P: We don't know where this place was because they came and took us by a black car and they never bring us back after the blood tests. We spent two weeks at that place after we had the kidney operation. We were locked in the apartment. We were forbidden to go out of the apartment at all.

S: Do you know where the operation was performed? Was it in a hospital?

P: The operation took place in an apartment, in the basement. I remember, we were going down by stairs. At the beginning when we came to the operation, we were locked in the apartment and no one was allowed to come out. They told us, we will bring to you anything you want, if you want water, food, juice, smoking, girls, drinks, anything they would bring to us into the apartment. We weren't allowed to come out at all, we were forbidden to come out. They brought two bodyguards who were standing at the apartment door at all times to make sure we were locked in.

S: Everything was guarded?

P: Yes, but everything we wanted they brought for us in the place. They would bring to us foods, drinks, girls; everything we wanted they would bring to us.

S: How long did they keep you there before the operation was performed?

P: We stayed in the apartment for about a month.

S: And after that?

P: A car came after we had done everything, like tests, they came by black car and you can see out, but no one can see inside [tinted windows]. When we dropped out from the car, we went downstairs. We didn't went upstairs. We entered a white room.

S: Did they bring you into a different apartment or the same one?

P: It wasn't the same apartment—we had gone far away. We drove all night to arrive in this place of the operation. We slept in a car, until we woke up from sleeping in the morning [and] the car was moving.

S: What happened then?

P: They took us one by one. Any one of us who entered this room, he spent about 6 to 7 hours in operation. After that my turn came and I entered the operation room; there came two doctors who were women. They change my clothes and they made me lie down on the bed and they injected me with some drugs. After that, voluntarily, you are going into sleep and you go out of the consciousness [general anesthetic], and you never woke up, unless they took the kidney and closed the operation wound after it had been taken.

S: Did the doctor explain what was happening? Did anyone give you information about the surgery itself?

P: The two doctors who changed our clothes, they explain to me how the operation will be done, they told me, kidney side will open easily and then it will be closed after they open, and it will be done smoothly.

S: And did they pay you afterward?

P: After the surgery they took us back to the apartment. We went back into the same apartment we were staying at. The money came in the next day. Everyone they gave an envelope and told everyone to find his name on envelopes and take his money.

S: Full $5,000?

P: $6,000, big ones.

S: More than you had agreed?

P: $6,000. Yes.

S: You were happy with this?

P: When I got the money, of course I was happy [laughing].

S: Did it last for long? How did you use it?

P: No.

S: What happened?

P: I sent $1,000 for my uncle back in Eritrea; they bought a home there. My sisters are coming here to Egypt in two months. I used $1,000 to rent an apartment for myself. I spent money in shopping, I used on clothes, watches, hats. Having fun.

S: How are you doing now?

P: My situation right now, I went back to work again.

S: What are you working at?

P: I'm working at car washing.

S: Is that OK?

P: Somehow.

S: Do they pay you fairly?

P: They give us E£400 [Egyptian pounds, about $22] a week. That's OK.

S: What happened with your asylum claim? Have you told anyone else about this [selling kidney]?

P: I spoke with the UN, and they gave me a yellow card, and nothing happened until now. UN just give a yellow card and just write protection on the card, but they never really provide protection. Sometimes they send you to a church in Zamalek called All Saints. They gave me food for a month, and going back to Caritas that gives medication, and some assistances like that. But only Dawitt knows about this [points to abdomen] and you. He said you are a good guy. I think you are.

S: Thank you. How have you been feeling since the operation? Your health.

P: After the kidney was taken, I cannot work, sleep well. I cannot play football with my friends. There are many things I cannot do it right now.

S: Do you [Dawitt] feel the same?

D: Yeah. I feel the same. I cannot lift something heavy, I cannot go to gym, and I cannot take the stairs.

P: I noticed yesterday you [Dawitt] looked so tired.

D: Yeah, I was really tired. I don't know about you [Petros], but I want to leave. I want to leave by boat and I want to go to Australia.

S: Would you stay here, or would you consider going a different way?

P: I would like to go somewhere else. For several times, I go to Alex [Alexandria] to go somewhere else by smuggling but I couldn't make it. I have been trying to go to Libya, to get to Europe by sea. Every time I went on sea by boat, the coast guards catch us and then send us back.

S: Can you tell me more about the boats?

P: The coast guards ask about our ID. If you have a Sudanese passport, they deport you to Sudan, but we gave them our UN cards, so they released us in Cairo. The police call UN and tell them that here there are some who want to escape by smuggling, what should we do, and the UN response: just release them in Cairo.

S: Do you pay the smugglers in advance?

P: So you don't pay in the beginning. You have to make an agreement with the smuggler and give him half of the money, and you will leave the rest of the money with your brother or friend. When you arrive there, you going to call that someone that you had left the money with, and tell him, I had arrived, and then he going to give him the rest of the money. In case you didn't make it and you didn't arrive, when you came back you going to take the rest of, half of, the money from him. Some people they don't give your money back; some people they tell you it's not our problem you came back, so you lost your money.

S: Do you have to know someone in particular?

P: You don't have to know some particular you can deal with anyone, but you don't have to give all your money to someone.

D: You just give him half of the money.

S: Was it better in Sudan?

P: In Sudan, of course was better. Even if there was some harassment, but they will never beat you or hustling to take your money. And they don't put you in prison like they do here and beat you.

D: Here they beat you and take your phone and your money. One day I was walking on the street, someone came with knife, and after I ran they cut me on my legs so they could take my phone. We are facing injustice, racial discrimination. That's why people want to leave Egypt. Not just us. The Egyptians want to leave too.

S: Can you tell me a little more about this network, this broker from Sudan? He was working with an Egyptian and you mentioned there were people guarding the apartment.

P: The Sudanese broker talks to you, and the Egyptian come after to talk and convince you. After the operation, someone will come to the apartment to knock on the door to give you the money. You don't have any communication with them [brokers] at this time. You only talk with someone who is in charge of the apartment. He is the only person you can talk to, and this person is always an Egyptian. And the Sudanese [brokers] just talk to you by the phone. They don't want to have nothing to do with you after the operation.

They [broker network] only give him about $500 to recruit a person, and then he keeps silent after that.

S: What about the doctor?

P: The doctor, also you don't see them. They drug you [general anesthetic], and you don't see them after that. You only see the two nurses before and after the operation, but you will never see the doctor even before or after.

S: Is this still happening?

P: Yes, it happens now without papers [consent forms].

S: Really?

P: Yeah, it's happening right now. It's like a network, a mafia. All just word of mouth, to speak, to know, through the people. This is the only way to know what they are doing. Because now some who donated their kidney is scared to talk about these issues. He [the organ seller] will be in a bad psychological situation. He doesn't want anyone to know this case. Only if you met someone who have the courage to talk and tell you that he has done a kidney operation. People feel ashamed to talk about this, what they have done. I am glad I can tell you this and you can know, and others will know because of you.

S: I will do my best. . . . How many nationalities are involved?

P: There are many nationalities involved: Somalia, Eritrea, Sudan . . .

S: What about Syrian, Yemeni, and other nationalities?

P: There are Yemeni involved.

S: But mostly Sudanese, Eritrean, and Somalis?

P: Mostly Sudanese, some Djibouti and other Africans, and right now there is a war in Yemen. Some people come from Yemen with money and others they come without money; and those who come with no money, they sell their kidney to survive.

S: OK, I think that's enough questions. Let's relax. Really, thank you for talking to me.

P: Thank you, man. I want that book when you're finished.

This transcript was recorded in English and Arabic. The respondent [Petros] could understand and speak some English but would revert to using Arabic when providing more detailed discussion. The interview was conducted with an interpreter from Sudan [Solomon]. The dialogue is repeated verbatim as it was recorded and communicated to me. The interpreter's first language is Arabic. The vernacular in the dialogue reflects this.

ACKNOWLEDGMENTS

This book is the culmination of several years of research examining the nature and extent of the organ trade in Cairo, Egypt. During my time in Cairo, I had the good fortune to meet and get to know some remarkable people. Their stories and experiences are at the core of this book, providing personal context and insight into an issue, or set of issues, that can easily become lost or underwritten by scholarly convention. In particular, I am greatly indebted to the hospitality and kindness of the respondents, from Sudan and South Sudan, Eritrea, and Ethiopia, who welcomed me into their homes and shared their stories with me. They have taught me the value of compassionate listening. I greatly admire their integrity and courage to reveal the truth regardless of the circumstances. Protecting their identities prevents me from naming them here.

Special thanks to Solomon, who acted as my translator throughout my time in Cairo. Without his friendship and assistance this project would not have been possible. Solomon accompanied me during interviews and offered me a place to live when I visited Cairo. His companionship—and patience dealing with an Irishman in the Cairo heat—is greatly appreciated. Thank you also to the many medical professionals, aid workers, journalists, law enforcement personnel, and general members of the public, whose names I cannot mention for reasons already stated.

Dr. Ninoslav Ivanovski arranged interviews with organ recipients in Skopje, North Macedonia, and Pristina, Kosovo, who had received kidney transplants overseas (i.e., in Egypt and Pakistan). His medical knowledge and personal insight into kidney transplantation have been an invaluable resource to draw on. Thank you also to the members of the ELPAT (Ethical, Legal, and Psychosocial Aspects of Organ Transplantation) Working Group on Organ Trafficking, in particular, Frederike Ambagtsheer for her stimulating conversations about the organ trade.

In between research visits to Cairo in 2017 and 2018, I was a visiting scholar at the Centre for Criminology and Socio-Legal Studies at the University of Toronto. Thank you to all the members of the Centre who attended my research seminar, where I had the opportunity to present two draft chapters from this book. Thanks to Audrey Macklin, Matthew Light, and Leon Kosals for your feedback and encouragement.

The writing of this book has also benefited from the support of other academic colleagues. Thank you to Ciara Kierans, Sandra Walklate, Jennifer Bryson Clark, and Federico Varese for their intellectual generosity and advice. Anastasia Tataryn read numerous drafts of my chapters, proofreading and providing valuable feedback. Her criticism has always been constructive, considered, and illuminating. I would also like to thank Graham Ellison for helping me to develop as a researcher during my years as a doctoral student at Queen's University Belfast. Thanks also to my colleagues at the School of Law and Social Justice, University of Liverpool. I was fortunate to receive institutional funding as well as a year of research leave that allowed me to complete my fieldwork in Cairo. I would also like to thank my students for their contagious enthusiasm and for their unyielding ability to challenge me to think in new ways. Thanks to Laura Burns for helping with some last minute fact checks.

Warm thanks to Michelle Lipinski at Stanford University Press for believing in this project from the beginning and for guiding me through the publication process. Marcela Maxfield stepped in to assist me in the final weeks before publication. Thank you also to the excellent production and editing team who worked on this book. Gretchen Otto and her team at Motto Publishing were beyond helpful during the final revisions.

Finally, I would like to thank my parents, John and Theresa; my sisters, Dominique and Niamh; my close friends (you know who you are); and my extended family. There were many times during the writing of this book and while I was away on fieldwork when I became disillusioned and/or needed a friendly ear to vent my concerns and frustrations. I am grateful for the all the encouragement and support that I received. Special thanks to my mother, who has never failed to lift my spirits and to inspire confidence when it is most needed. This book would not have been written without you.

TRADING LIFE

1

EXCAVATING THE ORGAN TRADE

PETROS, WHOSE INTERVIEW IS FEATURED in the preface, was not recognized as a victim of human trafficking. On the contrary, in the absence of a valid residency permit, his status was considered "illegal," leaving him subject to arrest and/or deportation. It was from within this precarious context that he was exploited for his kidney. In 2010 the Egyptian government made it a criminal offense to buy or sell an organ. Fearing arrest, Petros was reluctant to report the broker who solicited his kidney to the Egyptian authorities. Petros received $6,000 in exchange for his kidney, but his circumstances did not change, and he remained determined to leave Egypt in search of better living conditions and employment opportunities.

The purchase or sale of organs is prohibited worldwide, with the exception of Iran. This means that in most states where the sale or purchase of organs is illegal, people who have "consented" to sell a kidney can be held liable for committing a criminal offense. Following this logic, people who sell an organ can be considered complicit in their own exploitation. Although it is unlikely that organ sellers,[1] who are perceived to have been victimized in some way (e.g., they have been trafficked), will be prosecuted, arrest and detention is a real possibility for people marked out by their "illegal" migrant status. In this regard, the exploitation that organ sellers experience is recognized only in the context of human trafficking, categorically defined as a criminal offense against a victim-citizen. This narrow emphasis on criminality overlooks important intersections of agency, culture, identity, and politics, diverting critical attention away from the environments and circumstances that predispose people toward organ sale. Criminal measures do nothing to offset demand for illegal transplants. The prevailing law enforcement response does not capture or respond to the empirical reality. Conversely, crime and immigration controls have produced an anomic environment that fosters a subculture of organ sales among migrant populations in particular. In Egypt the organ trade has developed from the informal economy as part of the "service industry" of organized crime, orchestrated by a network of intermediaries operating across the illegal-legal divide.

Drawing on the experiences of African migrants in Cairo, Egypt, in this book I bring together seven years of fieldwork (2014–2020), charting the development of the organ trade from an informal (unregulated) economic activity into a structured criminal network. The narratives that I present forge new insights into the structure and activities of organ trading networks and the impact of current legal and policy measures in response to the organ trade. Moreover, the findings demonstrate how investing financial and administrative resources in law enforcement and border security at the expense of social services has led to the convergence of illicit networks (i.e., smuggling and organ trading networks) in the informal economy and the development of organized crime.

Conceptualizing the Organ Trade

In the past 20 years the organ trade has gained international attention and notoriety as a form of human trafficking. Intergovernmental reports, academic articles, and media exposés speak to the egregious nature of organ sales and/or organ trafficking, two distinct terms that are used interchangeably, and point to the existence of an illegal underworld that traffics body parts within and between countries (see, e.g., Scheper-Hughes 2001; OSCE 2013; and UNODC 2018). A common narrative is constructed in which organ brokers or traffickers manipulate, deceive, and coerce vulnerable individuals into selling their organs. Victims are trafficked to a medical facility, where they are forcibly detained, if necessary, before having their organs removed by nefarious medical professionals.

> Traffickers may persuade victims that trading one of their kidneys is the only way to cope with poverty. Traffickers abuse these vulnerabilities, specifically targeting unemployed rural workers or homeless people who are in desperate

situations, and deceive them into trading their organs for money that will not be paid at the end of the surgery. . . . Traffickers collude with medical professionals, relying on corrupt and fraudulent practices. (UNODC 2018: 30)

The World Health Organization (WHO) has estimated that 5–10% of organ transplants take place illegally each year (Shimazono 2007). In a 2018 report the United Nations Office on Drugs and Crime (UNODC) collected data on more than 700 incidents of organ trafficking, primarily from North Africa and the Middle East.[2] Global Financial Integrity, a Washington, D.C., based nonprofit organization, ranks the global trade in organs in scale and profit alongside the illicit trade in drugs, wildlife, and weapons, with an estimated annual profit of $1.7 billion. How exactly this figure was established is unclear. Nevertheless, the global trade in organs is believed to be among the most lucrative forms of human trafficking (UNODC 2018).

Influential voices within the transplant profession have condemned the unethical payment of vulnerable donors, advocating for a worldwide prohibition of organ sales to combat the threat of organ trafficking. Meanwhile, states have been urged to increase their altruistic supply of organs to offset the demand for illegal transplants (Danovitch and Leichtman 2006; Delmonico 2009). Legislative responses reflect this interpretive bias by concentrating efforts on increasing the donor pool by legitimate means and by applying formulaic criminal prohibitions against organ sales.

In 2000 "the removal of organs" was listed as a form of exploitation under Article 3(a) of the United Nations Protocol to Prevent, Suppress, and Punish Trafficking in Persons (hereafter, the Trafficking Protocol; UNODC 2000b).[3] According to the Trafficking Protocol, organ trafficking occurs when there is evidence of an act (e.g., recruitment) carried out by illicit means (e.g., threat or use of force or other forms of coercion) to exploit a person for the removal of one or more of their organs in pursuit of profit. How exactly the "removal of organs" becomes a criminal act or how an ostensibly consensual agreement to sell an organ becomes exploitative and subsequently a trafficking offense is not elaborated.[4]

In drafting international guidelines in response to the organ trade, it was assumed that organ sellers would inevitably come under the control of traffickers. Therefore prohibiting all instances of "transplant commercialism" was necessary. In 2004 a World Health Assembly (WHA) Resolution (WHA 57.18) called on member states "to take measures to protect the poorest and vulnerable groups from transplant tourism and the sale of tissues and organs, including attention to the wider problem of international trafficking in human tissues and organs" (WHA 2004: 57). This resolution was accompanied by a news bulletin that warned that "the international trade in human organs is on the increase fueled by growing demand as well as unscrupulous traffickers" (WHO 2004: 1). A 2007 WHO report identified Egypt, Pakistan, China, the Philippines, and India as "organ exporting countries" where "organs from local donors are regularly transplanted to foreigners through sale and purchase" (Shimazono 2007: 957). At an international summit convened by the Transplant Society and the International Society of Nephrology, political leaders were called on to prohibit all instances of transplant commercialism (i.e., organ sales). Under threat of organ trafficking, states were urged to develop their transplant infrastructure to accommodate deceased organ donation: "In countries without established deceased organ donation or transplantation, national legislation should be enacted that would initiate deceased organ donation and create transplantation infrastructure, so as to fulfill each country's deceased donor potential" (International Summit on Transplant Tourism and Organ Trafficking, 2008: 135).

In an update to its *Guiding Principles on Human Cell, Tissue, and Organ Transplantation* the WHO encouraged all states without a regulatory framework governing transplant practice to prohibit organ sales: "Payment for cells, tissues and organs is likely to take unfair advantage of the poorest and most vulnerable groups, undermines altruistic donation, and leads to profiteering and human trafficking" (WHO 2010: 5). In 2014 the Council of Europe established the Convention Against Trafficking in Human Organs, expanding criminal sanctions for offenses related to the "illicit removal of human organs." Paradoxically, the Convention allows for both the prosecution and protection of organ sellers. As outlined in Articles 4(a) and 4(b) criminalization is contingent on a lack of informed consent and the exchange of money. This means that individuals who have "consented" to organ sale are potentially liable for prosecution, "where in exchange for the removal of organs, the living donor has been offered or has received financial gain or comparable advantage" (Article 4(b)). According to the Explanatory Report to the Convention (paras, 29 53), the prosecution of organ donors and recipients is at the discretion of states parties to the Convention. States diverge widely with regard to the level of punishment to be administered for the offense of selling an organ and/or organ trafficking. Punishment can range from three months of imprisonment and/or a fine (e.g., the United Kingdom) to a life sentence (e.g., Egypt). Rather than address such inconsistencies, the Convention merely encourages states to adopt new offenses to prevent and combat trafficking in human organs.

The overarching rationale behind these combined ethical and legal guidelines is that a failure to prohibit organ sales and increase altruistic donations will result in organ trafficking. Yet existing international attention given to trafficking can address only a fraction, at best, of the issues that fuel and intersect within organ trading networks. As the narratives in this book demonstrate, the organ trade is better understood as an informal economic activity, as opposed to a human trafficking offense. It is economic pressures and the demands of survival rather than *traffickers* that force people into exploitative arrangements (i.e., organ sale) that they would otherwise avoid. To move away from a trafficking paradigm toward what might be termed an exploitation paradigm, I examine the background rules and legal structures that position people as sellers, buyers, and brokers.

To be clear, I do not deny that organ trafficking takes place. On the contrary, many of the narratives in this book demonstrate that it does. What I am contending is the way the trafficking label has been used to support a selective criminal justice agenda reproduces the conditions of exploitation it purports to prevent. The discursive framing of the organ trade as a trafficking issue has diverted critical attention away from the structural factors that underpin the organ trade. A narrow focus on criminality fails to take into account the role that the transplant industry has played in producing the economic rationale for organ markets. At the same time, the threat of organ trafficking is used to galvanize support for punitive policies (e.g., increased border controls and criminal penalties), ostensibly established to eradicate human trafficking or what is increasingly referred to as "modern slavery." These policies are increasing the level of harm that undocumented migrants, in particular, are exposed to by criminal actors who profit from their circumstances and by state forces who curtail their movement and entrench their suffering. The reasons that people sell or are coerced into giving up one of their organs are not determined by a criminal act, that is, trafficking for the purpose of organ removal. The choices people make are shaped by their personal histories and are mediated by legal rules and political decisions played out over time and space.

Because of their precarious legal status, migrants, asylum seekers, and refugees are being solicited for their organs by brokers with connections to transplant clinics and hospitals in Egypt. The exploitation they experience is exacerbated by political instability across the Middle East and North Africa and the political indifference of the international community.

The Politics of Exploitation

As a neutral technical term, *exploitation* refers to the action of making use of and benefiting from resources, skills, assets, or opportunities. Accordingly, a person exploits a thing or resource by making use of it. There is nothing particularly controversial or morally problematic about this.[5] It is when we consider exploitation in relation to other people that its normative rendering takes on a more pejorative connotation (Munro 2008). This relational distinction is apparent in the *Oxford English Dictionary*, where exploitation is defined in both its neutral (as above) and relational capacity: "the action or fact of treating someone unfairly in order to benefit from their work." It is in this pejorative sense that exploitation has developed, in legal parlance in particular, as a feature or purpose of "trafficking in persons" (UNODC 2000b). Human trafficking is defined broadly as an action (e.g., recruitment) by illicit means (e.g., force, fraud, or coercion) for the purpose of exploitation (e.g., removal of organs). The trafficking label can be applied to any conduct considered harmful or immoral (Campana and Varese 2016). Theoretically, this has enabled anti-trafficking legislation to develop beyond sex trafficking. In practice, the legal concept of exploitation has been used in instrumental terms to rationalize the expansion of the law enforcement apparatus over a wide spectrum of activities that invite moral condemnation, e.g., migration, sex work, organ sales (see Chuang 2014). Nevertheless, it is only the most exceptional claims to exploitation, classified as human trafficking or slavery, that are recognized at the judicial level (see Farrell et al. 2014). Following what was nominally termed the migrant crisis in 2015, the concept of exploitation entered the political discourse as an object of national security. Speaking as the U.K. home secretary in 2016, Theresa May stated, "It is only by working together, taking responsibility and fighting criminality that we can stop the misery of exploitation and enable everyone in society to work without fear" (Home Office 2016). In January 2019 Donald Trump, acting as president of the United

States, declared a national state of emergency, claiming, among other things, that "human traffickers exploit our borders to traffic young girls and women into prostitution and slavery" (White House 2019). The implication is that in order to stop exploitation, whatever that may be, criminalization of suspect activities, individuals, and/or groups is necessary.

Deployed in this way, the concept of exploitation operates as a kind of indeterminate moral compass that (re)directs acrimony toward specific harms (actual or invented) and finds resolution in criminal punishment. Hence the normative scope of exploitation as a legal concept has been limited to state-centric concerns over selective nonstate actors and activities considered a threat to national security. Little consideration is given to ways in which law and policy can combine to produce vulnerability to exploitation by private or state agents (Marks 2008; and Mantouvalou 2018). Rather, political action is developed around a retributive desire to punish the individual perpetrators who are held responsible for the personalized suffering of victim-citizens. The hypervisualization of specific harms linked to exploitation rationalizes penal policies and obscures more subtle forms of exploitation and background rules implicit in legal structures.

Most of the people I interviewed for this book were compelled to consider organ sale because of their socioeconomic status. Categorized as illegal and formally barred from legal employment, they were exploited for their kidneys. The exploitation they experienced was implicated in and contingent on their particular circumstances and environments, subject to which they were unfairly treated for the material benefit of others, that is, brokers, organ recipients, and/or corrupt transplant professionals. In this book I use the term *exploitation* in the pejorative sense, to denote unfair treatment manifest in the poor bargaining position of people targeted for their organs. More broadly, I use *exploitation* as an analytical concept to explain how people are positioned in exploitative relations, where their bodies are subject to the kinds of individualized harm generally associated with human trafficking or serious crime. Building on insights from Marxist accounts of labor exploitation and structural unfairness (Roemer 1989; G. A. Cohen 1979), I understand exploitation as an oppressive process played out on the bodies of an economic underclass that is systematically cut off from legal protection. I explore this process and the legal structures behind it through the narratives of people who have been exploited for their organs in Cairo, Egypt.

Selling Kidneys in Times of Revolution

In 2010 Egypt introduced the Transplantation of Human Organs and Tissues Act (Law 5/2010), which prohibited the sale or purchase of organs. The law was established in accordance with the Law of Trafficking in Persons (Law 64/2010), which extended liability for organ sales to include trafficking offenses. Before its drafting, the Egyptian government had deferred the passing of a national transplant law for over three decades (see Hamdy 2012). Plans to bring the stated provisions into force were abandoned with the onset of revolution, however. On January 25, 2011, thousands gathered in Tahrir Square to demand the resignation of then-president Hosni Mubarak. After decades of spiraling unemployment, rising food prices, police abuse, and endemic corruption, Egyptian citizens and noncitizens, supported by a disillusioned military leadership, forced Mubarak into political exile. In the first democratic election since Mubarak came to power in 1981, Mohamed Morsi and the Muslim Brotherhood were elected into government. Morsi's reign lasted less than a year; a military coup, led by General Abdel Fattah al-Sisi, seized power after accusing Morsi and the Muslim Brotherhood of betraying the revolutionary mandate of the Egyptian people. In the absence of an elected parliament, a series of draconian decrees restricting freedom of expression, association, and assembly were issued unilaterally by the Supreme Council of the Armed Forces (Ketchley 2017). New laws were enacted banning protests, expanding military jurisdiction over large public spaces (e.g., roads, bridges, universities), and granting political control over universities (Rutherford and Sowers 2018). In the same month, June 2014, al-Sisi was inaugurated as president of Egypt. In the revolutionary aftermath, the Egyptian people had once again found themselves living under a military dictatorship. A sustained period of economic decline followed, as military funding was increased in an effort to consolidate control over the population and to ward off the threat of insurgent Islamic groups (Rutherford and Sowers 2018).

In this political climate, policing the organ trade was no longer a priority. Although a law prohibiting organ sales had been established and subsequently enacted into the Egyptian penal code, in practice the trade was tacitly accepted as an unregulated market solution to the surplus demand for organs (see Chapter 2). Political indifference, particularly with regard to the bodies of predominantly black migrant donors, facilitated the development of organ trading networks along ethnically stratified lines. It was in this postrevolutionary context of political instability, economic decline, and divergent social and cultural norms that the organ trade emerged as an informal economic activity, for migrant populations in particular.

A number of scholars, largely in the field of anthropology, have studied the challenges of organ donation from moral, cultural, and ethical perspectives (see Hamdy 2012; Lock 2002; and Sharp 2006), but evidence-based research into the legal, social, and political factors that underpin organ markets and the networks that supply them is scarce. Furthermore, critical engagement with the implications of current legislative and policy mechanisms in response to the organ trade is lacking. Despite the growing interest in what has been described as "a fatal form of exploitation" in a "fast and expanding black market," there remains a critical deficit of evidence-based research into this area. The existing commentary on the organ trade is dominated by expert opinions of professional practitioners working in the field of transplant medicine. In contrast, the experiences of organ sellers and organ brokers have largely been discounted or bypassed by a narrow bioethical debate contesting the pros and cons of a regulated market in organs (see Erin and Harris 2003; Danovitch et al. 2013; and I. G. Cohen 2013).

This is not a book about organ donation or the ethics of organ sales. This is a book about the emergence of the organ trade in the Egyptian context and the wider impact of crime and immigration controls at the international level. The trade in organs has developed alongside these controls, generating revenues for the transplant industry and creating economic opportunities for illicit networks. The core aim of this book is to demonstrate how law and policy produce and construct vulnerability to exploitation in organ markets and to explain the theoretical and practical implications of the prevailing law enforcement model in response to the organ trade. In this regard the organ trade acts as a heuristic device, providing broader insight into and commentary on human trafficking and the deep dynamics of legal marginalization, social exclusion, and exploitation. I chose Cairo as the key research site for this study because of its reputation as a hot spot of organ trafficking. Conducting fieldwork in Cairo provided an opportunity to assess the implications of criminalization and the politics of exploitation in a period of political upheaval and social change.

I first traveled to Cairo in May 2014. I wanted to learn from people who had bought, sold, or brokered kidneys. Why did they sell and/or arrange for the sale of their organs? How was this trade facilitated and organized? From a theoretical perspective, I was interested in how law and policy produce vulnerability and how the social experience of exploitation differs from the legal definition outlined in Article 3 of the Trafficking Protocol. More specifically, I wanted to examine how organ markets emerge in a given context and to what extent the trade in organs is controlled by organized crime groups. On a more personal level, I wanted to connect with people whose lives had been shaped by political and social violence and bear witness to their stories. I was aware of the limitations of my research and my position as an academic, but I was nevertheless motivated by a desire to do something helpful in my capacity as a researcher. With these motives in mind, my inability to directly assist the people I had grown close to played on my conscience throughout my fieldwork. Nevertheless, it was because of these personal connections that I was able to gain access to otherwise inaccessible social networks among Cairo's migrant community and forge new insights into organ trading networks. After preliminary discussions and inquiries with local nongovernmental organizations (NGOs), it became apparent that undocumented migrants in particular were being targeted for their organs.[6]

Researching the Organ Trade

This book is informed by 63 in-depth narrative interviews carried out between 2014 and 2020 with people involved in various aspects of organ trading. Interview respondents consisted of thirty-one organ sellers, seven organ brokers, nine organ recipients, seven medical professionals, two international law enforcement officials, and seven NGO staff members. Because of the sensitive nature of this research, it was not possible to interview Egyptian law enforcement officials. Seventeen of the organ sellers were female; fourteen were male. Of the organ brokers, six were male and one was female. The ages of the organ sellers were 18–36 years old for the male respondents and 19–42 years old for the female respondents.[7] Further interviews were carried out with organ recipients who traveled overseas (i.e., to Pakistan or Egypt) for organ transplants. In Chapter 2 I draw on interviews with transplant professionals and organ recipients who traveled to Cairo for kidney transplants. I examine how the illegal trade in organs emerged among migrant populations in particular. In doing so, I link the commercial expansion of the transplant industry to the development of organ trading as an economic activity. The chapters that follow draw on the experiences of African migrants who sold and/or arranged for the sale of organs in Cairo. The analysis in this book is grounded in and developed from the situated perspectives and experiences of these respondents. I have used pseudonyms throughout to protect their anonymity.

During my first three months in Cairo I developed a close relationship with Solomon, a Sudanese national who acted as an interpreter throughout my fieldwork. Solomon was my initial gatekeeper, connecting me with key members of the Sudanese community who had information on the organ trade. Data collection involved a combination of participant observation, informal conversations, and semistructured interviews. Much of my time in Egypt was spent waiting and talking to different people in informal street markets in the Greater Cairo region. Interviews with organ sellers were largely arranged through personal connections and introductions. Interviews with organ brokers followed periods of observation based on information received from organ sellers who had sold a kidney. In some cases, personal introductions were arranged through preexisting contacts. At other times, I approached the brokers on my own and requested interviews subsequent to and contingent on the tenor of informal conversations and personal observations.

The narratives of organ sellers and brokers featured in this book are predominantly from Sudanese nationals (Sudan and South Sudan) who normally reside in Cairo. Other respondents were from Eritrea, Ethiopia, Somalia, and Chad. Many of the people I interviewed were escaping violent regimes and the economic aftermath of ongoing conflict, characterized by high unemployment and inflation. Some had come to Cairo to claim asylum and seek resettlement outside Egypt. Others had traveled to link up with family members, to advance their education, to find employment—in general, to build a better life. They were at once economic migrants, asylum seekers, and refugees depending on their circumstances, which changed over time and space. Accordingly, I adopt different terms (migrant, asylum seeker, refugee, undocumented, irregular, illegal) throughout this book to emphasize the (arbitrary) legal status of respondents at the time of interview, and to reveal the social consequences that these legal categories produce (see Macklin 2005; 2007). I use the term *migrant* broadly to refer to people traveling and living outside their country of origin. This includes people who have been denied state protection as asylum seekers and refugees.

Through conversations with different members of the Sudanese community, I learned that the organ trade was something of an open secret among migrant populations residing in Cairo's low-income neighborhoods, for example, Ard El-Lewa, Faisal, and Shubra. In a context devoid of financial opportunity, the organ trade was a recognized economic activity, albeit with a high degree of social stigma attached. Selling a kidney was considered *haram*, forbidden by Allah. Yet the intermediaries brokering organ sales were tolerated as legitimate market players in an otherwise illegal trade (see Chapter 3). In a (global) environment where access to health care is increasingly defined by social status and relative wealth, exchanging money for a kidney is a logical conclusion to organ donation. According to this logic, the existence of brokers makes sense; that is, they are not perceived as deviant. In contrast to reports of rogue surgeons and traffickers kidnapping people for their organs, organ sellers (with some notable exceptions) exercised a degree of agency that is missing from the one-dimensional portrayal of trafficked individuals in government and media reports. Selling a kidney was an economic option of last resort as opposed to a forced act of aggression imposed by a nefarious criminal order. The people I interviewed were keen to communicate this, explaining how it was that they had come to sell a kidney, as opposed to speaking about the act of organ removal in and of itself. I was surprised by their candor and encouraged by the importance they attached to the work I was doing. They were angry with the political indifference to their welfare and wanted someone to listen to what they had to say. In this regard, they viewed me as a potential ally, someone who could convey their personal experiences and speak truth to power.

Interviews with organ sellers took place in their homes, public spaces (e.g., bars and cafés), and occasionally at the apartment where I stayed with Solomon. More often than not, respondents interviewed me before I interviewed them. They would ask questions about my personal and professional background and read my body language in response to more pointed questions regarding the purpose of my visit. I approached interviews as I would any other conversation, leading with questions and developing the discussion as the narrative unfolded. Depending on the dynamic and/or level of rapport I developed with the person I was interviewing, we would talk for hours at a time, often over food or in some cases over copious bottles of Stella, Egypt's national beer. Although initial interviews were often short and inconsistent in detail, with some people providing contradictory statements with regard to the manner in which they were recruited or the level of remuneration they had received, people gradually became more comfortable speaking and narrating their experiences. Follow-up interviews were arranged where possible, to allow time for respondents to think over different aspects of their experience that may have been withheld or simply forgotten during the initial interview. All but two of the interview narratives presented in this book were from repeat interviews with people who I would draw closer to over the course of my fieldwork. I formed a strong bond with many of the people I spoke with and found it increasingly difficult to extricate myself from the emotional ebb and flow of our conversations. What I refer to here as interviews, for the sake of academic continuity, were often intimate conversations animated with laughter and/or weighed down with tears and long silences, at times both awkward and profound. The ability and opportunity to engage and interact with different members of the community was fundamental to developing contacts and creating opportunities to speak with people who could provide information on the network members involved.

Seeking Truth in Violence

My first encounter with a broker was outside a café in downtown Cairo. At the time, the World Cup finals were being played and a crowd had gathered around a television set to watch a game between Brazil and Germany. Solomon gestured toward a man in his early to mid-30s, sitting with his legs crossed and holding a cigarette in his hand. Kariem had been mentioned by an organ seller we interviewed two days earlier. I took a seat next to him and introduced myself, engaging in casual conversation and talking my way into a discussion about the organ trade. I explained that I was interested in hearing his point of view and wanted to learn from his perspective. Satisfied with this explanation, he revealed how he had become involved in the trade, recruiting donors and linking them up with other intermediaries connected to analytic labs and transplant clinics in the Greater Cairo region (see Chapter 3).

The social networks I developed with members of the Sudanese community, in particular, were critical to my efforts to establish contact with brokers. I had no set method of identification. Contact was initiated after inquiries, personal introductions, and chance encounters in different social venues where brokers were said to frequent. On one occasion I was introduced to a young Sudanese man at a restaurant, doubling as a nightclub, in Maadi, a suburban district on the lower east bank of the Nile. Shaker recognized Solomon and waved us over to join him for a drink. We talked about music, and after a few drinks he told me he had a young daughter living with his ex-partner in Khartoum, Sudan. I asked him whether he knew anything about the organ trade, and he explained how he entered the "business" on the recommendation of a friend. Soliciting kidneys from migrants supplemented his income as a musician, enabling him to send remittances back to his daughter. Sensing my unease, he insisted he was no longer in the business. He smiled at me affably and ordered another round of drinks.

After speaking with organ sellers, it was difficult not to carry my affective bias into conversations with organ brokers or other intermediaries (e.g., pimps, smugglers, money lenders, housing agents, recruitment agents) who profited at their expense. I was also concerned about the potential threat of violence should something go wrong. Yet I realized the significance of these encounters as unique sources of information providing insight into organ trading networks and as a reflective lens into the personalities of individuals collectively vilified in the press. From an observational perspective, my encounters with brokers (and smugglers) helped me to understand how they rationalize their involvement in harmful activities and the limited effect of criminal deterrence (see Chapters 3, 5, and 6). For the most part, interviews with brokers were as congenial as one might expect. However, there were occasions when the balance of my questions leaned too close to an unspoken truth or when the uncertain tension that comes with interviewing people with a criminal background threatened to spill over. In one encounter with Ali, a broker I interviewed at a café in Ard El-Lewa, I misjudged my line of questioning. I asked Ali how long he had been a broker. He had agreed to the interview in advance and was aware that I would ask him about his role brokering the exchange of kidneys. Nevertheless, he was adamant that he was not an organ broker; he was a "service provider." He slammed his fist onto the table and warned me to be careful who I speak to in the future, evidently offended by my choice of words. The interview ended.

In Chapter 3 I investigate and examine the different activities and actors that constitute organ trading networks in the Egyptian-Sudanese context. These networks are composed of diverse individuals (e.g., organ brokers, sellers, buyers, physicians), each with a different role and function, operating across the illegal-legal divide. Analytic labs used for blood testing and tissue typing between prospective donors and recipients are the key nodal points of activity where intermediaries link up actors in both the formal and informal sectors of the economy. In Chapter 4 I explore the links between migration patterns, labor market informalization, and organ markets. The diverse experiences of organ sellers and brokers demonstrate how a process of social exclusion and economic marginalization can lead to variable degrees of exploitation manifest, in this instance, in their involvement in the organ trade. Vulnerability to exploitation, I suggest, is due both to individual and structural factors.

Trading Life

I returned to Cairo for three subsequent visits in 2017 and 2020. I wanted to follow up with respondents, to check on their status and to see how the organ trade had developed, if at all. The legal architecture beneath the organ trade had shifted significantly since 2014. In response to persistent reports of organ trafficking, the Egyptian government extended criminal penalties prohibiting organ sales to include the death penalty. The decision to extend and increase criminal sanctions was part of a wider government strategy to restructure Egypt's anti-trafficking regime to include harsher sentences for offenses related to illegal migration and human trafficking (see Chapters 4 and 5). Between 2014 and 2017 thousands of sea crossings and migrant deaths along the Central Mediterranean Route (see map on page 90) were reported by the International Organization for Migration (IOM 2017a) and the international press (P. Walker 2014; BBC News 2017; Dehghan 2017). Following the outbreak of civil war in Syria together with the continued exodus of migrants from conflict zones in the Horn of Africa, the so-called migration crisis brought to bear a renewed focus on border security and illegal crossings. In an agreement with the European Union to reinforce border controls, and in accordance with requirements set out in Section 108 of the U.S. Department of State's "Trafficking in Persons Report" (2016) to comply with the "minimum standards for the elimination of trafficking," the Egyptian government established Law 82, Combating Illegal Migration and Smuggling of Migrants. The establishment of the National Coordination Committee for Combating and Preventing Illegal Migration and Human Trafficking brought the offense of people smuggling under the umbrella of human trafficking, extending culpability for crimes related to illegal migration (Stumpf 2006; Anderson 2013). The resulting criminalization of mobility has increased demand for smuggling services and increased the human and financial costs involved, as migrants undertake clandestine and circuitous journeys to avoid possible arrest, detention, and deportation. Suffering through a prolonged period of economic decline and living in fear of arrest and/or deportation, respondents were determined to leave Egypt by any means necessary. Several of the people interviewed in the coming chapters were referred by smugglers to organ brokers in Cairo who promised to finance their travel across the Central and Western Mediterranean Routes into Europe, in return for a kidney.

In contrast to my findings from 2014, the interview data collected in 2017–2020 are indicative of a much higher prevalence of physical violence and coercion, corresponding with the emergence of a criminal group recruiting people from Khartoum for involuntary organ removal in Cairo. The structure of the book reflects this process, charting the development of the organ trade in Cairo's informal economy (Chapters 2–4) into an organized criminal activity following the prohibition of organ sales (Chapters 5–7). In Chapter 5 I explore the relationship between people smuggling and the organ trade. Interviews with *samasira*, a local arabic term used to describe people who facilitate extra-legal migration, reveal how various intermediaries working in the informal economy collaborate to maintain profits when faced with regulatory challenges. In Chapter 6 I examine how emerging criminal synergies and a shifting political landscape have changed the dynamics of organ trading, increasing the need for secrecy and violent means of recruitment. In the concluding chapter I consider how decriminalization in the Egyptian context might alter the dynamics of organ trading, potentially limiting the level of exploitation that organ sellers and buyers are exposed to. Using the organ trade as a heuristic device, I consider how political violence maps onto social life, illustrating how, in the absence of state welfare, illicit trade and organized crime, broadly conceived of as a planned criminal activity (UNODC 2000c: Art 2), can develop from the informal economy. I revisit key themes discussed throughout the book (exploitation, shame, legal marginalization, violence), demonstrating how law and policy constructs vulnerability to exploitation in its various forms. Accordingly, I redirect analyses toward the legal barriers and policy decisions (crime and immigration controls) that produce circumstances and environments in which the business of selling organs has become a feature of economic survival.

2

THE ILLEGAL TRADE IN ORGANS

A 2015 NATIONAL GEOGRAPHIC DOCUMENTARY on the organ trade opens with a scene of an "organ trade boss" describing the business of organ trafficking. "Lakha" is wearing a black expressionless latex mask, resembling the mask worn by the fictional serial killer Michael Myers in the film *Halloween* (1978). He explains how he ties up his victims, "giving them five or ten blows to keep them in line." As Lakha speaks, the camera moves from a scene of what appears to be a transplant operation to a series of close-ups profiling random members of the public; the unsubtle suggestion is that anyone could become a victim. The documentary, part of a series titled *Underworld, Inc.*, comes with the tagline "In America, 14 people die each day waiting for a kidney transplant. Meanwhile, the black market organ trade is thriving, and gangsters with global reach are pocketing easy money."

Hyperbolic portrayals of abused victims and predatory traffickers, similar to the video footage just described, are typified and reproduced across the media, captured in documentary films, featured on NGO websites, and published in international government reports, characterizing the organ trade as a new and perilous form of human trafficking. This construction of deviance is a necessary prerequisite for criminal intervention, legitimizing draconian criminal measures that would otherwise be unacceptable. Representations of ruthless human traffickers speak to the "egregious" nature of the organ trade, leveraging political attention and gaining public support for policies that promise to crack down or get tough on the criminals responsible.

The illegal act of organ removal becomes the all-encompassing node of investigation, aligning political action with a punitive agenda remiss of the wider social, political, economic, and cultural factors that underpin organ markets.

The prevailing ethicolegal discourse on organ trafficking brings to mind Stanley Cohen's famous articulation of a "moral panic" (S. Cohen 2011). The global shortage of organs has been promulgated as a type of moral crisis, which has led to "the development of the international organ trade, where potential recipients travel abroad to obtain organs through commercial transactions" (Shimazono 2007). Organ trafficking rings composed of predatory brokers and unscrupulous surgeons are the folk devils of this global epidemic, threatening "to undermine the nobility and legacy of transplantation worldwide" (stated in the Declaration of Istanbul; International Summit on Transplant Tourism and Organ Trafficking 2008: 1227). Representing the organ trade in stark criminal terms has predisposed legislative action toward crime control and law enforcement. At the same time, linking a perceived global shortage in organs to the threat of organ trafficking has been instrumental in creating a sense of urgency around organ donation, particularly in countries where the concept of gift exchange has not been normalized as a feature of transplant practice.

The idea that donating an organ is a gift that does not require payment is part of a long-standing medical campaign to encourage altruistic organ donation (Parsons et al. 1972). In many Islamic countries, however, there is a reluctance to donate body parts because of religious concerns over the sanctity of the human body (Oliver et al. 2010; 2012). Criminal measures that prohibit organ sales do not account for cultural variations with regard to organ donation and/or the different health needs within and between countries. Rather, a narrow emphasis on illegal transplantation overlooks the social and economic arrangements that predispose people to sell their organs, further obscuring the role that the transplant industry has played in producing the economic rationale for organ markets. A dyadic division has been constructed between the legitimate domain of transplantation and the illegal underworld of organ trafficking. This rhetorical positioning deflects critical attention away from the transplant industry and suspends an interrogation into the processes of social exclusion and exploitation that have come to shape the organ trade as an illicit market.

In this chapter I examine how an illegal market in organs emerged in the Egyptian-Sudanese context. I argue that, contrary to the received wisdom of the international transplant community, the organ trade is not a direct consequence of a global shortage in organs. Rather, the trade in organs is causally related to the transfer of transplant capabilities to the global South. Accordingly, I link the commercial expansion of the transplant industry to the emergence of organ trading as an economic activity. The organ trade is an illegal subsystem of the transplant industry, a market solution to the surplus demand for organs. This is not an indictment of the transplant profession or a dismissal of the therapeutic benefits that successful transplantation can provide. In referring to the transplant industry, I mean the various parties—pharmaceutical companies, insurance companies, private transplant clinics, organ-sharing organizations, medical professionals, and so on—that have a commercial stake in transplantation. In Egypt a culture of organ sales has developed around the transplant industry. Unlike the narcotics trade, where the production and distribution of illegal substances violates long-established social and legal norms, the trade in organs has and continues to occupy a moral gray zone. The sale and purchase of organs was prohibited in 2010; nevertheless organ trading continues, albeit on different terms. Clandestine organ trading networks have developed, generating illegal profits from the bodies of migrant communities.

Transplant Tourism

The United Network for Organ Sharing (UNOS) defines transplant tourism as "the purchase of a transplant organ abroad that includes access to an organ while bypassing laws, rules, or processes of any or all countries involved" (UNOS 2007). At a 2007 international summit convened by the Transplant Society and the International Society of Nephrology in Istanbul, Turkey, transplant tourism was defined as "travel for transplantation" which "involves organ trafficking and/or transplant commercialism" (International Summit on Transplant Tourism and Organ Trafficking 2008: 1228). Hence transplant tourism refers to the purchase of a transplant overseas using an organ from a paid living donor who may or may not have been trafficked for organ removal. According to the World Health Organization (WHO), 5–10% of the organ transplants that take place annually are performed using illegally sourced organs from paid donors (Shimazono 2007).[1] This suggests that transplant tourism accounts for 1 in 10 transplants each year, compromising the health and safety of organ recipients and donors (Shimazono 2007). Patients travel for organ transplantation because the surgery is not available in their country of origin, because the facilities are inadequate, or because not enough organs are available. Patients or "transplant tourists" who are purchasing organs overseas are believed to be driving demand for organ "trafficking" in countries "with loose or no legal frameworks" for regulating transplant practice (Budiani-Saberi and Delmonico 2008: 928).

Yusef, an Albanian organ recipient who I interviewed in Skopje, North Macedonia, described the scene when he arrived at a hospital in Cairo, Egypt: "It [the hospital] was like a conveyor belt with maybe 10 or 15 transplants taking place each day. But everything was clean; this place was high quality. I had a room to myself, and it was very secure. This was a military hospital, so it was well guarded." Unable to find a suitable donor, Yusef made arrangements, through an intermediary in Turkey, to travel to Cairo for a kidney transplant in June 2010. A family acquaintance, Amir, organized his flights and accommodation and brokered a price for the operation with "one of his contacts in Cairo." The broker's fee for finding a donor and facilitating the kidney exchange was $5,000. "I know people from the Gulf [i.e., Bahrain, Iraq, Kuwait, Oman, Qatar, Saudi Arabia, and the United Arab Emirates] paid much more, between $80,000 and $100,000. People with more money, pay more," Yusef explains. "Amir knew my relatives in Turkey, so he understood my circumstances. He negotiated a fair price with the hospital: $57,000. My relatives, everyone, helped pay for this. They gave everything."

Yusef spent five days completing tissue typing, a blood test to check for compatibility with potential donors, at an analytic lab in downtown Cairo. He received a call from Amir shortly after the tests were completed, informing him that a compatible donor had been found. "There were at least 80 different donors at that time," Yusuf said. "I know because when I was getting the tissue typing done, I was told about the donors and their suitability. I met my donor when we signed the consent forms. He used a fingerprint for his signature." I asked Yusef to describe the donor: "He was black, an African," he says, shrugging his shoulders. "He was around 28 years old. I don't know exactly. The doctor told me that they do not use donors over 30."

Like other patients I interviewed, Yusef was advised against traveling to Egypt for a kidney transplant. He was nonetheless willing to risk his long-term health and personal safety to avoid a lifetime on dialysis, a procedure that removes toxins from the blood when kidneys stop functioning. He had been receiving dialysis treatment from the age of 15 at a clinic in Pristina,

Kosovo, where he was "hooked up to a machine for four hours at a time." His mother had offered to donate her kidney but Yusef refused, concerned that the procedure would compromise her health. "Let me tell you something, there was a donor here in Skopje," Yusef continues, "but they [the doctors] would not accept this. The physician wanted proof that we were related. If I had the option to receive a transplant here, I would not have gone to Cairo."

Yusef does not regret his decision: "When I was discharged from the care of the medical team, I was back to full health. The results were excellent. Before I went to Cairo, people were going to Pakistan or India. But the conditions there were bad, and some people died shortly after returning. If I were to advise anyone, I would tell them to go to Cairo."

Patients in need of a kidney transplant have been traveling overseas since the 1980s to purchase organs from paid donors, with the assistance of intermediaries. A medical study published in the *Lancet* found that between 1984 and 1988 more than 130 patients from the United Arab Emirates and Oman received kidney transplants in Bombay, India (Salahudeen et al. 1990). According to the study, patients were not properly instructed about their treatment, and little or no information about the surgery was provided to their acting physicians. Several of these patients had underlying medical conditions and were not suitable candidates for transplantation. Moreover, the transplants were completed in unsanitary conditions, exposing patients to serious infections, including human immunodeficiency virus (HIV) infection. Twenty-five patients died within a year of receiving an organ from the unspecified donors.

Recent studies suggest that, despite poor and in some cases fatal medical outcomes, there has been an increase in transplant tourism (al-Bugami et al. 2018) together with a concomitant rise in organ trafficking (Delmonico and Ascher 2017). A shortage of transplantable organs combined with weak regulations governing ethical transplant practice has been causally linked to transplant tourism and organ trafficking (Shimazono 2007; International Summit on Transplant Tourism and Organ Trafficking 2008). For this reason, states have been urged to prohibit organ sales and to develop the technical capacity of transplantation by "increasing altruistic and deceased organ donation to its maximum therapeutic potential" (WHO 2010: Guiding Principle 3). Even though demand continues to outweigh the supply of transplantable organs in countries with established organ procurement programs, this strategic intervention has gained political support by way of the perceived threat of organ trafficking.

The Transplant Industry

Kidney transplantation was regarded as a risky and experimental procedure until the 1980s. Advances in immunological knowledge and tissue typing and the widespread availability of the immunosuppressant drug cyclosporine, transformed transplantation into a routine medical operation that could be performed worldwide. According to the WHO, transplant units have been established in 91 countries (WHO 2010). Nevertheless, a growing incidence of chronic kidney disease has placed a heavy burden on existing transplant services. As the success rate for organ transplants has improved, with advances in surgical techniques and immunosuppression, transplantation has been performed for an increasing array of underlying diseases and conditions associated with organ failure. In addition, the ever-widening parameters created within the medical profession to determine who is eligible to receive an organ means that the demand for organs remains greater than the supply (Koenig 2003; Sharp 2006).

Despite a global increase in transplant activity, there is a wide discrepancy between those who need organs and those who receive them. According to statistics released by the Global Observatory on Donation and Transplantation, there were 135,860 organ transplants (89,823 of which were kidney transplants) performed worldwide in 2016 (GODT 2016).[2] This figure accounts for approximately 10% of global needs. In 2018 the United Network for Organ Sharing reported that out of approximately 114,000 people waiting for a transplant in 2018, only 36,527 organ transplants were performed (UNOS 2019). Similarly, in the United Kingdom 9,399 patients needed an organ in 2018, but only 4,990 organ transplants were carried out (NHS 2019). In the Middle East and North Africa, it is estimated that an average of 200 patients per 1 million of the population are in need of transplantation (Shaheen 2017).[3] Increased demand for kidney transplants in particular has been intensified by a lack of altruistic donations combined with restrictive access to transplant services. With wide variations in cultural views to organ donation and in access to transplant services, a surplus demand for organs has led to a reliance on informal organ-sharing networks.

The Euro-American transplant rhetoric representing organ donation as the "gift of life" does not correspond with the developmental trend of transplant technologies. Notwithstanding the therapeutic benefits of transplantation, the development of transplant capabilities is not an altogether altruistic endeavor. Rather, the expansion of the transplant industry is part of a wider trend of medical tourism and commercialized health care (Fox and Swazey 1992; Sharp 2006).[4] Although transplants produce high revenues for insurance and pharmaceutical companies, organ procurement organizations, medical professionals, hospitals, and their shareholders, the profits are largely remitted into the private sector at the expense of public health care provision (see Mahoney 2000; and Winickoff 2003).[5] Although transplant services are available through public health care systems, access is often constrained by the availability of specialist physicians and surgeons, partial or inadequately subsidized medical coverage for transplant procedures, and a lack of altruistic donations. These constraints are particularly acute in low- to middle-income countries where public expenditure is limited (Muller 2016). In comparison, the availability of (commercial) organs and the higher standard of care provided in the (globalized) private sector means that patients will pay out of pocket if and where they can afford it. Consequently, access to "life-saving" treatment is becoming a feature of one's ability to pay. This trend is no more evident than in the disparity of access to transplant surgery within and between countries.[6] The cost of a typical kidney transplant can range from $8,000 (e.g., Egypt) to $263,000 (e.g., United States) per patient, depending on where the surgery is performed (Barsoum 2016; I. G. Cohen 2014). In countries where universal health care is unavailable (e.g., United States), this cost delimits the benefits of transplantation to those who possess the necessary means to afford treatment (domestically or overseas), either out of pocket or through private medical insurance. More generally, for workers in the informal economy who are not covered by social security systems, access to transplantation is virtually nonexistent through legal, altruistic means.

Contrary to reports of wealthy patients traveling overseas to purchase organs from impoverished donors, patients who travel for transplant surgery are often priced out of treatment in their home countries.[7] In the United States the cost of kidney transplantation is covered by the Medicare public assistance program for patients diagnosed with end-stage renal failure. However, only one-third of the American population is eligible for Medicare or Medicaid coverage (I. G. Cohen 2014). Patients who are uninsured or underinsured (i.e., transplantation is not covered by their insurance plan) may find it is more cost-effective to travel overseas for transplantation (see Canales et al. 2006; Gill et al. 2008; and Wright et al. 2013). In countries with universal health care, long waiting lists for kidney transplantation are a major driver for transplant tourism (Wright et al. 2013; Prasad et al. 2006). Patients from countries where transplant services are limited or unavailable (e.g., South Sudan) have little choice but to travel abroad and pay out of pocket (see Chapter 4).

Many destination countries where the cost of transplantation is comparatively low (e.g., Egypt) do not have established organ donation systems and rely almost entirely on live donations, predominantly from paid donors. Hence foreign patients fuel demand for "illegal transplants" supplied by paid donors. At the same time, the commercial demand for organs undermines the supply of organs available through domestic public health care systems. That is, donors from poor socioeconomic backgrounds will not donate an organ altruistically when they can receive a payment in return. In a stratified medical landscape where access to health care is contingent on socioeconomic status, medical tourism and the commercial exchange of organs have become an inevitable feature of the transplant industry. Put differently, the commercial expansion of the transplant industry is dependent on illegal supply.

Organ Transplantation in Egypt

Organ transplantation relies on live donations across the Islamic world, where cultural (e.g., religious and/or ethical concerns over brain death) and practical obstacles (e.g., limited infrastructure to support deceased kidney donation programs) to deceased donation persist (Sharif 2012). However, contrary to Western altruistic norms situated in a context of relative wealth, most live donations are characterized by commercial transactions, predominantly organized through intermediaries who link prospective buyers with sellers. In Egypt organ transplantation has relied on live donations from "emotionally related" donors since the first kidney transplant was performed in Mansoura in 1976.

For decades legislators could not agree on how to provide a framework to regulate organ donation because of deep-rooted divisions over the legitimacy of cadaveric donations. From a medicolegal perspective the procurement of organs from brain-dead patients was considered unethical because the patients were not "legally" dead. According to the law, a patient could not be considered dead until all his/her organs had failed, that is, the heart of the patient had stopped beating (Paris and Nour 2010). Meanwhile, religious scholars argued that the soul of a brain-dead patient was still lingering and had not yet passed over to the other side (Oliver et al. 2010). According to Islamic custom, preserving the bodily sanctity of the dead ensures safe passage to the afterlife, preventing fragmentation and displacement of the soul. Although religious opinions differed, influential voices from the Muslim Brotherhood communicated a widespread concern that the body of the deceased could not complete its journey to the afterlife "in parts." The late Shaykh Ash-Sha'arâwî (1911–1998), for example, opposed organ transplantation in all its forms. He argued that "the body belongs to God and to God alone." Organ donation was therefore impermissible (*harâm*) and in opposition to *Sharî'a* law. This position was contested and overruled by a *fatwa* (Islamic decree) passed by the Grand Sheikh Mohamed Sayed Tantawy in 1997 permitting organ transplantation between Muslims (Hamdy 2012). Nevertheless, kidney transplants continue to be limited to donations from living donors.

Providing a more novel perspective, a transplant physician I interviewed in Cairo suggested that Egyptians have a cultural attachment to the dead going back to the time of the Pharaohs and the rituals associated with mummification. This, he argued, explained the cultural resistance to deceased donation in Egypt (personal correspondence, 2014). However, this cultural attachment to the bodies of the dead did not apply to the bodies of paid living donors and the realities of a society divided along lines of race, gender, and wealth. In the 30 years in which legislators remained at an impasse over the regulation of organ donation, the commercial exchange of kidneys became established as the primary means of donation.

Egypt's historical significance and geographic position at the center of the Arab world makes it one of the most influential countries in the Middle East and North Africa. Foreign patients seeking transplantation in Egypt are attracted by its geographic accessibility, a long-established medical fraternity, relatively low costs, and the availability of (paid) donors. In 2007 the Egyptian Society of Nephrology estimated that at least 500 kidney transplants are performed in Egypt annually, more than any other country in North Africa (El-Agroudy et al. 2007). In 2008 it was estimated that more than 70% of transplants are performed using living unrelated donors, with a significant number of patients coming from neighboring countries (Barsoum 2008; 2017). Foreign patients mainly come from the Arab states of the Persian Gulf and/or countries with a connection to the Islamic world (e.g., Kosovo, Albania, Lebanon, North Macedonia) (Shimazono 2007; Van Balen et al. 2016; al-Bugami et al. 2018). However, with a population of 95 million people, most organ recipients are of Egyptian nationality (Barsoum 2008; Shaheen 2017). About 20,000 new patients require transplant surgery or dialysis per year. Because of inflation and the rising cost of food (in the years before and after the revolution, 2008–2019), many Egyptians live on a diet of subsidized bread, oil, and sugar. Poor diets have contributed to obesity, diabetes, and kidney failure. Yet access to transplantation is inaccessible for most of the population. A report released by the Egyptian Initiative for Personal Rights (EIPR) estimated that out-of-pocket expenses account for 89% of the total spending on health in Egypt (EIPR 2009). According to the World Bank (2018), out-of-pocket payments in Egypt have been fixed at 61% of total health spending over the past decade, more than double the average of other countries in the Middle East and North Africa. Although transplantation is partly subsidized, state sponsored treatment is limited to people with the right connections and family members willing to donate. This effectively rules out most of the Egyptian population from having access to transplant services. The wider labor force working in informal sectors of the economy who are not covered by the social security system are even further marginalized (Roushdy and Selwaness 2017).

Organ Markets and Subjective Ethics

Although the official position of the Egyptian Ministry of Health has always been to procure organs from altruistic donors, it was clear from my conversations with transplant professionals and their patients that organ donation was premised on a commercial exchange. When I spoke to patients at a dialysis clinic in Cairo, it was apparent that, despite medical reports affirming the health of organ donors living with one kidney (see López-Navidad and Caballero 2003), patients continued to worry about the medical risks involved. They also feared the disruption of family ties and the guilt they would face for having accepted a kidney from a loved one. Similar to the patients I interviewed in North Macedonia (see my interview with Yusef earlier in this chapter), continuing with dialysis or purchasing an organ from a stranger was preferable to asking a relative for a donation. One patient receiving dialysis explained, "People will not donate their kidney if there is an alternative. If my daughter needed a kidney, I would rather pay to get it off someone I don't know rather than my other child." Another commented, "I don't want my family or anyone I know to donate their kidney. If I were to accept a donation from them, I would always be in their debt." According to one physician, Ahmed, at a transplant clinic in Cairo, "Intra-familial donations are often costlier than a commercial agreement with an unrelated donor. I mean this both psychologically and financially." He explained, "Related donors have a higher level of depression, due to pressure from the family and community to donate to a respected family member. On the other hand, there is often more money involved when a relative is asked to donate, because of inheritance requests, for example." Ahmed continued, "I know one patient who had to give his sister his inheritance in return for her kidney. I know of another who had to make his brother co-owner of his restaurant." He paused to make sure I was paying attention. "They say, 'I am giving you your life, so you should give me my livelihood.'"

Contrary to the "gift of life" rhetoric espoused by the international transplant community, organ donation in Egypt (and many other countries) is not viewed as a heroic or altruistic act. It is a calculated act of human survival in a precarious environment.[8] In Egypt organ donation is a source of social tension and contention, in large part, because of the absence of a culture of public organ sharing and the promise of reciprocity that such a system represents. In an environment marred by political malfeasance and socioeconomic decline, the organ trade emerged as an informal economic activity for significant parts of the population. The already negated lives of Cairo's urban poor were marked out as expendable and designated as donors. Whereas patients in otherwise socially and economically comfortable families had much to gain from organ replacement, the poor viewed it as yet another example of government exploitation and neglect. For relatively wealthy patients the organ trade offered a vital source of life beyond the oppressive needle of a dialysis machine. For others, it was a source of income, propelled by economic decline, forced displacement, migration, marginalization, poverty, and pervasive inequality. In 2011 more than 20% of Egyptians lived on $1 a day (Rutherford and Sowers 2018). According to a report by the World Food Program, 3.8 million people were classified as poor in the Greater Cairo region with limited access to education, food, housing, and health care (World Food Program 2013). In a context where large segments of the population were and continue to be deprived of basic health care, housing, and employment, the indignation of poverty has been normalized as a feature of society. A poor person selling a kidney is nothing out of the ordinary. It is part of the natural order of things, a legacy of decades of crony capitalism and structural inequality (Joya 2011).

In the first two decades of transplantation (1976–2009) impoverished sellers would frequent hospitals and dialysis centers to negotiate a price for one of their kidneys directly with patients and/or their physicians (Hamdy 2012; Barsoum 2017). Without any formal legislation regulating transplant practice, organs were legitimately sourced from a relatively large pool of living unrelated donors, most of whom were in financial hardship. Nevertheless, demand for kidneys continued to outweigh supply. Over time the compensation requested by donors increased beyond the purchasing power of the average Egyptian, leading to the recruitment of patients from neighboring countries who could pay a higher premium. A temporary nonlegislative ban on all unrelated organ donation was introduced in 1992 by the Egyptian Society of Nephrology, out of concern for Egypt's reputation as a destination for transplant tourism (Hedges 1992). The Egyptian Medical Syndicate, the professional association that licences doctors, formally rescinded the ban the following year after a decline in transplant activity was recorded. In the absence of a national transplant program, donor and recipient pairs were required to complete routine paperwork administered by the Syndicate to ensure that the donation was free of financial transactions. Although it was widely acknowledged that these agreements were commercial in nature, the level of oversight involved in this bureaucratic procedure helped achieve a minimal "ethical" standard, insofar as the transplants were carried out in legitimate hospitals by reputable surgeons. The medical outcomes were generally positive for both donors and recipients (Barsoum 2008). Under these circumstances, organ sales were considered wrong only when there was a perceived sense of exploitation, generally understood as an act of explicit violence, that is, forced organ removal or organ trafficking. This bounded sense of ethics was brought under close scrutiny, however, when the global media began reporting on "Cairo's black market in organs" (NBC/Associated Press 2009).

The Transplantation of Human Organs and Tissues Act: Egypt

As political and social tensions were coming to the fore, the organ trade served as a source of embarrassment and disrepute for the transplant profession and an indictment of a beleaguered Egyptian state (New Humanitarian 2011; McGrath 2009). Although organ sales between Egyptian nationals was broadly tolerated, reports of wealthy patients from the Persian Gulf purchasing kidneys from impoverished Egyptians was considered a national scandal. The Egyptian Society of Nephrology lobbied the state for a national transplant law to bring Egyptian transplant practice into line with international ethical standards (Hamdy 2012). Under pressure from civil society and partly in response to a growing sense of discontent with the Mubarak regime, the Transplantation of Human Organs and Tissues Act (Law 5/2010) was established in 2010.[9] The law, which prohibits the sale or purchase of organs, introduced a range of criminal penalties. It also established a formal waiting list and formalized a consent process that required organ donors and recipients to sign consent forms attesting to the altruistic nature of the donation. Significantly, the act provided for the development of a deceased donor program, ending the decades-long debate over the permissibility of cadaveric donation.

The legislative emphasis of the law is punitive in scope, bringing unethical transplant practices (e.g., the purchase or sale of organs) under the remit of criminal punishment. Subject to the provisions outlined in the act (Articles 16–26), intermediaries facilitating commercial transactions and doctors found to have performed illegal transplant procedures are subject to a maximum prison term of 7 years. Hospitals and medical facilities that host illegal operations can be fined up to E£100k (Egyptian pounds) and/or closed indefinitely. In cases where the donor dies as a consequence of illegal transplant activity, the people responsible are subject to life imprisonment (Article 18). In 2017 sentencing was increased to include higher fines, longer jail terms and the death penalty (see chapter 6).

In passing this law, the government assumed that the introduction of criminal sanctions would put an end to organ trading, promote altruistic donations, and thereby restore the public image of Egyptian transplant medicine. Against a backdrop of civil unrest, the Transplantation of Human Organs and Tissues Act provided the Mubarak regime with an opportunity to demonstrate strong political action against a recognized threat. Speaking to the national press, Assistant Health Minister Hamid Abaza declared, "This law will bring the organ trade in Egypt down to a minimum. . . . With a law like this, patients will not need to seek organs in an illegal manner" (New Humanitarian 2011). The WHO regional director for the Eastern Mediterranean, Hussein A. Gezairy, was similarly confident in his appraisal, commending the new law as a "significant step towards ending illegal organ trafficking" (New Humanitarian 2011).

The Transplantation of Human Organs and Tissues Act was not formally enacted until June 2010, several months after receiving parliamentary approval. In the years before the Egyptian revolution, during which time Mohamed Morsi and the Muslim Brotherhood were elected into government before being ousted in a coup d'état led by incumbent president Abdel Fattah al-Sisi, the momentum that had carried organ donation to the forefront of the political agenda had shifted toward a regime centered on military control. The enforcement of the law was further set back by a judiciary marred by corruption and scandal under the Mubarak regime and sent into administrative disarray following the coup in 2013 (Ketchley 2017).

More significantly, the substantive merit of the law suffered from a number of legal loopholes couched in vague and open-ended language. According to Article 3, transplants between Egyptians and foreign nationals other than spouses are prohibited. However, transplants can be performed between foreign nationals of one nationality "at the request of the State to which the donor and recipient belong." What this means is that, provided that a recipient and a donor receive approval by the relevant embassy, as evidenced by a letter declaring that the donation is consensual and altruistically motivated, the transplant can be sanctioned, "as determined by the executive regulations of this law." Article 4 allows for donation between non-relatives under exceptional circumstances, upon approval by a "special medical committee" nominated by the Minister of Health. As there is no guidance as to what these circumstances consist of the approving committee has wide discretion in making its decision. Rather than discourage foreign nationals from traveling to Egypt for transplantation, the law provides legal clearance for transplants between foreign nationals and non-Egyptian donors. Hence one major implication of the law is to shift the recruitment of organ donors or sellers away from Egyptian nationals toward migrant populations. Under Article 16 anyone who buys or sells a kidney is subject to prosecution. As a consequence of the ambiguous wording of the legislation, it is unclear how or when an individual who agrees to sell an organ (kidney, liver, cornea, etc.) might be recognized as a victim.[10] The lack of clarification suggests that it is only when organ sales occur in the legal, juridical context of "trafficking in persons" that the exploitation of organ sellers is recognized as a social wrong. This lack of clarity is particularly problematic for undocumented migrants, who, despite being exploited for their organs, sex, and/or labor, are branded "illegal" and excluded from state protection.

Prohibition and Symbolic Reward

Dr. Hassam was waiting at his desk. He invited me to sit down and asked his secretary to bring us two coffees. At the time of our interview, the transplant law had been in effect for four years, albeit subject to the setbacks outlined. I was interested to learn what effect the law had had, if any, on the organ trade. I asked Dr. Hassam whether in his opinion prohibition had been a positive development, reducing the exploitation of paid donors. He responded with a question: "How do you convince someone who has no employment, no access to education for their children, no support from the community or government to donate their organs for nothing?" His secretary returned with coffee. He waited for her to leave and continued. "How can I ask them [living unrelated donors] to donate an organ and get nothing in return? If that person was to accept, they would not be sane. No rational person would do this."

Part of the logic for banning organ sales is that commercialism undermines altruism and social solidarity (Satz 2015: 425). Yet it is unclear how banning organ sales will increase altruism in Egypt when there was never an altruistic system to begin with. If there was widespread altruism, commercialization would be unnecessary. However, in the absence of a reciprocal organ-sharing system, a market for organs is inevitable. Notwithstanding the illegal nature of the organ trade, the sale of organs is tacitly accepted and rationalized as a mutually beneficial transaction: The economic situation of the organ seller improves while saving the life of the organ recipient. Although the trade in organs is publicly maligned, in practice organ markets are considered a practical solution to the surplus demand for organs.

Dr. Hassam suggested that the health authorities in Egypt were in denial of the organ trade: "Global political pressure comes to nothing, because the public here in Egypt are not upset about this. People go to the lab and arrange payment. They are happy that there is availability. Business is good for the medical community, so they are happy." Two-thirds of the transplants performed in Egypt are between unrelated living donors (Barsoum 2013). Across the Middle East and North African region, living related and nonrelated kidney transplants account for almost 85% of transplant activity (Shaheen 2017). Despite the legislative prohibition on the organ trade and the establishment of an oversight committee charged with enforcing the strict provisions of the Transplantation of Human Organs and Tissues Act, organ sales have persisted.[11] Dr. Hassam explained further: "They [doctors] do not care where the organ source comes from, once they have work to do. The middlemen are also happy, because they can make a lot of money from this business. This is why there is no pressure. Why bring in an alternative for the sake of ethics? The moral argument does not accommodate the reality."

The continued reliance on organ markets suggests that the substantive merit of the law rests on its symbolic value, a rhetorical commitment to international ethical standards. As our meeting ended, Dr. Hassam shared some candid advice: "When it comes to selling a kidney, the importance of symbolic reward is immense. I always tell people to please never think you are selling an organ, you are donating. This is not selling and buying. You are being paid for your time and rewarded for your good deed."

Although the law sets out a normative position prohibiting the commercial payment of donors, it fails to address the conditions behind the organ trade in any meaningful way. On the contrary, it obscures the broader socioeconomic conditions that render individuals subject to the exploitation of others through the administration of a superficial consent process. This consent process ostensibly differentiates legitimate or altruistic organ donations from illegal or paid donations. If a consent form has been signed (by both the donor and the recipient) and approved by the Higher Committee on Organ Transplants, the transplant is considered legitimate. The overriding purpose of this administrative performance is to demonstrate that there is no commercial agreement between the donor and the recipient. The consent process protects medical staff and hospitals from accusations of organ theft and/or organ trafficking. It does nothing to improve the circumstances of organ sellers. Rather, it enables the transplant profession to distance itself from a scenario where a "consensual" organ sale results in explicit harm.

After the events of the Arab Spring (2011) spending on public health decreased, with a greater emphasis being placed on the military and internal security budget (Rios 2015; WHO 2016). Egypt spends 1.5% of its gross domestic product (GDP) on public health (WHO 2016; World Bank 2018). This is less than the average for countries of the same socioeconomic level (e.g., India, Morocco, Philippines, Pakistan). Consequently, government hospitals in Cairo are overcrowded, unsanitary, and critically underresourced. The financial burden currently imposed on the state budget by renal replacement therapy has added further pressure on government resources during a period of sustained economic decline (Barsoum 2013; Hamdy 2016). With little incentive to donate an organ altruistically and in the absence of a national organ procurement program, the organ trade has served as a market solution to the shortage of transplantable organs. In the same way that informal networks free formally recognized firms from the constraints imposed on them by social control and institutional norms, transplant clinics depend on informal networks to supply organs invariably sourced from individuals in financial hardship.

Prohibition is rationalized on the basis that purchasing an organ from an impoverished person takes unfair advantage of their economic circumstances and is therefore exploitative. It is presumed that prohibiting organ sales will prevent exploitation and eradicate trafficking for organ removal. Yet only the most exceptional claims of exploitation, where there is explicit evidence of nonconsensual harm against a victim-citizen, generate public outrage and/or receive legal recognition. This effectively creates a hierarchy of exploitive practices in accordance with the level of coercion and/or deception that precedes a commercial organ sale. The problem with this type of reasoning is that claims of exploitation are accepted as credible only in extreme circumstances (e.g., forced organ removal), after a violent exchange has taken place. This exceptionalism is politically and socially harmful, obscuring the legal structures and policy decisions that position people in exploitive relations manifest in trafficking claims. Under existing national (e.g., Egypt) and international (e.g., Council of Europe 2014a) legislation, any individual who knowingly enters into an agreement to buy or sell a kidney is subject to criminal prosecution. Organ donors who are perceived to have participated in a criminal activity are afforded little sympathy. Their claim to corporeal sanctity is forfeited when they "decide" to sell a kidney. Ethical concerns are further removed when an organ is sourced from a foreign body discursively associated with criminality.

When normative expectations are low, exploitation is no longer exceptional. Therefore the threshold for what is considered degrading, unfair, or intolerable is much higher for someone whose exploitation is taken for granted. For example, an employer might argue that paying an undocumented worker below the national minimum wage is not particularly exploitative. The employer is undoubtedly taking advantage of the worker's limited bargaining power. However, it could be argued that under the circumstances (i.e., illegal migration), the outcome is mutually beneficial: The employer benefits from cheap labor and the undocumented worker receives payment, albeit at a relatively unfair level of remuneration. Although there is a clear disparity of value with regard to the unfair working conditions, the wrongful use of an undocumented worker for said purposes is perhaps more tolerable than it would otherwise be for a victim-citizen legally entitled to a minimum wage. The tacit approval of organ sales from paid donors is rationalized in a similar way.

In the absence of a reciprocal organ-sharing system, intermediaries and other interested parties (e.g., hospitals) operate according to a human value dividend that is determined along lines of race, class, and gender, separating the donors from recipients, the sellers from buyers. Accordingly, when the sale of organs from impoverished Egyptians was called into question, recruitment shifted to migrant donors.

The 2016 Arab Development Index reports that 43% of Egyptians work in the informal economy. This figure does not account for the thousands of migrant workers who are not included in official records. Refugees and other migrant workers are the surplus labor force of the informal labor market. With expired passports, invalid visas, and no work permits, undocumented migrants, in particular, are at constant risk of arrest and detention and are in no position to negotiate the terms of their employment. Categorized as illegal and denied state protection, their bodies are marked out as expendable and subject to the exploitation of others. It is because of their structural vulnerability, created by law and policy, that migrants provide a preferential source of organs over citizens.

To understand why certain people or groups are positioned as organ sellers, we need to consider exploitation beyond its individualistic legal rendering as a feature of human trafficking or modern slavery. Conceptualized as a violent crime, exploitation is represented as a grave moral wrong inflicted by criminal perpetrators against passive victims. The social experience of exploitation, however, is much more variegated, contingent on particular circumstances and environments, and mediated by legal rules and political conditions. The people who feature in this book were compelled to consider risky medical procedures, carried out with little or no oversight, despite having no possibility of legal recourse should they be subject to any harm, medical or otherwise. Yet, in a context of legal marginalization and social exclusion, selling a kidney was widely considered the least bad option. None of the people I interviewed were recognized by the Egyptian authorities as victims of trafficking, forced labor, or slavelike practices. Nevertheless, they were clearly exploited.

A selective focus on the extreme suffering of individual victims, typified in governmental accounts of modern slavery, steers critical attention away from the systemic causes of victimhood toward specific abuses that have little or no connection to how exploitation is experienced over time and space. This singular focus on criminality lends authenticity and moral purpose to the pursuit of punitive responses that fail to locate suffering within broader political and structural contexts. Formulaic criminal responses follow that overlook important intersections of agency, identity, culture, and politics. In the next chapters I excavate and examine the processes of legal dispossession, criminalization, and marginalization that underpin the exploitative relations beneath the organ trade. In so doing, I interrogate the background rules and legal structures that produce vulnerability to exploitation by state and non-state actors.

The patients and transplant professionals that I interviewed for this chapter rationalized organ trading as a necessary measure: a vital source of organs for kidney transplantation and a source of income for impoverished donors. Public indifference and nonenforcement of preexisting criminal penalties allowed the trade to establish itself as part of the supply chain for the transplant industry. Ironically, although the patients I interviewed considered it ethical, even honorable, to refuse an organ donated from a relative or a friend, the conditions of poverty and indebtedness that compelled certain individuals to sell a kidney were accepted as a fact of life. Similarly, the transplant professionals I spoke with viewed the organ trade as a practical solution to the organ shortage. In contrast to their international colleagues, they considered it unethical *not* to pay a donor.

What these interviews reveal is not so much a resistance to organ donation but a legacy of social inequalities in basic health care and state welfare. A change in public attitude, following reports of wealthy Arabs purchasing organs from poor Egyptians, forced the issue firmly onto the political agenda. However, state intolerance and public concern over Egyptian organ sellers did not extend to the bodies of migrant populations, nominally cast off as illegal regardless of their actual legal status, that is, asylum seeker or refugee. Whereas transactions among Egyptian donors were condemned, trading from and among migrant donors increased. This trade was aided by legal loopholes and political indifference to the welfare of migrant groups. The prohibition of organ sales did not limit or prevent organ trading. What it did do was create the legal architecture for an illicit market in organs. It was at the point of prohibition that trading in organs ceased to be an ad hoc commercial activity that primarily involved impoverished Egyptians. Instead, the organ trade became an illicit market in its own right, generating illegal profits from the bodies of marginalized communities. Prohibition altered the dynamics of the trade, changing recruitment practices, increasing the role of intermediaries, and reducing the bargaining position of organ sellers. In informal street markets located in Cairo's marginalized neighborhoods, intermediaries gather in coffee shops to broker organ transactions and solicit kidneys from migrants looking for a source of income and a route out of poverty. It is in these marginal spaces of the urban economy that Cairo's organ trade developed into an extralegal activity coordinated by a network of brokers. In the next chapter I explore the actors and activities that constitute this network.

3

ORGAN TRADING NETWORKS

WHEN I ARRIVED IN CAIRO IN 2014, I contacted local NGOs that worked with "people of concern" on issues relating to forced migration and human trafficking. I was looking for information on the organ trade and was curious whether they had encountered anyone who had sold a kidney. A young man working as a translator for a charitable organization[1] assisting refugees claimed that the organ trade had ended with the revolution. "There were some issues before, but now everything is different. We have a strong government and good security," he reasoned. He reminded me of the new law prohibiting organ sales that had been passed in 2010, referencing this as evidence that there was no longer an active trade in organs. Before the meeting concluded, he offered some advice: "The organ trade is dangerous, and it is a subject best avoided. If I were you, I would not pursue this any further. Your nationality [Irish] won't protect you." At the time two journalists from Al Jazeera, a news broadcaster based in Qatar, had been arrested for reporting "false news with the aim of creating chaos" (Al Jazeera 2014; 2019).[2] As I was leaving the meeting, an Eritrean woman who had overheard our conversation tapped me on the shoulder and arranged to meet me the following day. Yasmin suggested we talk at a café in Talat Harp in downtown Cairo. She claimed that NGOs no longer had any autonomy in Egypt and that they could not discuss certain issues. The organ trade was one of them. "The government wants to protect the image of the country. The people you are talking to will not compromise their work by giving you information. This would

FIGURE 1. Street markets where brokers meet with organ sellers to negotiate organ exchange. Photo by author.

not look good for them." She leaned toward me, speaking in a whisper. "The Mukhabarat [secret police] are monitoring these organizations. The more questions you ask, the more you expose yourself to potential problems." Yasmin advised me to visit "street markets" in low-income neighborhoods where refugees and Cairo's poor reside. It was in these marginal spaces of the urban economy that organ traders gathered to broker and negotiate the price of organs, kidneys in particular. "If you want to learn about the organ trade," she said, "you have to go to the neighborhoods yourself and speak with the communities there."

I spoke with several people in an official or institutional capacity about the organ trade throughout my time in Cairo. In general, I was met with silence or issued unsubtle warnings about the limitations of conducting this type of research in Cairo. Most aid workers and representatives I spoke with claimed to have no knowledge of organ markets. Others insisted that they had only heard rumors of organ trafficking in the Sinai region, where armed groups were responsible for the trafficking of women, narcotics, and organs into Israel. The organ trade was cast as a border security issue controlled by criminal organizations and linked to illegal migration. The reasons that people might feel compelled to sell an organ were displaced by an emphasis on the criminal events unfolding in Egypt's border regions, namely, Israel, Libya, and Sudan. Although much has been written about the operations of "criminal syndicates" and "criminal enterprises" that are alleged to be responsible for the "global traffic of organs" (OSCE 2013; Scheper-Hughes 2000), there has been a critical deficit of empirical research into the social organization of organ trading networks in countries identified as having an active organ trade. Rather, tangential and generalized claims have been reproduced from a select number of cases at the judicial level (Medicus Clinic case 2011; *U.S. v. Rosenbaum* 2012; *The State v. Netcare Kwa-Zulu (Pty) Limited* 2010), reinforcing a partial conception of organized crime and organ trafficking at odds with the diverse experiences of individuals engaged, at various levels, in organ trading.

In contrast to the received wisdom of intergovernmental reports (Council of Europe and United Nations 2009; OSCE 2013; UNODC 2018) suggesting that transnational criminal groups recruit donors from overseas and coerce them into organ sale (primarily in countries with weak border controls), in this chapter I demonstrate how the organ trade in Egypt emerged as an informal economic activity. I draw on the perspectives of organ sellers and organ brokers to examine the implications of criminal sanctions following the establishment of the Transplantation of Human Organs and Tissues Act of 2010. Furthermore, I explore the development of criminal synergies in Cairo's informal street markets. To go beyond the media invective surrounding the organ trade, it was important to gain the perspective of organ sellers and organ brokers, in particular, to understand how they come to rationalize what they do. In doing this, my aim is to forge new insight into the different relations and activities that make up organ trading networks in the Egyptian context.

Whereas Egyptian, Syrian, Yemeni, and other nationals are involved in the organ trade, the findings I present in this chapter reflect personal encounters with Sudanese (Sudan and South Sudan) nationals who sold or arranged the sale of kidneys. Their accounts provide a unique insight into the social organization of organ markets in Cairo and the political and social arrangements that compel people to consider selling a kidney. The interviews presented in this chapter were conducted in 2014 before criminal sentencing was increased in 2017 (see Chapter 6).

Narrating the Threat of Organized Crime

Organized crime is an umbrella term used to refer to planned and coordinated illegal activities, of which there are different types, forms, and structures, carried out by multiple offenders in the pursuit of profit (see Varese 2010; Paoli 2002). The threat of *transnational* organized crime underpins the rationale behind the anti-trafficking framework. Various reports, academic commentaries, and media sources convey this threat and attest to the virulence and menace of an international criminal order, which threatens to undermine the integrity and survival of democratic governments (see, e.g., UNODC 2015a; Sterling 1994; and Shelley 1995). In this contemporary narration of organized crime, the conventional representation of criminal organizations, as hierarchically structured homogeneous groups, has been revised to include transnationality, suggestive of a widening domain of criminality under the control of a new global mafia (see, e.g., Galeotti 2014; and Nicaso and Lamothe 1995). Admonishing against the common threat to nation-states presented by transnational organized crime, the preamble to the United Nations Convention against Transnational Organized Crime (2000) declares:

> If crime crosses borders, so must law enforcement. If the rule of law is undermined not only in one country, but in many, then those who defend it cannot limit themselves to purely national means. If the enemies of progress and human rights seek to exploit the openness and opportunities of globalization for their purposes, then we must exploit those very same factors to defend human rights and defeat the forces of crime, corruption and trafficking in human beings. (UNODC 2000c: Preamble)

The language of risk and security associated with traditional organized crime has been augmented with an emphasis on the transnational, creating a sense of urgency around interventions that target the mobility of suspected criminals. Terms such as *transnational* and *cross-border* are indicative of an "alien conspiracy" with designs to infiltrate and corrupt the integrity of the nation-state (Ruggiero 2000). Problematized in this way, organized crime is conveyed as an external threat, acting on the state rather than within it.

Transnational criminal organizations are said to be responsible for all manner of social ills, resulting in the victimization of millions of innocent people (UNODC 2015a). However, it is the moral outrage associated with human trafficking that has elevated transnational crime to the forefront of the global political agenda. Allied with the transnational discourse of organized crime is the narration of threat advanced by the metanarrative of human trafficking (for further discussion, see Weitzer 2011; and Snajdr 2013). This threat is conveyed through the victimization of trafficked persons: "Human trafficking is a global problem and one of the world's most shameful crimes, affecting the lives of millions of people around the world and robbing them of their dignity. Traffickers deceive women, men and children from all corners of the world and force them into exploitative situations every day" (UNODC 2015a). A popular vernacular is composed through the suffering of idealized victims, exemplified in sensational accounts of human trafficking, for example, defenseless women being sold into sexual slavery or young children being kidnapped for their organs by unscrupulous traffickers. Yet as Weitzer (2011), Ellison (2015), and Steinfatt (2011) demonstrate in their studies of the sex trade, such macabre accounts apply only to a fraction of the reported millions of people who are trafficked. This singular emphasis on violent crime constructs a belief system at odds with the diverse experiences of individuals who are engaged in criminal activities and/or exploited for various purposes, obscuring the social context and relations within which criminality is situated. Critically, the perceived threat that this metanarrative represents lends credibility to policy interventions centered on cross-border policing and the apprehension of criminal perpetrators, policies that paradoxically contribute to the exploitation of the people they ostensibly protect (see Chapter 4).

The definition of trafficking outlined in Article 3(a) of the Trafficking Protocol (UNODC 2000b) advances a formulaic understanding of exploitation composed of three elements: an action (e.g., recruitment), a means (e.g., the threat or use of force), and a purpose (e.g., the removal of organs). States that have ratified the protocol, which supplements the United Nations Convention Against Organized Crime (UNODC 2000c), are encouraged to adopt a common definition of human trafficking to support coordinated efforts to "prevent and combat transnational organized crime more effectively" (UNODC 2000c: Preamble). However, in practice, it is not always clear when someone has been trafficked. For instance, individuals who sell an organ but do not clearly satisfy all three elements required to establish the offense of "trafficking in persons" are unlikely to be recognized as victims of trafficking (Yea 2010; Mendoza 2011). This might explain why relatively few cases of trafficking in persons for organ removal appear at the judicial level. Moreover, in most states where it is a criminal offense to buy or sell an organ, Iran being the exception, organ sellers who do not identify as trafficked victims are subject to prosecution. Hence individuals who have been exploited for their organs are unlikely to report any instances of abuse that they may have experienced as a consequence of their involvement in organ markets, making it difficult to determine the actual nature and extent of organ trading.

Organ Trafficking

Organized crime and violence are synonymous with illegal markets. Mafia groups such as the Italian Cosa Nostra, the Russian Mafia, the Chinese Triads, and the Japanese Yakuza are represented in the media as the archetype of organized crime. Films such as *The Godfather* and *Eastern Promises* depict large-scale criminal organizations composed of an ethnic brotherhood of callous mafiosi engaged in the provision of illegal goods and services, superimposed against a backdrop of murder and endemic vice. On-screen mafiosi typically trade in violence to gain control over territories, establish protection rackets, corrupt public officials, and monopolize illegal markets.

Empirical studies on illicit trade, however, present a different picture. As Letizia Paoli points out, though large-scale criminal organizations such as the Cosa Nostra and the Yakuza do exist, "they are neither exclusively involved in illegal market activities, nor is their development and internal configuration the result of illegal market dynamics" (Paoli 2002: 52). Although members are often successful players in the illegal marketplace, these organizations cannot be reduced to their involvement in illegal markets. Indeed, their existence predates the formation and expansion of modern illegal markets, most notably the trade in drugs, arms, human beings, and organs. Studies of drug trafficking, for example, have demonstrated that the supply of illegal commodities largely takes place in a disorganized way, because of the constraints of product illegality (Hobbs 1998). The illegal status of products constrains production and distribution, preventing the consolidation of a large-scale criminal enterprise. Moreover, a disaggregated structure makes it more difficult for law enforcement to detect illegal activities and seize assets. Accordingly, the supply of illegal goods and services is better explained by loose networks of people responding to opportunities as they arise, illegal or otherwise.

Even though the traditional mob boss model has been systematically challenged by a number of scholars (see Block and Chambliss 1981; and Hobbs 1998), it remains central to the working assumptions of many legal practitioners and law enforcement agencies (Farrell et al. 2014; Klerks 2001). Subscribing to a rigid crime-fighting doctrine, law enforcement strategies concentrate on the arrest and prosecution of professional criminals, the disruption of criminal networks, the policing of borders, and the seizure of assets (Klerks 2001; Ruggiero 2001; Chuang 2010). Yet, despite significant investment into zero-tolerance policies and the development of international agreements to coordinate efforts against transnational crime (e.g., the United Nations Convention Against Transnational Crime and the additional protocols), the operational capacity of these investigative methods is significantly limited (Weitzer 2011; Chuang 2010; Farrell et al. 2014). Moreover, there is little evidence to suggest that victims benefit from this approach. Rather, it would seem that this instrumental search for perpetrators is a way of managing public concerns, by rendering organized crime as something material, identifiable, and predictable, as something that can be controlled and countered (Garland 2001). This consequentialist response to organized crime relieves the state of its responsibility for the social inequalities that engender modes of criminality, deflecting critical attention away from failed state policies (e.g., around migration, public health, labor, crime control) and toward a narrow pursuit of criminal justice. The framing of the organ trade as a human trafficking issue orchestrated by sophisticated criminal organizations is a key example of this political misdirection.

Public anxieties over organ harvesting have been diffused into a moralistic debate over organ sales, collapsing a complex humanitarian issue into a narrow bioethical calculus that negotiates the ethical parameters of what can be considered good transplant practice (using organs sourced from altruistic donors) and bad transplant practice (using organs sourced from commercial donors). Organ trafficking rings are understood to be responsible for driving the trade in organs, recruiting people from poor countries and trafficking them into various destinations for organ removal (Shimazono 2007; OHCHR 2013). Destination states that host illegal transplants are encouraged to increase their domestic supply of organs by altruistic means; otherwise, they risk infiltration by organized crime groups that specialize in organ trafficking (Kishore 2004; Council of Europe and United Nations 2009; International Summit on Transplant Tourism and Organ Trafficking 2008; WHO 2010). Essentially, the organ trade is conceptualized as a perversely criminal phenomenon, a social aberration far removed from the ethical domain of transplant medicine. However, this unambiguous representation is a false dichotomy.

There is no clear illegal-legal divide. Organ transplantation is perfectly legal; it is the trading of organs that is contested and prohibited.

Organ markets exist to service the surplus demand for organs generated, to a large extent, by the commercial expansion of the transplant industry. The transfer of transplant technologies is contingent on the supply of organs (L. Cohen 2001; Mendoza 2011; Yea 2010). When this supply cannot be satisfied by legal channels, organs are sourced from commercial donors or, in some instances, from individuals who have been coerced into having one or more of their organs removed. The informal networks that support the organ trade are not isolated units possessing a purely criminal modus operandi. These networks cross various divides: legal, quasi-legal, and the blatantly illegal (Bruinsma and Bernasco 2004). The individuals who assume different roles in informal networks are rarely specialists in a particular criminal enterprise; rather, they respond to relative opportunities in a given context (Nordstrom 2000; Castells 2011).

In 2010 the Transplantation of Human Organs and Tissues Act (Law 5/2010) was established in Egypt. This act made it a criminal offense to buy or sell an organ. In accordance with the Egyptian Law of Trafficking in Persons (Law 64/2010), individuals who are implicated in organ sales are subject to trafficking offenses (EIPR 2010).[3] Yet, despite the legislative prohibition against organ trading and the establishment of an oversight committee charged with enforcing the strict provisions of the act, commercial transplants have persisted in Egypt. Significant cultural resistance to organ donation and logistical and infrastructural limitations that inhibit the successful operation of a nationally regulated organ donor program continue to place an overreliance on live donors, most of whom require payment (see Chapter 2). Whereas organ sales remained public knowledge, the process became more hidden. Private clinics and analytic labs (where most sellers are matched with buyers) proliferated. This made it increasingly difficult for transplant professionals to monitor the treatment of organ recipients and organ sellers. Furthermore, owing to their precarious legal status, undocumented migrants became a key source of organ supplies, with no legal recourse for harms committed against them. Although the organ sellers I interviewed were exploited, they were not recognized as trafficking victims by the Egyptian authorities, nor did they identify themselves as victims of trafficking. Rather, their exploitation was bound up in their migrant status and a lack of opportunities to generate an income.

Migrant "Donors"

When I first met Azim, he was smoking a cigarette outside the metro in Tahrir Square. He walked toward me and suggested we talk at a different location. We sat down in a corner of a nearby bar and ordered two bottles of beer. Azim spoke about the financial problems he had experienced since coming to Egypt from Sudan, circumstances made worse by a sustained period of economic decline in the years following the Egyptian revolution. "I wanted to send money home to my family, but I couldn't find any work." Azim had struggled to find employment and was in debt to a local money lender with a reputation for violence. Azim was looking for work when he was approached by two men who offered him a solution. "There were two guys, a Sudanese and Egyptian," he said. "They asked me if I would sell my kidney. They told me not to speak to anyone about this and they would arrange everything. It would make my situation better, they promised." He paused to light another cigarette. "They took my passport and I signed some papers at the hospital. The operation was at midnight. I stayed for three days. My head was spinning, and I was in a lot of pain after the surgery." Azim sold his kidney in March 2014 for $5,000.

Migrant populations provide a key source of organs for Egypt's transplant industry. Barred from access to the formal labor market, migrants have little choice but to accept precarious labor conditions. Furthermore, migrants compete with locals for limited job opportunities in an unregulated, uncertain, and often hostile environment (see Thomas 2010; Grabska 2006; and Jacobsen et al. 2014). Excluded from state protection, migrants rely on the strength of their social relations to gain access to job opportunities (Jacobsen et al. 2014). Although Sudanese migrants have strong social ties in Egypt, owing to a tradition of shared migration between the two countries, employment options remain limited and working conditions fall well below what might be considered reasonable standards (Grabska 2006). Faced with occupational barriers in both the formal and informal sectors, migrants have to achieve an extraordinary level of labor flexibility, responding to available market opportunities, legal or otherwise (Kleemans and van de Bunt 1999). In other words, the legality of their activities is shaped according to existing opportunities and demands.

Informal street markets are important sites of economic production for marginalized populations who are disconnected from the official labor mar-

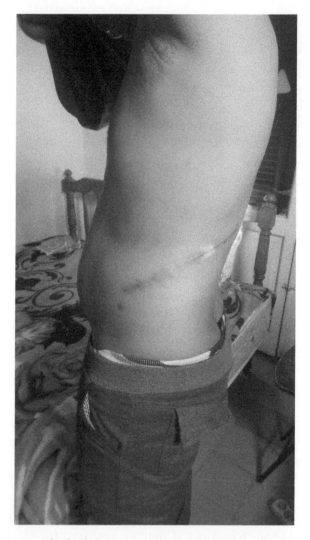

FIGURE 2. Azim after his kidney was removed in March 2014. Photo by author.

ket. Street markets provide a shared space to pool resources and organize economic activities. These markets consist of internally differentiated groups of stakeholders who routinely enter into associations, bargains, and partnerships, identifying demand and establishing supply chains (see also Kotiswaran 2008; and Meagher 2010). Responding to the surplus demand for organs, the organ trade has been identified as an alternative source of income generation for various stakeholders operating from Cairo's informal street markets.

Those who participate in one or more of the variegated activities that constitute organ trading networks are not professional criminals in the sense that they do not specialize in criminal activity. Nor do they cater to a specific market. Rather, this group represents an entrepreneurial core of migrants adapting to a challenging market environment, who "commute from illegality to legality and back again," to advance their own life choices (Ruggiero 2001: 42).

Numerous stakeholders are involved in the organ trade, each with different roles, functions, and identities that often overlap: transplant professionals, hospitals, brokers, service providers, corrupt officials. However, intermediaries, or brokers, play a key role in organizing and connecting the diverse networks that facilitate the continued expansion of the transplant industry. Critically, they occupy a strategic bridging position, linking up the various market players across the illegal-legal divide. The organ brokers I interviewed in 2014 explained how they worked in cooperation with other agents operating in Cairo's informal economy through a series of subcontracting arrangements and joint ventures, akin to formal capitalist structures (see Castells 2011). Brokers explained how they routinely exchanged services and knowledge with individuals or organizations in the formal economy, renegotiating and revising the boundaries of legitimate economic practice, along lines of mutual entrepreneurial promotion.

Organ Brokers

I met Solomon at a coffee shop in Ataba, a neighborhood in downtown Cairo mostly populated by Sudanese (from both Sudan and South Sudan) and Eritrean migrants. Solomon, a Sudanese national, had noticed me struggling to inhale smoke from a *shisha* pipe. We quickly developed a rapport and after subsequent conversations, generally while watching football during the World Cup tournament (2014), Solomon revealed some information about the organ trade: "Life in Cairo has been very difficult since the revolution, especially for people coming here because of the conflict in South Sudan. They sell everything they have to get here, and then there is nothing you can do: no help, no assistance. Egyptians cannot help themselves, so there is no way they can help us. With the way things are, the girl will sell her body to feed her family. . . . When you sell everything else, you sell your kidney." He continued, "There are secret places that we [migrant communities] know about. Coffee shops in Faisal and Ard El-Lewa, and here in Ataba. People come here to sell [a kidney]. The brokers make this possible. They are the ones who bring them to the hospital. Most of them are Sudanese."

The brokers were mediating on behalf of transplant physicians, acting as gatekeepers for patient-buyers and donor-sellers. Prohibition and the threat of criminal sanction changed the working conditions of the trade. What once was a self-regulating system with rudimentary oversight controlled by the Egyptian Medical Syndicate had become an extralegal activity loosely coordinated by a network of brokers with links to analytic labs and transplant centers in the Greater Cairo region. These brokers were responsible for soliciting and recruiting migrants for their kidney(s) and negotiating a price on behalf of profit-oriented transplant professionals. Their increased involvement in the coordination of organ trading has had a significant impact on the development of the trade from an informal economic activity into an organized crime.

In much of the literature on organ trafficking, organ brokers are represented as nefarious gangsters who prey on the weak and helpless (Scheper-Hughes 2000; Kumar 2003). These elusive criminals coerce passive victims into selling their organs. Or, in more fatalistic circumstances, they butcher and harvest body parts from innocent bystanders (Gutmann 2014). The overall image that is constructed is one of categorical deviance, inculcating an unambiguous image of brokers linked to criminal networks. My fieldwork, however, reveals a less sensational account of organ brokers, in sharp contrast to the one-dimensional caricature portrayed in the popular discourse framed around this issue. The brokers I interviewed (2014–2020) were part of a network of brokers and intermediaries with connections in both the informal and the formal economy. These intermediaries performed a number of different functions instrumental to the operation of organ markets. They were involved in the recruitment of organ sellers, the negotiation of fees, and the preparation of "official" paperwork, and crucially they were responsible for connecting buyers with sellers. The Sudanese brokers were generally involved in the recruitment of Sudanese migrants. However, depending on their relative skills and experience, they adopted more roles or functions that increased their level of involvement and subsequently their earning potential. Tissue typing and analytic labs emerged as the key nodes of activity linking up the various brokers in the networks.[4] Representatives from the labs formed partnerships with recruitment brokers, who operated both locally and transnationally. Organ sellers were recruited from the migrant community, whereas recipients were recruited domestically and internationally. When suitable donor-sellers were matched with recipient-customers, they were referred to hospitals or clinics where the surgery was performed.

This combination of flexible networking between local actors is more representative of the organ trade than the hierarchical structure of organized crime groups typified by the anti-trafficking discourse (Weitzer 2011; Snajdr 2013). In this way, more localized networks involved in the recruitment of migrants for organ sale can and do intersect with transnational networks through intermediaries recruiting buyer-recipients from overseas and/or smugglers moving people across national borders. It is this combination of flexible networking between local and global actors, within and between countries, that explains the transnational reach of the organ trade. The rudimentary structure of the organ trading networks described in this chapter did however evolve over time, largely in response to changing market conditions, with the development of an organized criminal group with a reputation for violence (see chapter 6).

Recruitment

In Cairo recruitment brokers operated in and around informal street markets spatially divided across different districts (e.g., Maadi, downtown Cairo, Ard El-Lewa, Faisal, Heliopolis, Nasr City, 6th of October), where they had links, either directly or indirectly through another intermediary, with tissue typing labs and/or hospitals with transplant facilities. Rather than compete for dominance over local territories, the various brokers or clusters of brokers were interconnected, exchanging information and adapting their activities accordingly. For example, brokers kept each other informed of the current market value of a kidney and exchanged information on potential targets considered more open to persuasion, often because of a particular individual's precarious circumstances. Brokers also referred sellers to other intermediaries when they were preoccupied with their regular occupations (security guards, street vendors, translators, etc.). Most of the Sudanese brokers I interviewed were primarily involved in the recruitment of Sudanese migrants and engaged with the trade on a temporary basis.

Shaker, a musician originally from Darfur, worked with a team of brokers recruiting organ sellers from Sudanese street markets in different locations around Cairo. He explained how he got involved in the recruitment process, after finding it difficult to secure employment.

I'm a musician but this work does not pay well. I needed to find another way to make money. I had a girlfriend, but she left me because I had nothing to give her. So, I started to ask people about their kidneys. I worked with some other guys in different places. One guy would stand by the corner every day asking about people, to know their situation and to see if they needed to find a way to get money. And then I would talk to them to see if they were interested in selling their kidney. If they were happy, I would bring them to get their papers stamped and then to a clinic for health checks. Maybe 10 people a week. . . . But, I don't do this anymore.

Shaker was quick to point out that he had done nothing wrong, explaining that he was "just trying to get by, like everybody else." He was uncomfortable referring to himself as a broker, insisting that he was providing a service: "This is just a service. If they want to sell, that is for them to decide. It is no problem to find people, but no one wants to talk about this. People want things. Sometimes this is the only way. They get paid what they are promised, and they are happy. Some of the people are stupid. I know one guy who sold his kidney because he wanted to buy a laptop and some speakers." According to Shaker most of the individuals that he referred to tissue typing labs had sought out his services: "You cannot go to a clinic by yourself. You have to be brought there by someone connected. This is the only way. Otherwise people will get suspicious, and that could cause some problems. Also, if people could go by themselves, we [the recruitment brokers] would lose business."

Kalib, a restaurant owner who occasionally connected recruitment brokers with tissue typing labs looking to increase their organ supply, provided a similar account: "Brokers have their own territories and work with specific labs and hospitals. There is no need to recruit people outside of Egypt as there is a plentiful supply of donors. But a lot of the buyers come from the Gulf."

However, conversations and interviews with people who sold a kidney suggest that in most cases they had only come to an agreement after a period of persistent solicitation, or, as outlined later, intimidation. Elaborating on Shaker's account of the recruitment process, several organ sellers commented on how brokers colluded with other "market dwellers" or "scouts," exchanging information on different individuals, particularly Sudanese asylum seekers who had recently arrived in Cairo. Zia, a Sudanese asylum seeker, age 22, explained: "Whenever you come to Egypt, people know that you are suffering. The brokers watch you and learn about your suffering. The Egyptian cannot come to you, but the Sudanese can approach you. He might say that we want to give you an idea to improve your situation; you will not lose anything. Then they offer you money. He offered me E£30,000 [about $2,000]."[5]

These scouts were usually Sudanese and had close ties to the community, working as street vendors, restaurants owners, housing agents, or hotel staff. In some cases they also acted as recruitment brokers. Hiba, a single mother with two children, was repeatedly solicited for her kidney while staying at a hotel shortly after arriving in Cairo. The hotel had been recommended by the smugglers who had organized her transport into Egypt. According to Hiba, hotel staff members had asked about her circumstances before she was solicited. After she left the hotel, she was pursued for over three months by two brokers, until she eventually relented and "agreed" to sell her kidney: "They don't give you time to think about what you want to do. They keep asking you, reassuring you. They say it is OK; it is going to be fine; this is good for you and your family. They introduced me to some guy who had already sold his kidney. They wanted me to see that he was happy. He said he was OK and that this was safe. But he did not look OK."

Other people who had sold a kidney reported similar experiences. Discussing his encounters with different recruitment brokers (Egyptian and Sudanese), Ahmed reflected on their unyielding perseverance: "I met these people in a coffee shop in Giza. They approached me several times. The first time I refused, and after that they were talking to me and talking to me until I agreed. I almost felt guilty for not doing it. . . . We met in different coffee shops. It was one guy from Sudan who convinced me. As soon as I agreed, he brought me to the lab for a health check and then I went for the operation. I didn't want to do this, but I needed to send money to my family. . . . The brokers knew about my situation."

Many of the people I spoke to felt that it was their responsibility to send money back to relatives who had supported them on their journey to Cairo and were dependent on their remittances. Men in particular expressed feelings of shame and guilt for failing to find gainful employment and to provide for their families, whom they had left behind in Sudan. Several people, male and female, cut contact with their families after selling a kidney. Ahmed explained, "I came to Cairo to help my family, but after maybe four months I still had nothing [money]. This is why I spoke to these people [brokers]. After I sold my kidney, I stopped calling home. I don't want to put shame on them."

This sense of shame was exploited by brokers as leverage to negotiate fees, to enforce compliance, and to maintain secrecy.

Negotiating Fees

Once an individual indicated that he or she was willing to sell one of their kidneys, the negotiation process began. This usually took place in an informal setting, such as a coffee shop or a restaurant, where a valuation for the kidney was deliberated between the prospective donor-seller and the recruiter. Often another intermediary, who has connections with a particular tissue typing lab or transplant clinic, was present. The initial recruiter would negotiate a price directly with the donor-seller before escorting the person to a lab for preliminary testing. Several people revealed that before any negotiation over a fee, they had consulted with an "adviser" to ascertain the current market value of a kidney. According to Mohamed, a 28-year-old Sudanese migrant, "There is a lady here [in Dokki] who tells people what they need to get paid. The price can change from year to year. It is going down now, as there are more and more donors. It is normal to donate your kidney this way. I met the brokers (two Egyptian and one Sudanese) in a coffee shop in Dokki to negotiate the price. One of them was from the lab; I think he was the secretary. After about an hour of talking, I negotiated a payment of $10,000. They tried to lower the price, but I knew what my kidney is worth."

The level of remuneration an organ seller received, or more pertinently was "offered," was contingent on his or her knowledge of the organ market. Depending on the seller's informational basis and subsequent ability to negotiate, the discrepancies in the level of payment received could be significant. For instance, the organ sellers that I interviewed in 2014 were paid between E£30,000 (about $2,000) and E£200,000 (about $14,000). That is a difference of E£170,000 ($12,000). This difference suggests a substantial divergence in market knowledge shared between organ sellers. Notably, the individuals who were paid the least were all relatively new to Cairo. The people who received the most had been living in Cairo for a number of years. Asylum seekers who had recently arrived in Cairo were not privy to this information nexus. Moreover, given the urgency of their particular set of circumstances, they did not possess the same bargaining power as individuals who had had more time to adapt to their migrant status. Disconnected from this local knowledge economy, they were at greater risk of exploitation. Yasmin, the NGO worker introduced at the beginning of this chapter, explained:

> When people come to Cairo, they go to the markets and talk to each other. They ask where they can go for assistance; how to register with the UN or where to go to look for work. But some people take advantage of their position. Let me give you an example: There is a hotel in Ataba where many people stay when they first come off the boat. I know what happens here. After they stay in this place, for one or two weeks, the people there convince them to sell a kidney. They say this is the only way they can pay them.

Other intermediaries involved in negotiations used their connections with various networks to influence proceedings. For instance, Kariem revealed how sex workers had been used to "sweeten the deal" in some of the negotiations that he was involved in. According to Kariem, most Sudanese migrants who sell a kidney are male. It is more difficult for them to find employment (Jacobsen et al. 2014; Grabska 2006); and without employment it is difficult to sustain an intimate relationship: "Sometimes I get a call and then I go to help people agree on a price. It can be difficult to come to an agreement. So, I offer them something more. . . . Some of these people I have seen in the nightclubs. I know what they want. They want to live the good life. They want to experience what they see [sex workers]. But this is not free. . . . If you come to the nightclub you will understand."

Kariem, who worked primarily as a pimp, used the services of sex workers as leverage when negotiating fees with both sellers and buyers. A night with a sex worker was offered as an extra inducement to sell. "Serviced" accommodation was arranged for organ donors after their operation: "After the operation they [organ sellers] are taken to an apartment for their recovery, for a number of weeks. The apartment is unfurnished, so they must pay for the rent and furniture. They are sent a caretaker to make them food, and they are brought women to make them feel good, but when they are ready, they must pay for this service. All of this is taken from their fee." Kariem did not comment on whether or not the sellers were made aware of these hidden charges during negotiations. Instead, he promoted the merits of his services, particularly his negotiation skills: "I help negotiate the price. There was a girl from France [who needed a kidney] whose father contacted me. I saved him a lot of money. He got the kidney for $45,000. Without me he could have paid more than $100,000." Asked how he made contact with potential recipients, Kariem declined to answer, simply stating that it was "a secret process." However, he did reveal (unintentionally) the name of one of the tissue typing labs that he was associated with. After searching for this particular lab online, using Google Egypt, a number of forum pages were located. On one of these pages a user posted a comment referring to the aforementioned lab and thanked an unnamed intermediary for his services. The recipient was from Saudi Arabia.

Enforced Compliance

It was common for organ sellers to undergo tissue typing and diagnostic testing in different labs before being matched with a suitable recipient. Such testing involved an ultrasound to determine the size and function of the kidney, followed by blood and urine tests (see Thiruchelvam et al. 2011; and He and Taylor 2014). For most people who had sold a kidney, this process was conducted over a period of two weeks. It is probable that donors were taken to several labs to expedite the tissue typing and matching process. Another possible explanation is that the brokers were looking to negotiate a higher recruitment fee, exhibiting their "merchandise" to different labs to elicit a higher price for their services. Furthermore, it is likely that the various tissue typing labs were working in partnership with different hospitals and transplant centers, which can pay more or less depending on the availability of donors. Certainly, the alleged payment structure of this illegal-legal interface would support such an inference.

Kalib, who had links to a number of labs, explained how payment was allocated between the different stakeholders.

> The hospital gets paid from the recipient via an intermediary, and then the money is allocated to different medical staff. The recipient can pay from $40,000 to $100,000. The hospital pays the lab around $6,000. Sometimes labs are separate from the hospital. Sometimes the hospitals and labs are one, so the payment can depend on this. The brokers gets paid around $3,000 from the lab and another $2,000 commission is taken from the donor. Most of the brokers work in teams so this money can be allocated amongst them.

All the organ sellers I interviewed were accompanied by at least one broker while attending the clinics. Apart from collecting their recruitment fee, the presence of the brokers ensured that the donors did not reconsider their "donation." Although most people did not experience any overt violence compelling them to donate, it was clear that once they had agreed to sell a kidney, they had little choice but to proceed with the operation. When asked whether an organ seller could in fact change his or her mind, Shaker bluntly affirmed that this was not possible: "They cannot change their mind. This is not an option. Once they agree, it is done." Pressed as to how exactly consent was maintained, given that a donor may wish to reconsider, he curtly restated that it was not possible.

The comments of some of the other organ sellers were more revealing. Six of the people I interviewed who had sold a kidney had expressed serious concerns before the operation. They had heard rumors that both of their kidneys would be taken or that other organs (e.g., heart, lungs, liver, cornea) would be removed while they were under anesthetic. These fears were escalated by the high volume of health checks that were performed in different clinics. Consequently, they expressed doubts as to whether or not they should proceed with the operation. These doubts were firmly dismissed by threats and warnings over the consequences that would follow if they were "dishonorable" and reneged on their agreement. Talia's narrative gives some context to the insidious nature of such threats.

Talia had decided that she no longer wanted to proceed with the operation, after being warned by a friend that she might lose both her kidneys. She informed the brokers (Egyptian and Sudanese) of her decision not to go ahead with the operation, but they insisted that it was too late for her to reconsider, as the health checks and surgery had already been paid for. They explained that Talia was in their debt and that she would have to reimburse them for their medical expenses if she changed her mind. Further, she was warned that it was better for her to come by her own volition. Despite such threats, Talia did not go through with the operation.

> I was going to do it, but I was worried when they would not let me take someone with me. I am afraid. People are talking about me now. They all think that I sold my kidney. I cannot walk around freely anymore because they will find me. These people have eyes everywhere. I did not take any money from them. I just did the tests because I wanted to help my kids. They told me that it is better you come yourself. They said, "All the people they know that you already sold your kidney so if we come and take your kidney nobody will care, and you will get nothing." The rumor is already out there.

Talia was forced to move to a new house and change her phone number after her door was kicked in several times in an apparent attempt to unsettle her. At the time of the interview, she was afraid to leave her house for fear of reprisal. She would not go to the police because she does not trust them. Although Talia's narrative should not be generalized, other respondents reported similar experiences. According to Patrick, "They [the brokers] told me that they would never let me change my mind. They said, if you change your mind, you will pay for all the health checks, and we will never leave you alone. We will take your money and your passport. We will never let you go. Every day they paid me E£50 or E£150. They told me that I owe them now. I couldn't pay them back, so I had no choice but to continue."

One of the respondents mentioned earlier, Hiba, had a particularly harrowing encounter when she was brought to a hospital that hosted its own tissue typing lab for diagnostic testing. When Hiba arrived at the clinic, she was welcomed by a member of the medical staff, Dr. Hakim, who conducted some blood tests to determine compatibility with the organ recipient. After the blood tests were completed, Dr. Hakim informed Hiba that she would receive E£40,000, significantly less than the $40,000 that she had been promised by her broker, Ali. Hiba did not accept this and refused to "donate" her kidney. However, she was prevented from leaving the hospital.

> They would not let me leave. He [Dr. Hakim] had my passport. They put me into a room, where they do the surgery, and locked me in. There were guards outside, so that I could not leave. After some time, the doctor gave me some medicine. I do not remember much after this. I was there for maybe four days. Then Ali [the broker] gave me E£40,000 [about $2,500] and asked me to leave. I spent most of this money staying at a hotel. I didn't want anyone to know what happened.

Hiba is adamant that security officials stood guard at the door of the operating theater, preventing her from leaving. Hiba never met the recipient and does not know anything about him or her. She was not provided with any information about the operation before being discharged from the clinic.

These narratives are indicative of the coercive nature of "consensual" organ sales, illustrating the thin line between a seemingly consensual agreement to sell a kidney and trafficking in persons for organ removal. However, although such cases underline the more nefarious elements of the organ trade, they should not be considered typical. Contrary to these accounts, other respondents experienced more favorable treatment. According to Kamal, a 21-year-old Sudanese migrant, "The doctor told me I could change my mind if I wanted. He asked me again before the operation. He said I am free to go at any time. I was not obliged to do this."

It is worth noting that such positive experiences were observed in transplant centers, as opposed to the tissue typing labs where donors were treated with a general sense of apathy and, in some cases, disdain. Most organ sellers had little if any direct correspondence with the medical staff at the labs. They were taken directly to a waiting room while the brokers spoke to a representative from the lab before undertaking the requisite medical tests. Nonetheless, experiences in the transplant centers were also variable, as Hiba's narrative confirms. In general, female respondents reported the most negative experiences. According to Mahmoud, a Sudanese community leader, this is because "women are easier to intimidate; the brokers use fear and shame to enforce their compliance."

Organ Laundering

It is important to reconsider here the division of labor between the different agents that constitute the organ trading network. Even though there is no fixed system binding the movements of the various stakeholders, there is a general pattern of activity evident from the interview data. In summary, recruitment brokers connect organ seller(s) to another intermediary, usually with ties to one or more tissue typing labs or hospitals. This intermediary negotiates a price with the donor, assuming a price has not already been agreed upon. Once a fee is agreed on, the organ seller(s) undergoes tissue typing. This usually takes place in several labs to increase the probability of finding a suitable match in the shortest time possible. Timing is important so that the seller does not reconsider selling their kidney. When a suitable match is found, the "donor" is referred to a hospital or transplant center, where the transplant is performed. Crucially, however, before the organ seller(s) is referred to the medical facility performing the transplant, the necessary paperwork alluding to the altruistic and consensual nature of the donation is completed. Once a "donor" has been received along with the requisite documentation (consent form, passport, medical records), the illegality of the transplant is concealed and rendered legitimate; normal procedure follows. In short, the illegal supply of organs is laundered by means of an arbitrary consent process, mediated by a segmented network of intermediaries. This process transforms what was an illegal transaction into a legitimate procedure. This process of "organ laundering"[6] disassociates the medical facility (transplant center or hospital) from criminal activity and negates any illegal activity on behalf of the recipient.[7]

According to Egyptian regulations established under the professional code of ethics and conduct[8] and reaffirmed and codified into domestic legislation under Article 9 of the Transplantation of Human Organs and Tissues Act (Law 5/2010), all transplants performed in Egypt must first be approved by the Minster of Health and the Higher Committee on Organ Transplants. Ostensibly this is to ensure that the integrity of the transplant procedure is upheld in accordance with internationally recognized guidelines (see WHO 2010). Before a transplant is approved, the medical facility where the transplant will be performed must submit all relevant documentation to a "special committee" (see Article 13 of Law 5/2010). This committee is comprised of an unspecified number of technical and legal experts (e.g. medical professors, lawyers, government officials) who are responsible for reviewing the documentation and confirming that "informed" consent has indeed been given. The documentation (passport, medical records) should include basic demographic information on the patient and the donor, confirming their age, gender, and health status. Moreover, it should include written testimony (letter from consulate office, consent form) to demonstrate that the donation is altruistically motivated. Furthermore, the donor is required to sign an affidavit before the committee declaring that their consent has been given freely, without financial reward or promise. In an illegal organ transplant, however, the affidavit is usually signed under the instruction of the brokers. The affidavit is then brought to a select committee member(s) to receive official approval.

As Shaker, the recruitment broker mentioned earlier, explained, "I took care of all the paperwork. I accompanied them to get their papers approved by the official and then later I would bring them to the lab for health checks before the operation. The doctors don't want to know anything. They take the money without question. This is their only concern. Once the papers are in order, everything is legal." When the affidavit is signed and the necessary health checks are performed, the tissue typing lab forwards the "official" documentation to the medical facility performing the transplant. Once the special committee has reviewed and approved the documentation, the acting physician makes a submission to the Higher Committee on Organ Transplants to obtain overall approval for the procedure. Further, the donor signs a second consent form at the facility where the procedure will be performed. This is to protect the facility hosting the transplant against any accusations of organ theft. Finally, according to Article 50 of the Professional Code of Ethics, the acting physician is obliged to confirm the donor's consent verbally, giving him or her the option to reconsider donating. Donors should also be informed of the medical consequences and risks to which they may be exposed as a result of the transplant operation.

On an evidential level the physicians are fulfilling their professional duties, provided consent has been confirmed. It should be noted, however, that medical practitioners are under no legal obligation to ensure the consent of the donor after a transplant has been approved by the Health Ministry's Higher Committee on Organ Transplants; this is merely a matter of professional ethics. In other words, although physicians or transplant professionals may be subject to disapproval from their peers, they will not be held in contravention of the law if they fail in their professional obligations (Ambagtsheer et al. 2013). Moreover, should a transplant professional suspect that an organ has been donated illegally, there is no legal duty to report this to the relevant authorities. According to the Hippocratic Oath, adhered to on an international level, medical professionals have a duty to uphold confidentiality of information shared by the patient and donor (see Edelstein 1943). This requirement grants transplant professionals the privilege of nondisclosure, meaning that they cannot be held to account for failing to disclose information related to a suspected organ sale, which may or may not have been sourced from a victim of human trafficking. Although in some jurisdictions doctors have a judicial requirement to report violent crimes, such as child abuse and crimes that could result in the death of the patient, no guidelines or bodies exist in Egypt, or anywhere else for that matter, for the reporting of organ purchases or sales. Without the testimony of transplant professionals, it is difficult to establish that an illegal organ sale has occurred.

In addition to a professional reticence to provide information that could lead to a successful prosecution, the organ laundering process presents a further challenge to the investigation and prosecution of organ trafficking cases. For instance, although it is illegal to buy or sell an organ, transplantation is a legitimate procedure. Therefore the proceeds of an illegal organ sale are reinvested without difficulty, into what is prima facie a lawful service. According to the information provided in interviews with organ brokers, the recipient's payment is, in general, allocated directly to the transplant center where the transplant surgery (nephrectomy) is performed and accounted for against the medical expenses a recipient might be expected to pay for a transplant procedure. The surplus payment that is received is allocated to the various agents involved in supplying the organ. Segmented in this way, it is difficult to trace the proceeds back to any one organization "existing for a period of time and acting in concert with the aim of committing one or more serious crimes or offenses" in order "to obtain, directly or indirectly, a financial or other material benefit" (UNODC 2000b: Article 3).

Further, the fact that there is no single structured group responsible for the illegal supply of organs makes it difficult for law enforcement agencies to investigate a human trafficking case, where evidence of the method and means in conjunction with an illegal purpose need to be established. Consequently, most "trafficking" suspects are charged individually with lesser crimes associated with human trafficking, for example, illicit organ sale, assault, battery, fraud, forgery, extortion, rape, fraud, or kidnapping (Farrell et al. 2014; *The State v. Netcare* case, in Allain 2011; and *U.S. v. Rosenbaum* 2012). New laws create problems for prosecutors because the elements of the crime that are needed to establish a prima facie case are unclear until tested in court (Farrell et al. 2014). Moreover, given the complications involved in establishing a human trafficking case, organ providers are more likely to be prosecuted for an organ sale than recognized as victims of human trafficking. Subsequently, many cases that would correspond to the legal elements of "trafficking in persons" are not reported. Hiba and Talia's experiences, described earlier, are indicative of this.

The interview data presented in this chapter suggest that the criminal sanctions introduced in response to reports of organ trafficking in Egypt have pushed the trade further underground. This has increased the role of intermediaries and reduced the bargaining position of organ sellers, leaving them exposed to a greater risk of harm. Although organ markets continue to operate, the process of organ trading has become more hidden, making it more difficult to assess the extent of the problem and to identify individuals targeted for organ sale. Analytic labs were the key nodal points of activity, linking actors in both the formal and the informal sectors of the economy. Reversing the logic behind prevailing attitudes on organized crime, which proceed from the assumption that crime infiltrates legitimate business, the interview narratives presented in this chapter reveal how analytic labs formed strategic partnerships with organ brokers to recruit individuals, usually from select ethnic backgrounds (in this case Sudanese), to meet a demand for organ supplies that could not be achieved by altruistic means. In other words, the criminal aspects (e.g., recruiting donor-sellers) associated with the organ trade were outsourced from legitimate businesses to individuals operating in the informal economy. Once a donor had been recruited, a process of organ laundering followed, disassociating the transplant clinic where the surgery was performed from any criminal liability.

The organ brokers and organ sellers that I interviewed were responding to the same set of circumstances and conditions. With limited access to employment, residency, and/or education, respondents were left with little choice but to find ways to help themselves. In this context, selling or arranging the sale of a kidney was an option worth considering. Contrary to popularized reports that link organ trafficking to the operations of transnational crime groups, the informal and formal relations that underpin Cairo's organ markets are based on modern modes of collaboration, trading, and communication across the illegal-legal divide. In this sense the organ trade is better understood as an informal economic activity, as opposed to a trafficking offense. Yet sensationalized global media accounts continue to overshadow a more nuanced analysis that considers the negotiated practice of organ trading, reorienting attention toward the macabre spectacle of organ trafficking. Rather than targeting the alleged criminal operations of transnational crime groups and suspected traffickers, legislative action needs to focus on addressing the legal barriers and policy decisions that leave vulnerable individuals exposed to exploitation of various kinds. To do this, exploitation needs to be resituated in its broader context and addressed at the domestic level where the effects of "criminal" behavior are experienced. In the next chapter I explore the social, legal, and political factors that compel migrant populations living in Cairo to consider and/or arrange the sale of organs.

4

DISQUALIFIED BODIES

I am Fatimah. I am 25 years old, from Sudan. I went to Egypt [in 2009] to claim asylum because there was no work in Sudan and the fighting was making it impossible to survive. My husband left me with three children. Without child support I was unable to keep up with house payments and we lost our home. I borrowed money from a friend and started working as a street vendor in Khartoum, selling tea and coffee. But the police closed me down because I couldn't pay them the [protection] money they wanted for permission to trade. They asked for sexual favors also, but I wouldn't agree to this. People would always harass me, asking for sex because I was a woman working on the street [in Sudan]. They thought I was a slut who would have sex with anyone. When you are working on the street, no one respects you. They think they can say or do what they want to you. One of my customers suggested that I go to Egypt. "You can go to Egypt and find work. There are more opportunities there for you and for your family," he said. From that moment I decided to go to Egypt, so I could send money home to help my children. When I arrived in Cairo, I registered with the UNHCR [United Nations High Commissioner for Refugees] as an asylum seeker. The only work I could find was as a housekeeper, but this was difficult for me because of health complications from when I gave birth to my last child. I'm not able to lift heavy objects because of this problem. I informed the UNHCR about this, and Caritas also, but they didn't listen to me. I left my children with my mother in Khartoum, but she couldn't afford to feed them or send them to school. I was worried about their condition; they were going downhill fast. So, I found work at an Egyptian house, where I was treated very badly. They let me work day and night without rest and no sleep for 15 days. I was like a slave to them. I was sexually harassed and insulted on a daily basis. I felt humiliated and I just wanted to get away; I left without asking for payment. But even if I did receive payment, it would not have been enough. Sure, I could buy some food, transport, and maybe cover my rent, but then I would have nothing left. I needed to send money home to my children. I am a divorced woman and I have a responsibility to them. You understand?

I never did get refugee status. I had the meeting [with the UNHCR], and after months of waiting I got notification that my file had been closed. I had no choice but to accept another position working as a housekeeper. Just like before, the work was hard and the hours were long. I was mentally and physically exhausted, frustrated by my own vulnerability and the situation I was trapped in. I was feeling worthless, like my life had no meaning. I had tried to work, but the work did not pay enough to cover my basic needs and to help my children. Then two [Sudanese] women came to me and asked me if I would sell my kidney. "This will improve the miserable situation you are in," they said. "You are working hard, and your children are suffering. You will never make enough money working as a housekeeper. It will be good to sell your kidney. You can start a business with the money," they suggested. They advised me to buy a tuk-tuk [motorized rickshaw]. "It will be a good investment for you and for your children. It will give you freedom to go back to Sudan, or, if you want, you could travel to Europe. We know some people who can help you with that," they said. I want you to understand that at the time I was in a desperate situation. I really needed the money. I was homeless, and my children were starving back in Sudan, so I agreed to sell my kidney. The women contacted a broker who took me to a clinic for a blood test. The results weren't great. The doctor told me that I had a fibrosis [damaged tissue] on one of my kidneys and it would be dangerous for me to donate. He said that he would consult with a specialist at the hospital and let me know if the kidney could be removed. The broker contacted me about a week later with a date for the surgery. I spent two days at the hospital. There was no contact with the medical team or the recipient. I just found myself in a room, alone and afraid. I was in a lot of pain, and I couldn't move my position in the bed. A nurse escorted me out of the building the next day. The broker called and told me to go home. "I will come to you with the money," he promised. When he came to see me, he brought papers for me to sign. He didn't give me any time to read them. He just told me where to sign, and then he took the papers and put them in his bag. Before he left, he handed me an envelope with $3,000. I sent some of the money back home to my children in Sudan, and I used what was left to rent an apartment. The broker called me about a week later and gave me an extra $2,000, followed by an additional $1,000 two weeks after that. But this was not the total amount we had agreed on. We had agreed to $8,000, but what could I do? It's not something you can report. They [government] don't care about you here, especially when you don't have papers.

FATIMAH, LIKE MANY of the other people I interviewed, had traveled to Cairo to earn a living and to escape ongoing conflict in her country of origin, Sudan. Life in Cairo was more difficult than she had imagined, and with a lack of options to support her family she agreed to sell a kidney. She was not trafficked according to the legal definition outlined in Article 3 of the Trafficking Protocol. Nevertheless, she was exploited as a direct result of her precarious migrant status. She experienced abuse, fraud, and deception, her wages were withheld, and her kidney was removed against medical advice. Yet, because of her "illegal" status, she had no grounds for legal recourse.[1]

The threat of organ trafficking has captured the imagination of political and legislative experts, as evidenced by the Council of Europe Convention Against Trafficking in Organs (Council of Europe 2014a). Relatively less attention has been given to the types of circumstances and environments that predispose certain individuals or groups to selling an organ. The life trajectories of the people I interviewed during my time in Cairo (2014–2020) revealed how processes of social exclusion and economic marginalization can lead to varying degrees of exploitation, manifest in this instance in the individuals' involvement in organ trading. Their experiences are illustrative of the types of legal arrangements, policy decisions, and social conditions that underpin the organ trade in the Egyptian-Sudanese context. Criminalization alone cannot address these dynamics. Accordingly, in this chapter I redirect analysis toward the legal barriers and policy decisions that shape the poor bargaining position of organ sellers in Cairo. The interview narratives in this chapter represent the perspectives of Sudanese (Sudan and South Sudan) migrants who were denied refugee status after claiming asylum. Their experiences demonstrate how labor market pressures and the demands of physical survival force people into exploitative arrangements (e.g., selling a kidney) that they would otherwise avoid. My focus here is on the background conditions and legal structures that underpin exploitative relations in organ markets. Although some of my respondents were physically coerced into organ removal, I argue that it is exploitation experienced at the structural level that ultimately induces people to sell an organ. In this regard, I explicate the oppressive processes of exploitation that position migrant populations as organ sellers in Cairo. I begin by exploring the social and legal context in which migrants, asylum seekers, and refugees have sold a kidney. I then consider the wider implications of legal measures established in response to reports of organ trafficking.

Conflict Organs

In a context of prolonged civil unrest, constitutive of poor labor conditions and limited access to public services, there has been a mass exodus of people traveling to the Greater Cairo region in search of better employment options and living conditions. Throughout my fieldwork I interviewed individuals from different nationalities, all with diverse backgrounds and experiences. Over the course of my research I developed a rapport with members of the Sudanese community in particular; they connected me with respondents in their immediate social network. For this reason, most of the people I spoke with were from Sudan and South Sudan. Other respondents had traveled from Eritrea, Ethiopia, Somalia, and Chad. Although many of them had come to Cairo "voluntarily" and were not "forced" into moving because of the direct threat of violence, they were nevertheless escaping the social and economic consequences of prolonged conflict and political instability.

Since the early 1990s, ongoing conflict in the Horn of Africa has led to large numbers of Sudanese, Eritrean, Ethiopian, and Somali refugees coming to Egypt (Jacobsen et al. 2014). Between 2006 and 2007 Iraqi nationals began to arrive, forced to leave their homes because of the insecurity and instability of wartime Iraq. Since 2012, Syrians have represented the largest migrant population seeking asylum in Egypt. As of August 2018, the UNHCR has registered 233,045 refugees and asylum seekers. Even though this number is considerable, it does not account for refugees with closed files and/or the increasing number of internally displaced people who have opted not to register with the UNHCR. In contrast to Syrians who have received priority resettlement outside Egypt, diaspora communities of Sudanese, Eritrean, and Ethiopian nationals who have been denied refugee status have settled in low-income neighborhoods, generally in the Greater Cairo region, for example, Faisal, Ard El-Lewa, Maadi, and Mohandeseen.[2]

Egypt signed a Memorandum of Understanding with the UNHCR in 1954, assigning responsibility for refugees to the UNHCR. As such, all procedures pertaining to refugee registration, documentation, and refugee status determination (RSD) are carried out by the UNHCR in Egypt. The transfer of responsibility under the Memorandum means that the UNHCR has assumed the state's primary role in providing health, education, housing, and financial assistance to refugees. This practice reflects a wider trend across the Middle East and North Africa, whereby the UNHCR acts as a surrogate state, substituting the state's role in administering key services for refugees (Kagan 2011). Essentially, registering with the UNHCR enables asylum seekers to apply for refugee status in the hope of being resettled in a third country, presumably with better living standards. From the perspective of asylum seekers, the possibility of resettlement represents an opportunity to rebuild their lives. However, most individuals who register with the UNHCR remain in Cairo, joining the ranks of the urban poor and occupying marginal spaces of the economy with limited resources and opportunities for social mobility.

In the years following al-Sisi's inauguration (2014–2018), the government institutionalized a securitization agenda built around punitive polices targeting illegal migration and human trafficking (see Chapters 5 and 6). Despite holding valid residency permits, many of the people I spoke with were targeted for arrest and deportation. As a consequence, they sought out the services of people smugglers to travel outside Egypt, in some cases to Europe, discussed in the next chapter. At the same time, sustained conflict and an escalation in violence following the fall of Muammar al-Gaddafi in Libya in 2011 rerouted migrant traffic into and out of Egypt. In addition, the de facto closing of Egypt's sea border in 2016 increased the number of internally displaced people looking to rebuild their lives in the Egyptian capital while seeking alternative migration routes. Most people ended up in low-income neighborhoods where already negligible resources were placed under additional pressure. This increased social tensions and conflict between subgroups of urban poor, leading to the fragmentation of communities and a loss of social controls (see Chapter 6). In a competitive environment where legal and social barriers to employment, housing, and education further entrenched conditions of poverty, trading in organs emerged as an economic activity, a pragmatic decision based on local realities.

Legal Barriers

The UNHCR headquarters are located in 6th of October, a remote satellite city poorly connected to Cairo's major metropolitan areas. Abido, a Sudanese asylum seeker in his late 30s, was waiting in line to inquire about his refugee status determination (RSD) meeting. He had slept outside the building the night before, hoping to avoid the large crowds seeking assistance. At 7 a.m. a disorderly line had already begun to wrap around the adjoining block of buildings. "It's like this every morning. Most of the people have to wait overnight because it's so far away from everything. Depending on traffic, it's about a two-hour drive on a microbus from Tahrir [Square]. Maybe that's why they built it here," he suggested. Abido claimed asylum in 2011 after he was accused of leading a protest against the Sudanese government. Upon registering, he was allocated a yellow card and given E£300 (about $33) per month, for a period of two months. After the two months had elapsed, the payment was canceled and his file was closed without explanation. "How can I survive on E£300 for a month? This will not even cover my rent. You register, get your card, and then you are forgotten. You have no real protection with the yellow card. It just means that your file is opened, and you are being considered for interview, to determine whether you will get refugee status." I asked him if he had tried calling beforehand, to find out why his meeting had not been scheduled. "I have tried many times to speak to them [UNHCR], but no one will see me. I do not exist for them. You know the Egyptians [government] and the Sudanese [government], they work together. I think this is why my file was closed." The line started to move, and I could see that Abido was anxious to get going. Before he moved on, I asked him whether he knew anything about the organ trade. He took several moments before replying: "If you cannot find work when you get to Egypt, you will not find mercy. This is why people sell their kidneys."

Sudanese migrants have historically shared a link with Egypt. Under the Wadi El Nil Treaty (1976) Sudanese nationals could enter Egypt without a visa.[3] Moreover, they were granted rights of residency, ownership, and employment, similar to Egyptian citizens. However, with increasing numbers of Sudanese nationals traveling to Egypt as a result of a succession of civil wars in the region, the Egyptian government made a request to the UNHCR in 1994 to begin processing "asylum seekers" (Grabska 2006; Jacobsen et al. 2014). Further restrictions were imposed when the Wadi El Nil Treaty was revoked after a failed assassination attempt on President Mubarak, allegedly performed by Sudanese Islamists (Turner 1995). Consequently, visa and residence permit requirements were introduced for all Sudanese nationals en route to Egypt, regardless of their reasons for travel. These restrictions remained in force until the Four Freedoms Agreement (2004) was established.[4] Thought of as a partial return to the Wadi El Nil Treaty, the Four Freedoms Agreement accords Sudanese nationals "special status," which exempts them from visa requirements and guarantees reciprocal rights of residence, work, and ownership of property (Jacobsen et al. 2014). However, an important caveat limits the scope of the agreement to Sudanese citizens. Under the agreement, "asylum seekers" are not extended the same privileges as Sudanese citizens, who are considered legal migrants. Like other African migrants (e.g., Eritrean, Ethiopian, Somali), their legal status and terms of residence remain subject to UNHCR registration.[5]

It is unclear who exactly qualifies as a "citizen," with most Sudanese nationals in Egypt labeled by border officials as asylum seekers regardless of whether or not they are actually seeking asylum. Yet those who have asylum or refugee status are often treated with the same disregard as "illegal" migrants. Conceptually, forced migration refers to individuals or groups that have arrived in a country without formal documentation, having been compelled by an element of coercion (e.g., environmental disasters, political persecution) to seek asylum (IOM 2011). Such individuals are normatively classified as asylum seekers. In contrast, labor migration refers to those who leave home for economic reasons in search of employment (IOM 2011). In practice, however, the distinction between forced migration and labor migration is blurred (Anderson and Rogaly 2005). The conditions that propel either forced or labor migration are interconnected; they are co-effects of the same environment in which social inequality and political and economic instability are embedded. Nevertheless, migrant workers who do not possess the necessary travel documents can be perceived to have committed a criminal offense (illegal immigration) unless they are claiming asylum (Coutin 2005; Dauvergne 2008; Thomas 2010; Hamlin 2014). Therefore migrants who are unable to obtain formal work or travel documents have a strong incentive to claim asylum, regardless of their purpose for travel. For example, for those fearing political persecution, it can be extremely difficult to obtain formal documents from the requisite officials in Egypt. Several of the people I spoke with suggested suggested that the Egyptian government was involuntarily repatriating migrants to Sudan and felt that they had no choice but to claim asylum (see later discussion). Hence, if there is any clear implication of the Four Freedoms Agreement, it is not the expansion of protections for migrant workers but rather the reduction of legal protection for Sudanese asylum seekers who are formally excluded from its provisions (Thomas 2010). Because they were formally excluded by the Egyptian administration, most of the Sudanese migrants I interviewed registered with the UNHCR, to avail themselves of whatever legal entitlements were available.

Constructing Vulnerability

To secure permanent residency rights, an asylum seeker must first register with the UNHCR, which then schedules an RSD interview. Upon registering, an asylum seeker is allocated a yellow card. The yellow card enables asylum seekers to stay in Egypt under the protection of the UNHCR until their RSD meeting takes place. This process can take several months to several years. Those who are rejected are entitled to appeal, but if the appeal fails, their file is closed permanently. They are no longer "people of concern" and are expected to depart the country (UNHCR 2016). As noted, most migrant workers whose files have been closed remain in Egypt, occupying a legal limbo with "illegal" status and limited access to rights and services. For those who qualify for a blue card, granting them refugee status, the benefits are marginal. The main difference between a refugee and an asylum seeker is that refugees are eligible for the UNHCR's "durable solutions": local integration, voluntary repatriation, or resettlement (Jacobsen et al. 2014). In practice, no mechanisms are in place to support local integration. For example, schools for refugees are not recognized by the Egyptian government. Therefore refugees cannot progress to third-level education. African migrants, almost universally classified as asylum seekers or refugees regardless of their reason for travel, are encouraged to attend UNHCR workshops where they can learn "essential skills." One 36-year-old woman from South Sudan, commenting on the educational programs provided by the UNHCR, claimed, "They only teach us how to be good servants. We learn how to cook the Egyptian way and learn how to read children's books so that we can read for their children.

They do not want us to be educated. They need to keep us in our place. We are only welcome here so that we can clean their homes and mind their children."

Although refugees can apply for a work permit, this is a difficult and costly procedure. To qualify for a work permit, refugees must first demonstrate that they are "uniquely qualified" for the position. Effectively, this means that refugees or their employers are required to prove that an Egyptian could not perform the work in question. The prospective employer must then purchase a work permit. If the employer refuses, the cost will need to be covered by the refugee. The cost of an annual work permit for a Sudanese refugee is E£200 ($15).[6] This may seem like an acceptable figure, but for someone with no viable source of income this fee can be a significant barrier to finding gainful employment. Should the requisite funds be raised, there is no physical office where refugees can apply for a work permit. According to one respondent working for an international organization, the UNHCR does not obtain work permits for its refugee staff interpreters, meaning that the agency given responsibility for refugees by the Egyptian government has to "illegally" employ refugees as interpreters. As a consequence, migrants, asylum seekers, and refugees seeking employment have no choice but to find work in the informal economy (see later discussion).

Voluntary repatriation is invariably involuntary, and only the most vulnerable cases are deemed serious enough to satisfy a resettlement request.[7] The criteria for resettlement is selective, arbitrary, and nontransparent. After talking to Abido, I had a meeting with a resettlement officer at the UNHCR. I asked how resettlement decisions were made and what "vulnerable" meant in the context of the resettlement process. "We cannot resettle everyone who is actually eligible because there are not enough places," she said, avoiding my question. "Resettlement places are being reduced all the time. There was a reduction by about 60% this year [2017]. At the moment we can only act on about 1% of our requests." She explained that resettlement figures do not account for the number of refugees who actually arrive in the country where they are being resettled. "When we say someone is resettled, this means that a country, for example the U.S., has agreed to offer the refugees rights of residence, subject to a security clearance. It can still take years before the refugee actually arrives at his or her destination." Therefore for most refugees a sort of de facto local integration occurs, with no substantive rights to employment, education, or housing. Asked about reports of refugees being arrested and deported by Egyptian police, she responded, "We cannot negotiate with

FIGURE 3. The Mogamma, in Tahrir Square, Cairo. Refugees line up to "regularize" their residency status. Photo by author.

the government, or any other for that matter. We are advocates for individual cases. It is the government's decision who enters and who remains."

Despite being signatories to the 1951 Convention Relating to the Status of Refugees, Egypt has placed several reservations on the implementation of the Convention, opting out of key provisions (Articles 12(1), 20, 22(1), 23, and 24) concerning personal status, access to education, labor rights, and social security.[8] For example, refugees residing in Egypt are not eligible to apply for Egyptian nationality. Their residence is considered temporary, and thus no real integration occurs. Under international law the possession of a blue card grants refugees a right to residence in the country where they have claimed asylum. Nevertheless, refugees in Egypt are required to reapply for residency permits every six months at the Mogamma, a monolithic administrative complex looming over Tahrir Square. Failure to do so results in their refugee status being revoked, making them illegal and subject to arrest and deportation. The application process is a time-consuming and debilitating experience for refugees, who start lining up at 4 a.m. to make sure that they can get inside the building. Once inside they have to complete an application form and provide personal and demographic information and a current address. The form along with identification (i.e., blue card) is then sent to the Egyptian Ministry of Foreign Affairs for a security clearance, which can take up to two months to complete. At any point during this process, their request for a residency can be denied and they can be detained. When this happens, the UNHCR is contacted to confirm refugee status. A letter is faxed to the Ministry of Foreign Affairs confirming that the person arrested is in fact a refugee and entitled to a permit. Refugees must then reapply or agree to "voluntary" repatriation. Like Abido, several of the refugees I interviewed were denied residency permits because of unspecified "security reasons." For this reason, they had decided to avoid Mogamma and forfeit their refugee status. "Illegal" or undocumented migrants are socially, politically, and economically subjugated, existing external to formal legal rules, and are therefore vulnerable to various forms of exploitation. In this way, the laws regulating refugee status and immigration can be seen to produce illegality and thereby construct vulnerability (Coutin 2005; Anderson and Ruhs 2010; Jones-Correa and de Graauw 2013). The organ trade is exemplary of this process.

Informalization, Precarious Labor, and Organ Sale

Migrants are commonly represented as passive subjects or victims lacking agency and control over their lives. On the contrary, the narratives contained in this book convey the experiences of resourceful people, willing to take risks and motivated beyond the norm to advance their life choices (see also Agustín 2007; and Isin and Nielsen 2008). Several of the people I interviewed had spent their life savings to get to Egypt, in hope of a better life. Their intention was to work, save money, and move on to another country with better job opportunities and access to services. Yet, registered by the UNHCR as asylum seekers, migrants cannot legally move beyond Egyptian territory. They have little choice but to remain and compete with Cairo's urban poor for limited employment opportunities while they await a decision on their refugee status.[9] Eight people I interviewed in 2014 had their files closed shortly after arriving, leaving them without legal protection and assistance. Speaking at length about her difficulties sustaining herself since emigrating from South Sudan, 28-year-old Nasrin explained:

I was forced to marry a man in Juba. He left me with one child. After that, I went to Cairo to find a job. I found work in the house [housekeeper], but they [UNHCR] closed my file. I went back to them [the UNHCR] many times after that, but they refused to listen. I would wait in line outside for 5 or 6 hours. No one told me how long I could expect to wait. I lost my job doing this. I was trying to get my file re-opened; I did not want to stay in Egypt. The only work I can find here is a house girl, or maybe I could work at a club. I was a nurse in Juba; I expected more from my life than this. They do not pay me the same as an Egyptian. I would like to go back to Juba, but I cannot afford this; and the UN canceled my passport when I came here. But I would not go back even if I could. I have failed since coming here. My family would know that I have shamed them. People like me are the easy ones to sell a kidney.

Anita, a 24-year-old Sudanese woman who traveled to Cairo to find work and advance her education, experienced similar difficulties.

The political situation in Sudan makes it impossible to work, and unless you have money you will not get an education. You cannot find employment here unless you know someone working with the government. I came here by secret. I paid someone to do the process for me. I went to Khartoum and then from Halfa to Aswan. I came here [Cairo] to find work and get an education, but it has not been like that. I had to sell my kidney to help myself. If I did not do this, who would help me?

Following the deregulatory trend of advanced capitalism, formal employment options in Egypt—and across the global North and South—are increasingly limited to high-skilled "professionals" with expertise in innovative sectors of the global economy, for example, the biomedical sector (Castells 2011; Daniels 2004). Conversely, global competition for lower skilled jobs has meant that the diffusion of labor across borders has coincided with a process of informalization (Castells 2011). With fewer employment options in the formal labor market low-skilled workers seeking employment often have no option but to accept conditions well below recognized labor standards (see Tataryn 2016). This has led to an expansion of informal labor practices, as people look beyond institutional means of income production in an effort to sustain themselves. The activities that make up the various sectors of the informal economy are unregulated by the social institutions that regulate similar activities in the formal economy (Castells et al. 1989). This absence of regulation affects the status of labor, lowering the costs of production by disregarding existing labor standards and regulations. In effect, workers' rights and protections are surrendered in a trade-off for increased production. Shifts to limit access to workers' rights and protections occur across all levels of employment and labor practices (Standing 2011). Yet migrants deemed "illegal," "irregular," or "undocumented" in informal economic arrangements are exposed and subjected to higher levels of work-related exploitation (Tataryn 2016; Bloch and McKay 2016).

According to Castells et al. (1989), the informalization of labor relations operates as a disguised form of wage labor that deprives workers of their bargaining power. Whereas jobs in the formal sector are relatively secure, informal workers lack access to formally recognized labor standards and protections, for example, minimum wage, collective bargaining rights, and safe working conditions (ILO 2012). Consequently, they are at greater risk of being taken advantage of. Notwithstanding the probability of abuse, governments tolerate or even stimulate informal activities as a way to resolve potential social conflicts while maintaining broader economic interests (Daniels 2004; Castells et al. 1989). For example, permitting the growth of squatter communities and informal settlements in the Greater Cairo region provides the government with a solution to the shortage of affordable housing and frees up resources to support the government's more vested interests, such as military power and consolidation of the security apparatus (Bayat 1997; Adham 2005). Similarly, excluding migrants (Sudanese or otherwise) from legal protection follows the logic of the state in reinforcing Egypt's migrant labor regime, supporting nascent sectors of the economy, such as the transplant industry.

The informal economy in Egypt is estimated to be valued at 69% of Egypt's GDP (ILO 2012). Given the inherent difficulties in measuring the economic impact of activities that are by definition hidden, such estimates inevitably betray a certain level of inaccuracy. However, considering that the informal economy largely consists of unreported income from the production of legal goods and services, the actual figure is likely to be even higher (Buehn and Schneider 2012; Nordstrom 2000). Thus, from an economic governance perspective, it would be disingenuous to invest resources in the protection of migrant workers, as this would potentially compromise the economic aspirations of the state. Rather, the classification of Sudanese migrants entering Egypt as "asylum seekers" underpins a regime of strategic neglect, marked by legal barriers to citizenship that position migrants as a source of captive labor in the informal economy. In 2007 the Egyptian Initiative for Personal Rights reported that only about 13,000 of the estimated 2–5 million Sudanese nationals (from Sudan and South Sudan) living in Egypt are officially recognized as refugees. Barred from entry into the formal labor market and with little chance of migrating beyond Cairo, undocumented migrants provide a source of captive labor with little or no bargaining power to negotiate fair wages or acceptable working conditions. In this environment selling a kidney is a survival strategy.

Migrant "Donors" and the Selective Limits of State Protection

Migrants without the recognized rights or entitlements to work guaranteed under Egyptian law have no legal recourse for the harms committed against them. Consequently, they are left little choice but to accept working conditions that would otherwise be unacceptable. Opportunistic employers often take advantage of this vulnerability, compelling migrants to work long hours for a derisory wage. All the organ sellers I interviewed in 2014–2015 reported working long hours for an insufficient wage. For those working as housekeepers, drivers, and security guards, a typical work week consisted of 12 working hours per day, 6 days a week. The average monthly wage for a (female) housekeeper was E£800 (about $50). The men I spoke with earned even less, making on average E£700 per month (about $45).[10]

Job security was also an issue. Seven people reported instances of arbitrary dismissal, lamenting their inability to challenge unfair working conditions. Abdal, speaking about his experience working as a security guard in Alexandria, without a work permit, explained his dilemma: "I travel from Cairo to Alexandria every day to do this job. Most of my money is spent on transport. I work for over twelve hours and some days I don't even get a break. If I complain, they will just ask me for my work permit. What can I do?" Another respondent, Joyce, was dismissed from her position as a housekeeper, for attending an RSD meeting, which she had informed her employer about, two weeks in advance. However, the employer claimed that she had never been informed of the meeting and consequently dismissed Joyce, insisting that she could not be relied on.

Unable to depend on a stable wage, most people had to supplement their income in other ways, engaging in several other economic activities in an effort to cover rent and daily expenses. For example, some of the female respondents supplemented their income earned as housekeepers by styling hair, applying henna tattoos, or engaging in sex work. Selling a kidney was another option. With limited opportunities to earn a living, the promise of a substantial cash payment in return for a kidney was a significant incentive for people with ambitions to increase their social mobility.

Another reason that migrants are targeted for their kidneys is that procuring an organ from foreign nationals raises less suspicion. Even though under Egyptian transplant law (Law 5/2010) it is illegal to receive an organ from a foreign national (altruistically or otherwise), law enforcement officials are less likely to investigate a suspected organ sale involving "illegal" migrants. This investigative apathy toward alleged criminal activity is sharpened by a cultural detachment to the affairs of foreign bodies, particularly asylum seekers and refugees who are not extended state protection. Owing to their precarious legal status, they are considered more expendable than other sections of the population. Therefore there is less pressure to open an investigation; it is of little concern to the authorities whether or not a migrant has been coerced into selling a kidney.

This selective indifference to the welfare of Sudanese migrants was a common theme in the narratives of organ sellers. Talia, a 23-year-old Sudanese migrant solicited for her kidney, revealed that she was subject to ongoing intimidation and threats from an organ broker after she informed him that she no longer wanted to proceed with the operation. Asked why she did not report this to the police, she explained, "The police don't care about you. They just file a report, but no one investigates. My door was broken because I am staying alone, and they know this. I went to the police to file a report, but they never even came to look at my house. I do not know what to do. I just lock myself in my room and hope they go away."

Experiences of hostility from the host community were interposed with reports of police brutality and state corruption. Tensions were evident between the Sudanese community and the domestic (Egyptian) poor, who were competing for work and opportunity in a context of social exclusion. From my interviews and general conversations with local Egyptians it was apparent that immigrants were blamed for the economic difficulties experienced by the urban poor, a convenient way to redirect attention away from failed state polices (see Bayat 1997). Stories of being robbed were common, as were accusations of corruption among various Egyptian organizations working under the auspices (and funding) of the government. Claims of direct physical violence and sexual abuse were common among female respondents, many of whom reported feeling unsafe living in Cairo and insisted that they were in need of protection. The police would not take their reports seriously, and local Egyptians would always defend their "own" regardless of the circumstances.

During my fieldwork in Cairo in 2014, a 19-year-old woman Sudanese migrant told me, "It is not safe for women here. Nobody will protect me when I go outside. I fear it. If they know that you are living alone with no man, they can come and break into your house and rape you and take everything valuable in your house, and nobody will protect you. The police, government will not protect you. They can't protect even themselves so how will they protect a refugee?" Another respondent, a 32-year-old male Sudanese migrant, said, "If you fight with an Egyptian, they will all gang up on you and beat you. Many people are arrested for having disputes with Egyptians. If you go to prison, you will be beaten unless you can pay money. When you are there, they can treat you like a woman."

Three people claimed that Egyptian nationals purchased refugee identity cards from UNHCR representatives in order to file a request for resettlement overseas, with Europe and the United States being the preferred destinations. One of them, a female migrant from South Sudan, said, "The UN is staffed by overprivileged Egyptians who do not care about our situation. They have no education of these issues. I know some of them use their position to make money. Others want to get out of here themselves. This is why they take this job."

Patrick, a 22-year-old Sudanese man, claimed to have been solicited for his kidney by law enforcement officials when he was arrested during a refugee protest outside the UNHCR in 2005: "When I was arrested, four different police were asking about kidneys. They said that they would release us if we agreed to sell our kidneys. Now you must understand why no one will go to the police about this." Patrick had been arrested a number of times before this and claims to have been beaten on each occasion. In this instance, he described being stripped naked, beaten with a metal pipe, and burned with cigarettes.

Another person who claimed to have been subjected to arbitrary arrest described the difficulties he faced after being released from prison. Mohamed, a 29-year-old Sudanese man, was arrested after getting into a confrontation with his employer over payment. Having no source of income upon release, Mohamed soon found himself homeless: "When you are homeless, people do not respect you and they treat you like dirt. Living on the street, I felt in constant danger.... When people feel you are weak and alone, they will take advantage." Mohamed was reticent for some time before revealing that he was offered $10,000 for his kidney. He claimed that the money he had received was taken from him by force shortly after the operation (by whom he did not say). Having lost his kidney, he expressed feeling a constant sense of shame and hopelessness: "I do not feel human anymore. I drink to forget about what has happened. Sometimes I feel like killing myself because of pain and depression. I do not know what to do with myself."

After his transplant operation Mohamed went to the UNHCR for assistance and was referred to its partner organization, Caritas. He was prescribed sleeping pills and discharged without further inquiry. He claimed that the medical staff working for Caritas were not trained professionals and routinely prescribed the wrong medication for refugees. He claimed to know of a gentleman from Sudan whose leg was amputated as a result of misdiagnosis. Mohamed attributed much of his misfortune to his perceived lack of support. At the time the interview took place, he was sleeping in front of the UNHCR building in Cairo, in protest against an institution he feels betrayed him. He explained how he had believed that once he made contact with the UNHCR, his problems would be over.[11]

Mohamed was not alone in his condemnation. Five people complained about the treatment they received from Caritas. One woman, a 32-year-old Sudanese migrant, explained, "This is not right how we are being treated. They keep postponing meetings. The UNHCR does not want to know about my kidney. If you go to Caritas, they tell you to pay first and then they will reimburse you for half. The whole experience is humiliating. They dismiss everything we [refugees] say and constantly delay meetings. We wait, and when we come after a month, they send us home and make us wait some more. When you call no one answers the phone."

In sum, with little trust in local authorities, migrants are less likely to report instances of abuse. Rather, they have to find ways to help themselves. Despite the many risks involved, selling a kidney was one such strategy.

The Social Determinants of Organ Sales

For most people, selling a kidney was not so much a rational decision but rather a consequential imposition, informed by the everyday challenges of sustaining themselves and/or their families. It was one of many circumstantial outcomes related to a variable set of factors negotiating the migrant condition. In this regard, involvement in the organ trade was not causally linked to the criminal operations of traditional organized crime groups or organ trafficking rings, as suggested by numerous media reports (see, e.g., Holmes 2016; and Pokharel 2015); rather, it was symptomatic of a kind of circumstantial criminality, an irregular adaptation to a challenging market environment. In an environment with limited resources, kidneys were often the most valuable resource people had in their possession. For some, with limited employment opportunities in either the formal or informal sectors, the organ trade was the only source of income available. For others, it represented an opportunity to enhance their labor market prospects. Joyce, a female Sudanese migrant, said, "When you are suffering and short of money and you need to help your kids, you can donate your kidney." Kalib, a young Sudanese man, said, "It is better to sell a kidney than live on the street. I have to help myself. This was the only way for me. But the money was finished after 6 months."

Most women who had sold one of their kidneys were single mothers. They described the challenges of raising children on a low budget. Despite working long hours as housekeepers, their remuneration was wholly insufficient to meet the costs of running a household. The women who were interviewed had between two and five children. They explained that with their limited budget they could not afford to send all of their children to school, if any. Moreover, they could not pay for childcare. Often a number of families would live together in the same household, splitting costs and sharing responsibilities. Yet, there was not always someone available to watch over the children, which meant leaving them alone for extended periods of time. Hiba, a single mother working as a housekeeper, described an incident where a child who had been left on his own for the day had fallen from a balcony and died. Notwithstanding this apparent danger, Hiba insisted that she had little choice but to continue working, even when her children were unsupervised. Her immediate concern was the more probable risk of losing her job, falling deeper into arrears, and being evicted from her home. Struggling to keep up with payments and concerned for the well-being of their children, women viewed the sale of a kidney as an opportunity to transform their lives. Amirah, a Sudanese sex worker, explained how she had hoped to use the money she received from selling her kidney to improve her life choices: "I do not want to work in clubs, but this is better than working as a cleaner. I cannot feed my family any other way. I thought that if I sold my kidney, I could start my own business selling clothes. This would be a better way for me."

These respondents were motivated by a desire to advance their life chances. For most women, it was their hope that in selling one of their kidneys they could send their children to school, start a business, or relocate to another country with better labor options and/or conditions. Men were similarly motivated. Three men described feeling emasculated by their joblessness (see also Jefferson 2002; and Yea 2015). They were uneasy staying at home with their children while their wives were out working. Musa, commenting on his unemployment, explained that in South Sudan "the man must provide for the family. You cannot have a wife unless you have something to give them." For Musa the sale of his kidney was the ultimate sacrifice, a way to reestablish and verify his male identity. It was better to be an organ seller than an impotent husband.

> I cannot find work here, so I stay at home and take care of our children. I wanted to sell my kidney to make a new life for my family. It is my responsibility to make sure that they are OK. Back then we had no home. We were staying with other people, but I knew their generosity could only last for so long. The children were crying with hunger. So, I went to Ataba and I told one guy about my problems, and he suggested that I sell my kidney. I had to make this sacrifice for my family.

Unplanned events were another factor that predisposed people to selling one of their kidneys. Living on the margins of society, circumstances can change from bad to worse in an instant. After his mother was involved in an accident that severed her spinal cord and broke a thigh bone, Kamal sold his kidney to cover her medical expenses.

> I could not find a job here [Cairo] for three years. It was very difficult. I stayed with some people, but they treated me very bad. They made me sleep outside on the balcony. They did not respect me because I had no job. I stayed with them for a year. All this time I was looking for work. I was very worried because my mother was sick, and I needed money for her treatment. I eventually found work with a ceramic company in Maadi. I was only paid E£10 (about $0.62) per day. I worked around 9 hours per day. I was 16 and could not negotiate a higher wage. They did not take me seriously because they knew I was desperate. I had to find money to help my mother. No one approached me

about my kidney. I needed money. I spoke to someone who told me this was very safe and that I would make a lot of money. I was offered $7,000. I agreed to do this for my mother. My mother is very sick and needs an operation for her leg and back. This will cost $25,000. But the money was not enough. She still has not got the operation.

He added, "After selling my kidney, I lost my appetite. I am not strong like before. I stayed with a friend after the operation, because I did not want my mother to know what I did."

Others sold a kidney after losing their jobs under circumstances beyond their control. Two of the respondents had fallen ill and were subsequently dismissed by their employers. Another respondent from South Sudan had been arrested for driving without a license, and lost his job while in prison.

> I was driving to Suez with my niece and nephew when they stopped me. I had a yellow card, but the police wanted to see my license. They told me to leave the car and go, but I refused because this car was my responsibility. So, they arrested me and the children also. Relatives had to pay the police not to abuse me. They beat me with a stick and would put water over me and kick me to get up. I was just given halawa and cheese to eat—if your family do not bring you food, you don't eat. They held me there for three months. I never spoke to a lawyer, no one. During this time the UN closed my file. This was in 2008. My relative had to pay $3,000 so that I could be released. We had to pay more so that the children would receive favorable treatment. After I was released from prison, I could not find work for a year. I lost my job after I was arrested. So, when I was released, I had nothing, and I needed to pay my relative for his help. This is when I decided to donate my kidney [2010].

Najla, age 23, traveled to Cairo to advance her education. She took all of her savings with her but what little money she had when she arrived was stolen: "I was staying at a friend's apartment. One night someone broke into our home and I lost everything. I had no money. Then I met some guy. He is in the jail now. He said that I would get the money the easy way, a lot of money. I was promised $40,000 to sell my kidney. He told me that this was a safe procedure that would benefit everybody." Najla received E£40,000 upon completing the surgery, which when converted to U.S. dollars amounts to about $2,600, significantly less than what she was promised. As soon as she received the payment, Najla was asked to leave, without receiving any information about the procedure or the type of postoperative care that was needed.[12] Najla felt too ashamed to tell anyone about her experience and spent a significant portion of the payment covering the costs of a hotel room while she recovered. Najla frequently experiences sharp pains in her lower abdomen and can no longer perform tasks that involve heavy lifting.

Although most of the people I interviewed were aware that they were agreeing to sell a kidney, some of them were physically coerced and/or deceived into having their kidneys removed. Two people had been taken to a local hospital on the pretense that they were receiving medical treatment. Zarif was suffering from a severe intestinal disorder and required urgent medical attention. He claimed that he could not find work until he received treatment. At the time he was staying with the smuggler who had arranged for his entry into Egypt. The smuggler, or *samsar* (as Zarif described him), known as Rashad, agreed to bring him to a clinic, provided that he was compensated once he had started working. According to Zarif, Rashad took him to a number of clinics where preliminary blood tests were conducted, which he understood were to diagnose his medical condition. After he went to four or five clinics (Zarif was vague on the details), he eventually spoke to a doctor who assured him that he could perform a successful operation. When Zarif regained consciousness, he noticed a large scar across his abdominal area and his lower back. He was told by a nurse that this was where an endoscope entered to perform intestinal surgery. An ultrasound later confirmed that one of his kidneys had been removed.

According to Zarif, he had no prior knowledge that his kidney would be removed. Yet, having revealed that his intestinal condition had also been treated, it would not be unreasonable to question whether Zarif had in fact traded his kidney in return for treatment and, more pertinently, for Rashad's services. Considering that Zarif claims to have visited several clinics for blood tests before his donation, it seems rather dubious to conclude that his suspicions were not aroused at any point during this process.

Other cases were less ambiguous, however. Grace explained how she had been deceived by her then partner into selling her kidney.

> After three months living in Cairo, I met a man and I moved in with him shortly after. At the time I was working as a house girl. When I was working there, I hurt my back and then I lost my job. My boyfriend took me to the hospital to get my back fixed. The doctor never spoke to me. I saw the doctor who

did the operation on my back, but my boyfriend spoke to another doctor. The operation took around 12 hours. The back operation cost E£30,000. After the operation I noticed a large scar.

Grace continued, "He gave some money [amount not specified] but this went on rent, children, and food. School is E£1,000 per month for preschool. After three months all the money was finished. Now, I feel tired most of the time, and I cannot do any heavy work." According to Grace, this particular man had sold his kidney earlier and was working for the clinic as an organ broker. Subsequently, Grace was informed that her former partner had moved in with another woman shortly after her operation. This woman, Grace claimed, had her kidney removed also.

The Failure of Crime and Immigration Controls

The selective categorization of people as asylum seekers, refugees, and illegal migrants enables state authorities to shift and indefinitely defer the legitimacy of claims to legal entitlements, for example, under the Four Freedoms Agreement, and/or international protection under refugee law. The interpretation and application of refugee status at the local level reflects national interests and priorities, which change over time (Crawley and Skleparis 2018: 51). Rather than advance legal protections, the label *refugee* was used by Egyptian authorities to identify and manage migrant populations residing in and entering the country. The Sudanese nationals interviewed in this chapter traveled to Egypt in search of better employment options and living conditions. Nevertheless, they were classified as asylum seekers and subject to the UNHCR registration process. For those who were granted refugee status, the protections "guaranteed" under international refugee law were not recognized by the Egyptian state. Others lost their refugee status for failing to "regularize" their residency permits. More generally, African migrants were identified and designated as illegal or undocumented by law enforcement officials because of their skin color and ethnicity, regardless of their legal status or reasons for travel (see Chapter 5). With limited access to employment, residency, and/or education, marginalized people have to find ways to help themselves. In this regard, selling or arranging the sale of a kidney is a survival strategy necessitated by a difficult economic environment. Although most of the organ sellers I interviewed regretted selling a kidney, it was not the horror of organ sale that they wanted to communicate. Rather, it was their lack of support in a precarious environment with little or no opportunity for social mobility. Mahmoud, a 21-year-old Sudanese construction worker, explained, "I do not regret this. If I had some support, I would not have to do this [sell a kidney]. We need protection here. I was robbed when I came here; my passport and money was all taken. We are targeted by everyone because they know that we are suffering. There is no protection for us from the government or anyone."

Although some people had their kidneys removed under fraudulent or coercive circumstances, most sellers were under no illusion as to what they were agreeing to. Fatimah, whose narrative introduces this chapter, was prepared for the extremity of death and was willing to forfeit her life if it meant helping her family. Considerations of legality or consent held little meaning for her: "The person [broker] who convinced me had sold his kidney, but now this man is dead. He told me that everything was good, that if I sell my kidney, your life will be good. You will get money to help your family. How could I change my mind? I have to support my family. This is not any kind of choice. My children will suffer if I do not do this."

There is little to suggest that law enforcement measures against the organ trade are of any tangible benefit to people targeted for organ sale. On the contrary, criminal sanctions have pushed the trade further underground, increasing the role that organ brokers play in facilitating illegal transactions. Similarly, tighter controls around migration have the paradoxical effect of increasing the market for people smugglers and/or traffickers in the migration process. Although it is debatable whether or not the Egyptian state has either the capacity or the interest to enforce legal provisions against the organ trade, it is unlikely that criminal sanctions will have a significant effect on the existence of organ markets. The organ trade cannot be reduced to a singular criminal act. It is a particular expression of violence linked to a process of exploitation experienced over time and space. With regard to the exploitation of migrants, understood here in the narrow pejorative sense, political attention has largely focused on the activities of smuggling networks and human traffickers (Aronowitz 2001; Salt 2000). There has been relatively less attention paid to the laws and policies of transit or destination states where people are ultimately exploited. Even though some European leaders have claimed that smuggling and trafficking organizations are behind the increased flow of migrants attempting to cross the Mediterranean, it is the closing of regular and safe routes that are producing demand for their activities (De Haas 2008; Brachet 2016).

In 2017 the European Union signed an agreement with the Egyptian government to manage migrant populations attempting to cross the Mediterranean into Europe. This agreement, discussed in the next chapter, correlates with the further erosion of refugee status to the extent that African migrants who had been residing in Egypt for years were being arrested and threatened with deportation (see also Macklin 2014). Claims for asylum by African migrants were increasingly turned down as more asylum seekers arrived from Syria and Yemen following the outbreak of civil war. At the same time, the United States, under the Trump administration, cut resettlement places by more than 40% (UNHCR 2018).

Several of the people I interviewed had taken significant risks to come to Cairo. Most did not intend to travel onward to Europe but decided to leave because of a combination of political and economic factors, a lack of access to legal entitlements, and human security. As conditions worsened in Cairo, large sums of money (between $3,000 and $8,000) were needed to pay smugglers and secure travel, often under cramped and unsafe conditions. Female respondents in particular faced brutality and hardship along the way. Selling a kidney was another aspect of this journey, part of a wider struggle to survive in a hostile environment. In the next chapter I examine the fallout of the 2015 migration crisis from the perspective of African migrants residing and/or seeking asylum in Egypt. Drawing on their experiences, I explore the relationship between people smuggling and the organ trade.

5

EXODUS

ON SEPTEMBER 6, 2014, a boat carrying 500 migrants from Egypt to Italy capsized in the Mediterranean Sea. There were only nine reported survivors. A Palestinian man interviewed by the Geneva-based International Organization for Migration (IOM) recalled boarding the boat in Damietta, Egypt, along with migrants from Sudan, Syria, and Eritrea. He explained how during the voyage they had been ordered to board another smaller, less seaworthy vessel.[1] When the passengers refused, the smugglers who were onboard a second larger vessel, rammed into the side of their boat, causing it to capsize. Almost all the passengers were reported missing, presumed drowned after the boat began taking on water. A spokeswoman for the Sicilian coast guard, interviewed by the *Guardian*, said they had no information about the incident and no contact with any survivors (P. Walker 2014). The area had been searched, but there was no trace of a boat or of any bodies. On the same day another boat heading toward Italy and carrying 250 people capsized off the coast of Tripoli, Libya (P. Walker 2014). Months later two boats sank off the Maltese coast and the Greek island of Rhodes (Kirchgaessner et al. 2015). An emergency meeting of EU interior and foreign ministry officials was called in response to reports that several hundred migrants had been killed (European Council 2015c). Afterward, the European Commission announced plans to coordinate "a systematic effort to capture and destroy vessels used by the smugglers" in Libya (European Council 2015a).[2]

On September 21, 2016, a vessel carrying 600 migrants from Egypt to Italy overturned in the Mediterranean Sea. The boat was dangerously overloaded and sank 8 miles from the port city of Rosetta, in northern Egypt. The dead included Egyptian, Sudanese, Eritrean, and Somali nationals. The incident was reported to be "the largest smuggling operation ever detected in Egypt" (Kingsley 2016). In November 2016, Egypt's Parliament passed Law 82, known as the Law on Combating Illegal Migration and Smuggling of Migrants.[3] Law 82/2016 set out prison terms and fines for individuals who were found guilty of smuggling migrants, acting as brokers, or facilitating migrant journeys. Shortly after the law was approved by Parliament, 56 people received sentences of up to 14 years in prison for convictions including murder, manslaughter, and negligence in relation to the September 2016 incident (Kingsley 2016; BBC News 2017). The speed and severity of the sentences were intended to act as a deterrent, underlining the Egyptian government's commitment to cracking down on people smuggling and human trafficking.

Egypt's law on smuggling was established as part of a joint EU-Africa strategy to "prevent and address irregular migration and to fight related organized crime, such as migrant smuggling and trafficking in human beings" (European Council 2015c: 12).[4] Figures released by the European Commission in 2018 claimed that there was an 80% reduction in "irregular" arrivals entering European territory via the Central Mediterranean Route since the height of the "crisis" in 2015. The successful interdiction of migrant vessels was credited to the coordinated efforts of European leaders and African heads of state to manage migration flows originating from Africa (European Commission 2018a). However, the policies and practices that constitute the EU's migration strategy in Africa have had some unintended consequences (see Frelick et al. 2016). Although the number of migrants, asylum seekers, and refugees crossing the Central Mediterranean Route has decreased, the de facto closing of borders has pushed people to further extremes, increasing the hold that criminal networks have over their mobility. In this chapter I engage with the narratives of African migrants who attempted to make the journey to Europe using irregular routes into and out of Egypt and Libya. Unable to finance the cost of travel, *samasira* (intermediaries who facilitate extra-legal migration) encouraged them to sell a kidney to raise the necessary capital to pay for travel overseas. Drawing on the experiences of the Sudanese, Eritrean, and Ethiopian migrants I interviewed in Cairo between 2017 and 2020, I examine the impact of crime and immigration controls on informal market dynamics, exploring the convergence of smuggling and organ trading networks in Cairo's informal economy.

Securing Borders

Ongoing conflicts in Syria, Libya, Somalia, Yemen, Afghanistan, and Iraq, repressive regimes in Ethiopia, Eritrea, Sudan, and South Sudan, and political instability following the Arab Spring (2011) have coincided with an increase in attempted crossings, shipwrecks, and fatalities on the Central Mediterranean Route. Figures released by the IOM in 2017 estimated that more than 22,500 migrants died or disappeared while attempting to cross the Mediterranean from North Africa between 2014 and 2017 (IOM 2017a). Although these figures are high and undoubtedly a cause for concern, a relatively small percentage of total migration figures account for people attempting to reach Europe by extralegal means (see Trilling 2018; and De Haas 2008). Nevertheless, in the years following the so-called migration crisis, the European Union tripled its spending on border management controls, technologies, and policing to prevent extralegal migration (Anderson 2017; D. Stevens and Dimitriadi 2018). European governments have discussed the need for a humanitarian solution to the crisis unfolding at Europe's borders. At the same time, the spectacle of death in the Mediterranean Sea has been appropriated into a political narrative that rationalizes the expansion of a security framework against "illegal" (or irregular) migration. Exceptional measures have become the norm, rooted in a criminocentric approach to migration management that reproduces the irregular patterns of migration it sets out to destroy.

Political leaders have suggested that the activities of people smugglers and human traffickers are responsible for luring migrants onto vessels making dangerous journeys overseas. Politicians, largely representing groups aligned with the political right, have suggested that, to protect jobs and livelihoods, people need to be deterred from migrating, whether or not they are seeking asylum (see S. Walker 2018). Framing migration as a national security issue in 2016, the Hungarian president Victor Orbán claimed that "every single migrant poses a public security and terror risk" (Kroet 2016). Mateo Salvini, acting as Italian interior minister in early 2019, argued that his hardline policies against immigration have saved lives by preventing "migrants, and smugglers, from making the deadly crossing" (see Horowitz 2019). Speaking in

2019, the United Kingdom home secretary Priti Patel claimed that "ruthless gangs of criminal people smugglers" are putting lives in danger (Ford 2019). What these statements suggest is that, to protect lives and preserve the national interest, borders need to be controlled and suspect activities, individuals, and/or groups, including people seeking refuge, involved in irregular migration need to be punished.

Writing in 2006, Judith Butler noted that this trend of securing borders as a way to manage migration accelerated after the events of September 11, 2001. In the post-9/11 period immigration was normatively linked with criminality and terrorism and U.S. state policy took a decidedly punitive turn, placing an emphasis on border security and protection (Butler 2006; see also Macklin 2014). Under the Trump administration, the U.S. Department of Homeland Security (Witsman 2019; Martin 2017a; Martin 2017b) has taken efforts to step up border and interior enforcement further, in an attempt to deport all unauthorized persons regardless of their reasons for traveling. Similarly, in Australia Operation Sovereign Borders (OSB) has been praised for successfully intercepting and detaining people smugglers, traffickers, and irregular maritime arrivals in offshore locations (Dutton 2017).

Whether intentional or not, there is a fundamental misconception between people smuggling and human trafficking in governmental approaches to migration management. Trafficking is primarily an offense against the person; smuggling is a violation of state sovereignty that involves crossing borders illegally (see UNODC 2000a).[5] People smuggling is an illegal form of trade in which the commodity exchanged is the illegal entry of a person into one or more countries. In human trafficking the commodity that is exchanged is the control over a person for profit (see Bilger et al. 2006; and Kleemans 2009). The level of exploitation involved in human trafficking is significantly higher (see Campana and Varese 2016). Conflating smuggling with trafficking legitimizes the expansion of the law enforcement apparatus, bringing any cross-border movement considered irregular within the scope of criminal sanction. Criminalizing irregular migration, broadly interpreted as any movement that takes place outside the regulatory norms of the sending, transit, and receiving countries, is rationalized as a necessary measure to prevent human trafficking (see IOM 2017b). However, tighter controls around migrant mobility and the increased threat of punishment for immigration offenses are preventing people from claiming asylum and creating demand for extralegal migration. It is in this context that the clandestine routes from

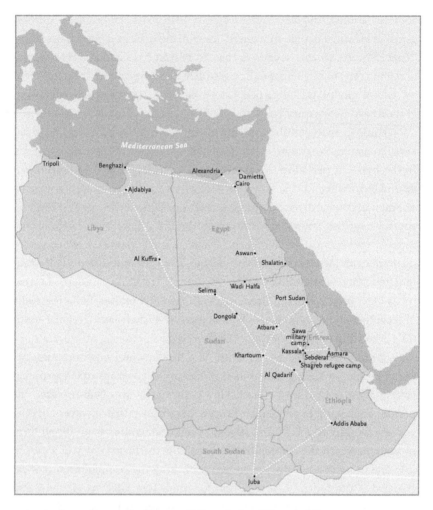

MAP 1. Smuggling routes between Eritrea, Sudan, Libya, and Egypt.

North Africa have developed as an extreme response to economic turmoil and closed borders.

The EU Emergency Trust Fund for Africa

In 2012 the president of the UN Security Council articulated a concern about "cross-border trafficking and movement" as a threat to international peace and security and suggested that it "can be addressed by improving Member States' abilities to secure their borders" (United Nations Security Council 2012: 2). The following year, the Israeli government constructed a security fence along the Israel-Egypt border. Quoted in the *Times of Israel*, the Israeli prime minister Binyamin Netanyahu lauded the construction of the fence for "making a significant contribution to tackling the dual threat of illegal migration and terrorism in the Sinai" (Fiske 2013). The return of the Egyptian military to the Sinai Peninsula, after the inauguration of Egyptian president Abdel Fattah al-Sisi in 2014, created additional barriers that obstructed the mobility of migrants. Although migration into Israel from the Sinai Peninsula was significantly reduced, the closing of borders had a displacement effect, leading to increased migration into and out of Egypt and Libya along the Central Mediterranean Route. To put this into perspective, there were 34,586 Eritrean migrants intercepted by border patrols in northern Egypt and Libya in 2014, up from 2,604 in 2012 (Frontex 2015).

Concerned by the level of maritime arrivals coming from Africa and the Middle East, the European Union (EU) invested heavily in the development of extraterritorial deterrence measures. These measures include training and support for border forces, the construction of security fences and detention centers, and the development of advanced coastal radar systems (e.g., the EUROSUR system) to detect and intercept people smugglers or traffickers (United Nations Security Council 2015).[6] Following the Valletta Summit on migration in 2015, the European Commission established an emergency trust fund for Africa (EUTF) to address "the root causes of instability, forced displacement, and irregular migration" and to protect migrants "from violence, abuse and exploitation" (European Commission 2015). The political declaration from the summit calls on EU member states and their African counterparts to respond decisively and to work together to "manage migration flows in all their aspects" (European Council 2015b). This involves enlisting the help of African partners (governments), identified for their strategic importance along migrant routes as countries of origin, first arrival, and transit, to prevent "irregular migration and fight against trafficking of human beings, smuggling of migrants, and other related crimes" (European Commission 2015). The assistance provided by the fund is framed in terms of capacity building and development to support the rule of law, human rights, and conflict resolution in Africa. In practice, the outsourcing of Europe's security agenda encourages and supports the apprehension and return of migrants, irrespective of their legal status.

In a Joint Action Plan signed in March 2016, the European Union announced an agreement with Turkey to build cooperation with Frontex, the European Border and Coast Guard Agency, with the aim of reinforcing the patrolling and surveillance capacity of the Turkish coast guard in the Aegean Sea (European Council 2016). The agreement committed Turkey to shelter Syrian refugees and readmit irregular migrants deported from Europe. In return, the EU paid Turkey €6 billion and promised to resettle one Syrian refugee for every irregular migrant readmitted to Turkey. A statement released by the European Commission in April 2018 claimed that irregular arrivals from Turkey to the EU had been reduced by 97%. However, this measure of success has come at a significant human cost. Given free rein to prevent migrants from crossing into European territories, the Turkish coast guard has been involved in several violent incidents. In November 2017 gunshots were fired at a migrant vessel heading toward Greece, forcing its occupants back into Turkish waters (Sea-Watch 2017). At the Turkish-Syrian border there were reports of migrants being beaten and killed (Human Rights Watch 2016; McKernan 2017). Migrants entering or being readmitted into Turkey have faced further abuse: from being denied the right to apply for asylum to arbitrary detention (Bosworth et al. 2018; Freedman 2016; D. Stevens and Dimitriadi 2018).

The readmittance agreement that underlies the EU-Turkey deal presents a clear violation of the principle of nonrefoulment, prohibiting the expulsion of a refugee to "territories where his [or her] life or freedom would be threatened on account of his [or her] race, religion, nationality, membership of a particular social group or political opinion" (UN 1951: Article 33(1)). Nevertheless, the agreement has served as a platform for similar agreements with Libya and Egypt under the EUTF for Africa. Shortly after the trust fund was announced, Libya received €90 million to strengthen coordinated efforts to "disrupt the business model of people smugglers and human traffickers" as part of Operation Sophia (see European Commission 2015; and European Council 2015a). Further funding was provided in 2017 to support the creation of a "protection space" for migrants and refugees.[7] This involved the construction of detention centers to contain migrants, asylum seekers, and refugees who had been forcibly returned from Europe. In 2017 Egypt received €11.5 million as part of a program called "Enhancing the Response to Migration Challenges in Egypt" (European Commission 2017). This was in addition to funding received from Italy and Germany to facilitate the return of Egyptian nationals to Egypt.[8]

EU support has strengthened Egypt's policing and surveillance capacities by providing training and funding for its security forces operating under the National Coordinating Committee for Combating and Preventing Illegal Migration (NCCPIM). It has also provided the Egyptian government with political legitimacy at a time when its oppressive state apparatus has come under scrutiny for perpetrating human rights abuses (Human Rights Watch 2017b). In Libya, EU funding has created a situation in which migrants are being detained for profit by dissident militia groups (see also Boffey 2019). These partnerships and agreements have effectively given license for already repressive regimes to control populations by force (see Statewatch 2019a; Statewatch 2019b). Obstructing the mobility of migrants has reduced regional labor mobility options and has discouraged people from claiming asylum out of fear of arrest and deportation (Koser 2010; Anderson 2012). As a consequence, clandestine and hazardous routes are being used by migrants in attempts to evade authorities and the threat of detention or repatriation. For smugglers, fewer opportunities to travel translate into a reduction in profits. To minimize their losses, smugglers raised their fees from a high of $1,500 in 2014 to a minimum of $3,500 in 2018. One implication of this is that prospective passengers unable to finance their travel are being referred to organ brokers for kidney sale.

Intersections of Violence

Nuredin Wehabrebi Atta was arrested by the Italian police in 2014 and given protective custody in return for information on the activities of key members of a criminal network that smuggled people, arms, and drugs. In his testimony, obtained from the Office of the Liaison Magistrate in Rome, Atta described his role facilitating smuggling operations in Libya. He explained how different smuggling groups were working together in Libya, Egypt, and Tunisia, sharing information (e.g., travel routes) and resources (e.g., arms). Four individuals were identified as coordinating the activities of network members.

> The four smugglers I told you about are the guys leading the main part of human smuggling from Libya. There are minor groups operating in Egypt and Tunisia, but they cannot be compared to the others when you look at the number of trips and the financial gain involved. All four of these guys have a group of trusted men who work for them, between six and ten. Apart from that there

are numerous men working for them who earn a lot less. The groups are not in conflict but collaborate. All these groups have arms at their disposal: Kalashnikovs, Makarovs, and other arms. The four groups are active in Tripoli, except for Walid [smuggler], who is also active in Bengasi.

Before his arrest Atta was managing a bar in Tripoli, where he negotiated travel costs with migrants seeking passage across the Mediterranean. Migrants, he explained, are collected in the Kufrah region of Libya in towns bordering Sudan. They are then transported by microbus to Tripoli before departing from the North Libyan coast. Atta would collect and deposit cash payments to the smugglers in advance of any scheduled departures overseas. In his testimony he claimed that migrants who were unable to pay for smuggling services were transferred to organ "traffickers" in Egypt to sell their organs: "Sometimes the migrants do not have money to pay for the trip they made over land. . . . I was told by Khaled and Walid [names have been changed] and some of the survivors that these persons who cannot pay are handed over to Egyptians for their organs, which are sold in Egypt for around $15,000. Sometimes they are even killed."

Atta's testimony led to the arrest of 23 individuals believed to be involved in human trafficking (Tondo and Scammell 2016). A further 15 warrants were issued for suspected members of the organization, including nationals from Eritrea, Ethiopia, and Italy. The reports of organ trafficking were never confirmed by the Italian authorities, and the arrest warrants remain outstanding. Although it is possible that the veracity of Atta's testimony was compromised under the implicit duress of police questioning, it did provide insight into the structure and activities of smuggling networks in Libya. His account is consistent with empirical studies that suggest that rudimentary hierarchies exist within smuggling networks, which coordinate activities with smaller localized units, which operate at different stages of the migrant journey, overland and overseas (see, for example, Campana 2018; and Pastore et al. 2006). Atta's testimony also suggests that there is a connection between people smuggling and the organ trade in Egypt.

The interview narratives presented in this chapter reveal the extent of this connection, demonstrating how organ brokers working in tandem with smugglers encourage people to sell a kidney to finance transport overseas. In contrast to Atta's account, I did not find evidence of people being killed for their organs. Furthermore, the smugglers and organ brokers who I interviewed were not part of a single criminal organization "trafficking" people. Nevertheless, they shared a common interest to maintain their revenues in the face of new regulatory measures introduced as part of the government's anti-trafficking regime. *Samasira* working at the intersections of criminal networks formed key links between different groups and facilitated mutually beneficial arrangements. This relationship or pattern of economic exchange developed alongside punitive immigration controls and containment strategies established as part of the EUTF. The narratives of the people I interviewed in this chapter speak to the violence of the migration policies and law enforcement strategies played out on the bodies of migrant communities.

Indefinite Detention

The assassination of former Libyan president Muammar al-Gaddafi in 2011 created a power void in Libya. The subsequent lack of political oversight and judicial accountability facilitated the development of smuggling activities on the Libyan coast. Without a recognized political leader in Libya, the EU was unable to establish a formal readmittance agreement similar to the deal struck with Turkey. In theory, this gave migrants traveling from Libya a better chance of reaching Europe and claiming asylum. At the same time, the gap in governance enabled militias, armed tribal groups, and smugglers to establish pockets of control across Libya's Mediterranean coast. These networks, described by Atta in the testimony, established a monopoly over smuggling operations across the Central Mediterranean Route. Accordingly, they have become the focal point of international border security policies and joint investigative teams with a mandate to disrupt migrant smuggling networks on the Mediterranean coastline (Europol 2018; Amar 2013).

Notwithstanding the lack of a formal agreement with the Libyan government, EU member states have proceeded to cooperate with an ambiguous collective of Libyan militias who control migrant populations in their respective territories (Brachet 2016). In 2016 Italy pledged assistance to the Libyan coast guard by providing funding, boats, and intelligence to facilitate the interception and "voluntary" return of migrants to Libya. This agreement has materialized into an economic opportunity for criminal groups to intercept, detain, and exploit people with impunity (Mannochi 2017). According to Amnesty International, migrants intercepted at sea are detained without legal recourse in clandestine detention centers on the borderlands of Libya and Egypt (Amnesty International 2017). Many of these centers, ostensibly under the control of the Libyan Department for Combating Illegal Migration (DCIM), are reportedly managed by the same networks that are responsible for smuggling migrants from the Sudanese border to Libya's northern coastline (Flynn 2017; Mannochi 2017). Arbitrarily detained in covert locations for indefinite periods of time, migrants can be exploited with impunity.

Samir, a 19-year-old Sudanese national, was detained in a Libyan detention center after boarding a vessel he believed was heading toward the Italian coast: "There were around 70 people in the boat, of all ages. Most of them were men. We were on the boat for 4 or 5 hours when all of a sudden, the engines cut out. Nothing happened for a long time. Then a larger boat came, and we were told to get on board. They had guns, so we knew they were serious." Samir, along with the other passengers, was taken to a warehouse on the eastern Libyan coast. They were put into a dark room and told to give up all their belongings. The men who had taken them there appeared to be Libyan militants.

"After they took our belongings, they told us to call our families and tell them to send money for our release. Some people called and were taken away after that, but I refused. I did not want to cause trouble for my family. But also, I could not remember their phone number." The militants threatened to sell anyone who did not get the requested money to the "organ mafia" in Egypt. Samir tried to call a friend in Sudan, but the number had been disconnected. Hungry and tired, he feared that his kidney would be taken and his body discarded into a mass grave. He had been forewarned of this possibility before leaving Cairo. "They took an Ethiopian man and stole his kidney. He was gone for three days. He was very weak and tired when they brought him back, always drinking water. He would not speak with anyone after this."

The Libyan army raided the warehouse and took Samir along with the captive migrants to an "official" detention center at the southern Egyptian border. The living conditions offered little improvement over the squalor they had experienced at the warehouse. Food supplies were rationed and delivered by representatives of UNICEF and the Red Cross. A blanket and a meal were provided, to be shared between groups of three. "We had pasta every day and one bottle of water, a liter for three people. The detention center was worse than a prison. It was overcrowded and dirty. We all had to eat and shit in the same place every day, like animals. No beds, no light, only darkness. There were many people there with large scars, from where their kidneys had been taken."

Samir was released on September 14, 2017. He spent three months in detention before being deported back to Sudan. The IOM arranged his transport at a cost of $105. He was smuggled back into Egypt four months later by way of the Wadi-Halfa port. I asked him what he would do next: "I will try again; I don't give up. But next time, I won't go to Libya," he concluded. Libya remains the most active point of embarkation in North Africa. However, the increased military presence off the Libyan coast and the risk of detention by armed militia groups has increased smuggling activity into and out of Egypt. This shift or rerouting of migrant traffic into and out of Egypt has coincided with the imposition of criminal sanctions targeting irregular migration and people smuggling.

Building on existing anti-trafficking measures established in 2010 (see Chapter 2), Egyptian Law 82 outlines specific penalties that target criminal groups responsible for people smuggling. The penalties range from fines of E£50,000 to E£500,000 to life imprisonment, if the offense was carried out by an "organized criminal group" and/or resulted in the death of smuggled migrants (Article 7).[9] The establishment of the National Coordination Committee for Combating and Preventing Illegal Migration and Human Trafficking brings the offense of people smuggling under the umbrella of human trafficking, extending culpability for crimes related to illegal migration. The law signals Egypt's intention to get tough on organized crime, people smuggling, and illegal migration by reinforcing the punitive trend of existing anti-trafficking legislation. Significantly, the crackdown on trafficking comes at the expense of commitments to safeguard the rights of asylum seekers and refugees. Article 27 provides for "the safe return of migrants to their countries, after confirming their nationalities or residency in such countries . . . provided that they have not been convicted of any criminal charges." Considering that migrants residing in Egypt without up-to-date resident permits, travel documents, or personal identification are categorized as illegal, it is difficult to see how this provision will provide for the safe return of people intercepted at sea. Notably, Law 82 does not include the term *refugee*. This omission elides any responsibility Egypt has to adhere to the UN Convention Relating to the Status of Refugees. Absent any guarantees to uphold the right to claim asylum or to protect against refoulment, the law serves to criminalize the mobility of migrants and to legitimize their detention and subsequent deportation. This failure to protect refugees has produced more demand for smuggling services and increased the dependency that migrants have on illicit networks.

Clandestine Migration

Ibrahim was waiting outside a café on a narrow street corner near Tahrir Square. He waved me over, gesturing to an empty chair. A television was playing footage of street demonstrations in the Sudanese capital, Khartoum. Protests in opposition to the ruling military regime were sweeping across the country. "Most of them will be killed," he explained calmly. "The regime will want to send a message, to prevent more demonstrations." Before coming to Egypt, Ibrahim was conscripted into the Sudanese Presidential Guard, a military unit responsible for protecting the Sudanese president, Omar al-Bashir. "I was with the army for about a year," he recalled. "We were given orders to demolish a village [in Darfur] believed to be a rebel stronghold. They told us to destroy everything, to burn it all down, to kill everyone, even the animals."

After the peace process broke down in 2014, military troops were dispatched to Darfur to eliminate the rebel militias and establish control over the region. Ibrahim was among a group of mutineers who refused to carry out their orders. "Some of us joined the rebels. Others were killed for disobeying direct orders. I was one of the lucky ones who made it to Egypt." Ibrahim claimed asylum and was granted refugee status in 2015. His refugee status was revoked a year later, for failing to provide the authorities at Mogamma with a permanent address. "It was impossible to find work [in Cairo] and without a job I couldn't eat or find anywhere to sleep. For months, I was sleeping on the street. Then a friend introduced me to an Egyptian guy who was looking for a driver."

For over half a century, nationals from Sudan and the Horn of Africa have traveled relatively freely into and out of Libya and Egypt (Hüsken 2017). These journeys have always been "irregular" in the sense that they are navigated and mediated by a collective of drivers and guides who know the desert terrain, physically and socially. These informal transport networks became professionalized as more border officials and security agencies were stationed at checkpoints, asking for bribes to cross state boundaries (see also Brachet 2018). The system of illegal taxation that emerged made cross-border travel an expensive undertaking for migrants. Moreover, it became a significant source of income for corrupt officials—police, military, custom officers—and drivers (known as *Muharib(in)*) specializing in the irregular movement of people. During his time in the military, Ibrahim acquired a detailed knowledge of the borderlands within and between Sudan, Libya, and Egypt. Ibrahim referred to himself as a *samsar*, being careful to distinguish his place in the historical tradition of cross-border movement.[10] His job, he said, was to organize transport and negotiate service fees as part of a clandestine network operating along the north Egyptian coast. "People come to me to organize their transport and to make the payment. I confirm the payment, and then I bring people from Cairo to Alexandria. They stay in warehouses, on chicken farms, and wait there until the time is ready to go to sea."

Smuggling networks have adapted their recruitment strategies in response to increased border controls along the Mediterranean coast. Passengers are collected in small fishing boats from different embarkation points (e.g., Damietta, Mersa Matruh, and Rosetta) along the north Egyptian coast and ferried out to sea. They are transferred onto larger vessels midway through the voyage, making it difficult for border patrols to identify and seize any one vessel. "When we get out to sea, we transport them into a large ship. This ship has a fishing license and can go anywhere. The police and coast guard are given prior warning, and an agreement is made for an emergency rescue, when the ships arrive into international waters. In the end they [the passengers] are taken the legal way. When they make land, they [the passengers] are given food, medication, and some money to keep on going into another country," Ibrahim explained. The smuggling networks, he claimed, involve members of the Egyptian, Libyan, and Italian coast guards, who exchange information on migrant vessels and the location of border patrols. The smugglers accept that a quota of migrant ships will be seized, allowing border authorities to document their success preventing illegal migration. In return, a limited number of ships carrying migrants will be permitted to enter international waters.

More established smuggling networks with the financial clout to pay protection money to border officials have the highest success rates. "These smugglers are working under officials. The official gives them protection to do their work. They are paying these officials a lot of money, let me tell you. I'm talking about Italian, Libyan, and Egyptian officials," Ibrahim clarified. Since 2014 smugglers operating out of Egypt and Libya have raised their fees from approx. $1,500 to $3,500 to compensate for a loss in profits. I asked Ibrahim how people could afford to pay this amount. "People can pay less than the asking price ($3,500), but if you do this, you're like a third-class passenger," he said. "These ones can end up in detention centers, where they will only be released if they agree to work or sell their bodies for sex." Ibrahim shifted in his seat uncomfortably, reaching for a cigarette. He inhaled slowly, taking his time to consider what he wanted to say next. "There are some people who only care about getting the money. They don't care if you arrive to your destination or end up dying at sea. This is why I advise people to make the payment in advance, even if that means selling a kidney."

Ibrahim drew my attention to bullet holes clustered over the door frame, a relic of the revolution where shots were fired at protesters during the demonstrations on January 25, 2011. He knows what he is doing is illegal but suggested that the government is at fault. "I do not see my work as bad because I am helping people to change their life for the better. Here they can die, because they wouldn't find help or protection."

In exchange for financial aid and economic cooperation, Egyptian and Libyan authorities agreed to implement EU-mandated sanctions against irregular migration. The objective from a European perspective was to limit migration across North Africa, on the false assumption that all trans-African migration routes ultimately lead to Europe (Andersson 2016). Under international pressure Egyptian and Libyan authorities began targeting irregular entries, with or without bribes. Arrests and deportation became more common, creating demand for more specialized and clandestine transport networks—in effect, transforming irregular migration into a clandestine activity. As Ibrahim's narrative demonstrates, travel arrangements are segmented between localized groups of actors who coordinate their activities at different stages along smuggling routes (see also Campana 2018). In an effort to avoid contact with state actors, migrants take longer circuitous routes that bring them into contact with a wider range of intermediaries, whose actions have a critical influence over their safety and well-being. The longer the journey, the more indebted and/or dependent migrants are on *samasira* for information and guidance, exposing them to a higher risk of harm. Some *samasira*, along with the network actors they are connected to (e.g. *muharibin*), are more reliable than others, delivering passengers safely on a relatively consistent basis. Others are more reckless, abandoning people along desert routes (Le Monde and AFP 2016), trading people for ransom (Van Reisen 2017), or overloading boats equipped for a maximum of 50 people with over 300 passengers (Grey and Ismali 2016). Others have developed working arrangements with organ brokers.

The Road to Cairo

Dawitt, a 19-year-old Eritrean national, was smuggled into Sudan in 2012. He crossed the border on foot by way of a mountain pass near Sebderat, eastern Eritrea, into Kassala, a city on the Sudan-Eritrea border. From there he was taken to Khartoum in a pickup truck along with other Eritrean men and women fleeing indefinite military service. In recent years, 2014–2019, Khartoum has become a transit hub for Eritrean, Ethiopian, Somalian, and Sudanese migrants traveling to Libya and Egypt. *Samasira* are often well known to migrant communities and can be found in cafés and restaurants, generally in areas of the city with large immigrant populations, for example, Al Amarat, Al Daim, Gabra, and Al Sahafa. Dawitt paid a *samsar* $300 to take him across the Sudanese border at Wadi Halfa, into Cairo. He paid less than the asking price of $500 because of his age; he was 16 at the time. However, the $200 difference was not forgotten by the *samsar*. Dawitt spent his first few nights at a hotel in Ataba, downtown Cairo, before beginning work at a factory producing glass in the 6th of October district. The work, which had been prearranged by the *samsar*, was unregulated, with little or no oversight involved in the operation of machinery or the control of chemicals and gases. Dawitt worked 12-hour shifts six days a week for E£2,500 (about $140).

> I was really stressed out and the guy who brought me here wanted his money back [$200]. Someone I was working with told me that I could sell my kidney. He said it was safe and that it was an easy way to make money. I thought that it would be a good way of getting money fast and traveling to Europe.... I was worried, but he convinced me that it is a very easy operation and you can live a normal life with one kidney. I saw that he was looking normal [healthy], and I did some research on the internet about organ donation. This guy was very sure that the operation was safe and performed in a good hospital.

He continued:

> At the time, I was thinking about killing myself. I just wanted my life to end. I didn't really care what happened, and I was thinking that it is better to sell and take the risk than to continue working like a slave in this factory. If I am

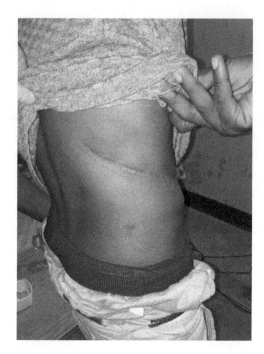

FIGURE 4. Dawitt after his kidney was removed, May 2018. Photo by author.

going to die anyway, why not sell my kidney? The only thing I was worried about was my family, especially my mother. I didn't want her to know about this. That was important to me.

Dawitt agreed to a payment of $5,000 in exchange for his kidney. Before the operation he was instructed to sign an affidavit declaring he was a Sudanese national and that the donation was being made on a voluntary basis. Under Egyptian law, transplants can be performed only "among foreigners of one nationality at the request of the State to which the donor and recipient belong" (translated from Article 6 of the Egyptian Transplant Law of 2010). This means that transplants cannot be performed between individuals of different nationalities. Brokers sidestep this requirement by dealing with select members of the Sudanese embassy who provide "approval of kinship" forms for a nominal fee of $1,000, paid by or on behalf of the broker. Dawitt had been concerned that the operation would not go ahead because he was of Eritrean nationality and the recipient was from Sudan. He was also underage—only people over the age of 25 are permitted to donate an organ in Egypt. The broker assured him that there was no need to worry about identification papers: "'It's very easy,' he said. 'You just say you are Sudanese at the hospital, and then you are going to sign the papers and it's done.'" In an agreement signed by the Arab League in 2017, the Sudanese government passed a law allowing any Arab national from an Arab state in conflict to claim nationality in Sudan. Brokers have used this law to their advantage to purchase passports and retrieve the requisite paperwork from the Sudanese embassy to solicit kidneys from undocumented migrants who cross the border into Egypt from Sudan (see Chapter 7).

When Dawitt was discharged from the hospital, he was taken to an apartment to convalesce: "After they gave me permission to leave the hospital, I asked them [medical staff] for my money. No one answered until Ali [the broker] came to collect me. He told me to go to the apartment and I would get the money when I was feeling better. We took a taxi to an apartment in Mohandessin, Shehab Street. He said I could rest there, and he would take care of everything." Dawitt received an envelope with $2,000 when he arrived at the apartment. Ali promised to pay him the remaining $3,000 once he had recovered from the surgery. Concerned that Ali would not honor their agreement, Dawitt reiterated his desire to travel to Europe, underlining how important it was for him to receive the payment ($5,000) in full. "I was very honest with him, I told him I sold my kidney for going out from Egypt, to make the journey to Europe. I told him about my dream, to one day go to America, to study at Harvard so I could be like Nelson Mandela. He [Ali] seemed like an educated guy, so I thought he would understand. But he just told me to rest, and that we would talk later. After about a week, he introduced me to his friend, Isaac, who he said could help me."

Isaac offered to take Dawitt to Alexandria, where he would board a vessel to Lampedusa, Sicily. He convinced Dawitt to make an immediate payment of $3,000, claiming that he needed the money up front to reserve a place on the next boat to leave from the Mediterranean coastline. Ali agreed to pay Isaac the $3,000 he had been "keeping on hold" for Dawitt. "I felt very comfortable with him [Isaac] after talking. He was Eritrean, and he didn't look like a thief. He told me that he smuggles hundreds of people every month and that he doesn't need the money. He made me feel like he was the one doing me the favor. He gave me his number and told me to call him when I was ready. So, I told Ali that he could give him the money. And I told him that I would make the journey as soon I was feeling stronger. I was very clear about that."

As reported by several other respondents, brokers often provide accommodation after surgery, keeping the donor-seller in a controlled space to limit the risk of police attention and/or to further exploit organ sellers for profit. Nine people I interviewed between 2014 and 2020 revealed connections between organ brokers and intermediaries involved in other illicit markets, such as the sex trade, people smuggling, and the drug trade. In each case the organ broker used his connections to provide additional services for an undisclosed fee, which was deducted from the price that had been agreed on in exchange for the organ. In Dawitt's case, he had been offered transport overseas to Europe without any assurances as to when, or if, the boat would depart. Without any alternatives Dawitt had no real choice but to place his trust in Ali. Feeling his strength return, Dawitt called Isaac several times, but there was no response. After several phone conversations, Ali, who had declined to visit since introducing Dawitt to Isaac, arranged to meet him at Marghani Square, downtown Cairo, along with Isaac.

> I waited for hours and I called him many times. He told me that they were on the way. Every time I called, he told me that they were coming, but they never arrived. His [Ali] mobile was turned off after that. . . . I took my phone and smashed it against the ground. I remember watching it break into small pieces and then I could feel it, the regret hitting me. I sat down crying, thinking about how I have sacrificed everything since leaving my family and I have nothing to show for it. Those motherfuckers have gone away with my money and my kidney.

When Dawitt reported the incident to the police, he was threatened with deportation. In the months that Dawitt was recovering from his surgery, he was unable to register his address at the Mogamma and regularize his status. In failing to provide the requisite paperwork, he was identified as an illegal migrant and refused assistance. From the perspective of the police Dawitt was not entitled to protection. When Dawitt protested, he was verbally insulted by police officials and warned that he would be deported if he refused to leave. The next time I met Dawitt, he introduced me to Petros, whose narrative features in the Preface. They were part of a group of young Eritrean men who were smuggled into Egypt and targeted for their organs in Cairo.

In contrast to the moral outrage occasioned by the spectacle of death on the Mediterranean Sea, public debate with regard to the dehumanizing effects of migration policies on everyday life has been considerably muted. This silence and lack of recognition for the lives of disqualified others is being exploited by state and nonstate actors alike, normalizing the violence of migration management (De Vries and Guild 2018: 3). In this context of political indifference and social exclusion, selling a kidney has become an economic reality for people living on the margins.

Exploiting Mobility

I met Ibrahim for a second time at a café in Taalat Harp, near Tahrir Square. He wanted to introduce me to a friend of his, Anisha, who was considering selling her kidney to pay for travel overseas. As discussed, *samasira* are important figures in migrant communities, maintaining and perpetuating migrant networks and social capital within and between countries of origin, transit, and destination. Accordingly, the people I interviewed often placed more trust in the words of *samasira* than those of government officials or representatives from international organizations, including the UNHCR. In navigating the uncertain routes into or out of Egypt, migrants base major decisions about crossing borders and raising the necessary capital to finance their journey on information and guidance they receive from *samasira* and their associates. This information is often incomplete and misleading and can lead to increased debts and exposure to unnecessary harm. According to Ibrahim, smuggling networks employ informants (e.g., border agents) to collect information on migrants on the road to Cairo. They exchange this information with other intermediaries, who target new arrivals for different illicit services, for example, guidance crossing borders, accommodation, identification, and organ sale.

> People call me before they come to Egypt, on the way from Sudan. They tell me how many people are coming and what they have paid. Unless you pay, you will never go to the microbus. You will have to go back across the border by yourself. People need to get the money somehow. . . . I know a Syrian who sold his kidney to pay a smuggler so that his family would be brought over from Syria. But listen, you sell the kidney by yourself. Bring the money and you can go. Smugglers don't want to get involved in this kind of business [organ trade].

Ibrahim was keen to stress the value of his work, perhaps sensing some disquiet at the direction the conversation was taking. He commented on the economic and social circumstances behind people-smuggling.

> Refugees and immigrants are not afraid of dying on the sea because they face death here or in their home country. They will take the risk even if they know they are going to die at sea. For me, I do not see my work as bad because I am helping people to change their life for the better. Here they can die, because they wouldn't find help or protection. In the next few days there is a bus coming from Sudan. All of them are coming to me. They called ahead to prepare for them housing and a trip into Europe. . . . But please, speak with Anisha. I want you to understand this better.

Anisha had contacted Ibrahim through a mutual friend who had recommended his services. She was determined to leave Egypt by any means necessary, giving up on the promise of resettlement. I interviewed Anisha at her home, a small apartment in Heliopolis. She shared the apartment with her parents and three younger sisters.

> We came here from Darfur in 2012. We sold everything we had to pay for the travel. Our house, clothes, jewelry, everything. On the way it was terrible. We were raped many times. My sisters are only children, 12 and 14. But the people who take you to the border they can do anything, it is their right. They beat my father and my mother also. . . . We continued our journey so that we could claim asylum and get out from here.

After months of waiting for an interview with the UNHCR, Anisha and her family were granted refugee status. Anisha was hopeful that they would soon be resettled outside Egypt. However, after four years of waiting, their case for resettlement has not progressed. In the intervening years Anisha's father was involved in an accident with a tuk-tuk driver, which led to serious health complications that have prevented him from working.

> The driver drove over his foot and crushed it. There was blood everywhere, but he never stopped to help. I think it was deliberate. I went to the police to report him, but the guard didn't take me seriously. He made fun of the situation and told me that he didn't think he should file a report. When I argued with him, he told me he would do something for me if I did something for him.

After the accident Anisha's father was taken to Caritas for medical treatment. His foot was bandaged, and he was advised to keep the wound clean and to change the bandage on a daily basis. Nevertheless, the skin around the wound started to discolor and her father began convulsing. He was suffering from sepsis, a potentially fatal form of blood poisoning, sustained from the injury to his foot. Subsequently, he was diagnosed with anemia and liver disease. Struggling to keep up with payments, Anisha approached a local money lender to request a loan of E£10,000 ($558). She found employment as a housekeeper in an effort to manage rising debts. As with the other respondents I interviewed, Anisha lamented the lack of employment opportunities in Cairo. She explained that the only work available to a female refugee was housework or sex work, neither of which provided any physical or financial security.

> The housework is very bad. The husband of the woman I was working for used to touch me inappropriately. I was not paid properly. The payment I received would change from week to week. I was working long hours, and I could only see my family at the weekend. When my father's condition got worse, I had to leave this job so that I could take care of him. And now I need to pay back the money I owe.

Anisha claimed to have received death threats from the money lender, who is demanding a weekly repayment of E£1,000 ($55). He has advised her to sell a kidney to pay off her debts. She could also use this money to go to Europe, he suggested. Ibrahim informed me that Anisha had already been in contact with a broker and had arranged to meet him. I asked her if she had negotiated a price with the broker and whether she would consider changing her mind.

> The lender threatened to kill me if I don't pay him back. He wants E£9,000. I can't pay this right now. Selling my kidney is the only way. I have to do this for my safety and the safety of my family. But really, I need to get out of here. There is nothing for me to do. If I get the money I have been promised, I can pay for a boat to Europe, and even if it is just me, I can find work to help my family. I will work there and send money back to them, so they can go to school and live like normal people. . . . Ibrahim, I hope you can help me achieve this.

The moral panic generated by the "migration crisis" combined with the perennial specter of human trafficking and organized crime has rationalized and reinforced the punitive logic behind border controls. These controls exacerbate the level of abuse and exploitation that migrants, regardless of their legal status, are exposed to (Anderson 2013). In the current global political climate, criminal policy has become synonymous with migration management.

In the United States, for example, immigration offenses outnumber all other federal offenses (Chácon and Coutin 2018). In Europe the EU migration partnership framework provides a formal and legal basis for discriminatory and coercive border practices that contribute to the exploitation of already marginalized populations. According to Boltanski and Chiapello (2005), the exploitation of mobility keeps some people immobile to support the mobility of more privileged others. Susan Marks (2008) elaborates: "The capacity to move about, network and multiply the settings in which one acts and interacts, is a key element in the accumulation of social (and actual) capital" (288). It is therefore in the interests of global hegemonic powers to maintain the status quo, to protect and limit access to capital networks by excluding people from less developed countries. However, the bifurcated purpose of crime and immigration controls to maintain internal order and exclude unwanted populations (i.e., migrants) is creating subspheres of criminal influence outside state control. The coercive power of state policies enables criminal entrepreneurs to exploit the inability of migrant populations to maintain a livelihood. This engenders a process of exploitation and social exclusion that can manifest in trafficking in its various forms.

Far from deterring criminal behavior, Egypt's anti-trafficking framework has stimulated criminal synergies and increased the influence that criminal actors have over "illegal" populations. This has led to increased violence and exploitation. Disillusioned with the UNHCR resettlement process, several people I interviewed turned to *samasira* for assistance relocating to another country. Their exclusion from state protection was a determining factor in their exploitation, compelling them to take risks they would have otherwise avoided: selling a kidney, risking death at sea under the threat of indefinite detention and/or deportation, trusting strangers, and traveling along unknown routes patrolled by armed militias. Significantly, their lack of valid identification and/or legal status reduced their bargaining power and increased their dependency on intermediaries who coordinated activities in the informal economy.

The second time I met Azim (introduced in Chapter 3), he was sitting outside a café on Tahrir Square smoking a *shisha* pipe. He greeted me with a broad smile and gestured for me to sit down beside him. During my previous visit in 2014, Azim told me he was approached by three men who convinced him to sell a kidney for $5,000. He was unemployed at the time and needed the money, so he agreed to the sale. "Things have changed since you were last here," he said, reaching for his cigarettes. "What's changed?" I asked. He inhaled deeply, taking his time to answer my question. "Life is more difficult than before. Everyone is struggling, the Egyptians also. There is no work for anyone, and everything is more expensive. This is why people do things they do not want to do." I waited for him to continue. "You know, the last time you were here I didn't tell you everything." He looked around the room to make sure no one was listening. Satisfied, he edged his chair closer to the table. "A few months ago, someone came to me and told me that he wanted to sell his kidney. I put him in contact with the broker, and they negotiated a price together. He was offered $4,500, but he wouldn't accept. This man, he disappeared after that and I never saw him again. I don't know where he is now."

Azim had been working with the brokers who recruited him, soliciting kidneys from the migrant community in Ard El-Lewa. "They offered me $100 for every person I convinced to sell a kidney. A lot of people who sell their kidney end up working with them. They are ashamed, but there is nothing else they can do." He explained that it was common for organ sellers to work as recruitment agents for more established brokers with long-standing connections to analytic labs and physicians. "This is how the networks grows," he said, searching for another cigarette. Azim claimed that the trade had become more secretive and violent. For this reason, it was safer to work with brokers rather than risk being accused of being an informer. "This [organ trade] is controlled by Sudanese and Egyptians who have been working in this business for a long time. This is a mafia we are talking about." He looked at me sternly, making sure he had my attention. "In these times they have been taking people with no papers directly from Sudan. These people do not go to the hospital. They have their kidneys removed in apartments outside of Cairo. You do not want to talk to these people," he warned. "This is now a criminal society. I don't want to be involved in this, but there is no protection for me. I am afraid."

In Egypt, the organ trade has developed from the informal economy as part of the "service industry" of organized crime, orchestrated by a loose network of intermediaries operating across the illegal-legal divide (see Chapter 3). In the past decade (2010–2020) new criminal synergies have emerged, bringing different actors, activities, and dynamics together over time and space. In the absence of state protection there are signs that criminal groups are emerging as an alternative source of governance controlling informal market transactions. I explore these signs in the next chapter.

6

ORGAN(IZED) CRIME

IN DECEMBER 2016 Egyptian authorities arrested 45 people on suspicion of involvement in an international organ trafficking ring. The Egyptian Administrative Control Authority (EACA), the government's anti-corruption body responsible for the investigation, claimed that the network was "made up of Egyptians and Arabs taking advantage of some of the citizens' difficult economic conditions so that they buy their human organs and sell [them] for large sums of money" (BBC 2016). The EACA stated that millions of dollars generated from human trafficking in organs had been seized from the suspects, adding that the group was "the largest international network for trading human organs." A further statement issued by the Ministry of Health claimed that the network included university professors, doctors, nurses, medical center owners, and brokers involved in illegal organ trafficking. According to the statement, "The group's illegal operations resulted in the death of one of the victims and permanent disabilities in others" (Ahram Online 2017). The investigation, led by the Ministry of Health, focused on a group of private hospitals and health centers, licensed and unlicensed, where the illegal transplants had been performed (Mourad and Noueihed 2016). Following the investigation, the centers and hospitals were reported to have been closed down. Moreover, 41 defendants were referred to the Criminal Court under charges of profiteering, bribery, money laundering, dereliction of duty, and causing permanent disabilities (Ahram Online 2017). On July 12, 2018, a judicial statement from the Cairo Criminal Court was released through the government's news outlet, the Middle East News Agency, announcing the conviction of 37 defendants on charges related to illicit trading in human organs. The court documents from this case have not been made available to the public, nor have any details regarding the status of the victims.

The arrests followed a slew of media reports concerning Egypt and the organ trade. One media outlet in 2016 claimed to have revealed how "child migrants are being sold to the organ mafia, who harvest their organs and sell them for millions on the black market" (Christys 2017). Other news agencies picked up on the story, reproducing sensational accounts of infants being butchered by merciless mafiosi for their organs. The reports captured the imagination of the Egyptian public, placing the organ trade back on the political agenda and, at the same time, blunting public sensibilities to the issues behind the organ trade and feeding into a reactive desire for retribution. Despite the adoption of laws criminalizing the trade in 2010 and amendments to Article 60 of Egypt's 2014 constitution explicitly forbidding the commercial exchange of organs, Egypt has continued to be linked with organ trafficking. With a dramatic fall in tourism since the Egyptian revolution in 2011, the government has been determined to repair the country's reputation and dispel reports that link Egypt with the organ trade. A statement released by the Egyptian Ministry of Health claimed that the reports were "harming Egyptian medical tourism, as part of a systematic campaign to harm the country's national security" (Mada Masr 2017). In June 2017 the Egyptian parliament approved draft legislation to increase penalties for organ *trafficking* (Aziz 2017). Under the new legislation those who perform an organ transplant by deception or force will face life imprisonment and fines of E£1–2 million, with the possibility of a death sentence if the donor or recipient dies. Those who perform or help perform an organ transplant in an unauthorized or unspecialized medical institute or center will be subject to jail terms of up to 15 years, in addition to fines.

Because of their precarious legal status, refugees and undocumented migrants were identified as a source of organ supply and targeted by a loose network of intermediaries with links to analytic labs and transplant centers in Cairo. An informal market in organs had emerged with different brokers responsible for recruiting buyers and/or sellers, negotiating payment between the different actors involved, and organizing transport and accommodation (see Chapter 3). In 2014 I interviewed 15 people from Sudan (Sudan and South Sudan), Ethiopia, and Eritrea who had sold a kidney in Cairo. Although the individuals I spoke to were exploited as a consequence of their financial circumstances, most people were not coerced through physical violence into selling a kidney. In 2017–2020 I carried out a further 16 interviews with people who had a kidney removed between 2015 and 2020. In contrast to my findings in 2014, they experienced higher levels of physical abuse and exploitation, indicative of a change in recruitment practices and shifting market dynamics (see also Varese 2010; and Reuter 2009).

In this chapter I explore how changes to the regulatory environment influenced the level of physical violence involved in the organ trade and the organizational structure of a criminal group operating within and between Khartoum, Sudan, and Cairo, Egypt.[1] The criminal group described in this chapter should not be taken as representative of the organ trade as a whole as it exists in Egypt or elsewhere. It does, however, signal a need for policy change (discussed in Chapter 7) to prevent the development of more pernicious forms of organized crime.[2]

Arrested Development

Interviews with people who had sold a kidney between 2015 and 2020 suggest that one of the implications of harsher sentencing has been the development of more violent recruitment strategies. Okot, a Sudanese man in his late 30s, was introduced to the trade by his uncle in 2003. He described his role as an organ broker working as part of a group of intermediaries recruiting sellers from Khartoum, Sudan. "I work with people in Khartoum who find sellers and bring them here. We are communicating all the time . . . I'm talking about 20 or 30 [organ sellers] a week. I handle things when they get to Cairo." I asked Okot if reports of people being murdered for their organs were true. He shook his head in disapproval, neither confirming or denying the reports. "There are groups who bring people by smuggling. They work without the papers [consent forms; letter from consulate office; medical records; passport] and the operations are not done in the right way [at a hospital]. Anything can happen to these people because they are not in a position to bargain. They are at the mercy of the *samasira* who take them here [Egypt]."

There are different groups involved in the organ trade that are part of a wider interpersonal network sourcing organs illegally for transplantation. These groups are composed of established organ brokers with long standing connections to analytic labs and hospitals, who are willing to use physical violence to conceal their activities and maintain their revenues. Some of these groups are taking people to Cairo for forced organ removal. Although the threat of arrest has (according to government sources) led to fewer cases of organ commercialism, the experiences of the people I interviewed in 2017–2020 suggest that there has been an increase in organ *trafficking*, generating increased violence and exploitation. The literature on the narcotics trade reveals a similar pattern, demonstrating how under certain conditions law enforcement coincides with an increase in violence. Reuter (2009) has noted how intensified law enforcement in Mexico disrupted working relationships among criminal groups and corrupt officials, increasing intergang conflict and the targeted killing of officials. Similarly, in the United States a string of highly publicized drug seizures, spearheading the "war on drugs," drove up the market value of cocaine. This led to a sustained period of violent robberies and homicides between 1980 and 1998 (Bobo and Thompson 2006).

The upsurge in market-related violence described in this chapter correlates with the introduction of draconian penalties launched by the Egyptian government. These penalties were implemented in response to the perceived activities of people smugglers and human traffickers, discussed in Chapter 5, and what has been dubbed the "organ mafia" by the state-controlled press. As the narratives in this chapter demonstrate, the government crackdown on human trafficking and the organ trade in particular altered the dynamics of Cairo's organ market, increasing the need for secrecy and the use of violence as a means of control. Yet it was the effect that reports of organ theft and murder had on the affective relations between migrant communities and organ brokers that best explains a shift in market dynamics, whereby supply was constrained and market-related violence increased.

With added attention and sensitivity to the organ trade, the risk of police detection and arrest is higher than before. Although the intent and capacity of Egyptian law enforcement to successfully identify and apprehend the different actors involved is questionable, the perceived risk that an actual conviction represents has altered the terms of the trade, increasing the overall transaction costs. New payment arrangements have been made among brokers, buyers, sellers, and hospitals. According to the brokers I interviewed, bribes, or "service fees" as they call them, between consulate staff, police, and members of the special committees responsible for approving transplants (see chapters 2 and 3) have increased to accommodate the added risk of criminal sanction. Further, as the narratives in this chapter will show, new measures to manage secrecy have been introduced. This change of modus operandi has driven up costs related to protection and concealment. Operations have (in some cases) moved from private and public hospitals to apartments outside Cairo, adding significant costs with regard to equipment, transportation, and surveillance. In addition, more "enforcers" have been recruited to manage secrecy through blunt force and intimidation of sellers, who may otherwise threaten to report their activities. At the same time, the number of local residents willing to sell a kidney has also been reduced. Prospective sellers have become aware of the level of deception involved, in particular with regard to the asymmetry between the payment offered and the payment received. Meanwhile, macabre stories foreshadowing the gruesome end that awaits victims of organ harvesting have played on the social consciousness of migrant communities. This has discouraged people from entering into negotiations to begin with, regardless of their financial circumstances.

Damaged Legitimacy

On my third visit to Cairo (2017) I arrived to rumors of children being kidnapped and murdered for their organs. The authenticity of these claims has not been verified, but they have no doubt changed the way people perceive the organ trade. I visited Zarif, a Sudanese national I interviewed in 2014 who had sold his kidney to pay off his debts. When I last spoke to Zarif (see Chapter 4), he had been approved by the UNHCR for resettlement in the United States. However, his case was reviewed in September 2017, and he was notified that he no longer qualified for resettlement. No explanation was provided. Zarif was convinced that the decision to rescind his resettlement claim was politically motivated in an effort to silence him.

> The organ trade has become a taboo in Cairo; it's seen as damaging to the country's reputation. They [the government] don't want me leaving because they don't want anyone to know about this. If I leave and people know that my kidney was taken, then this becomes another bad story for Egypt. They don't want that to happen. Nearly everyone working for the UN are working for the government also. They trade information with the Mukhabarat [secret police] about certain people, like me, and then deport them. The UN is a black market; they take people in and offer no protection. They get money for this, you know. We are supposed to receive $300 when we register, but they keep it for themselves.

Zarif was a former government minister under the Sudanese president Omar al-Bashir, but after falling out of favor, for reasons he would not reveal, he fled to Egypt seeking asylum. He changed accommodation frequently, convinced that the Mukhabarat, a local Arabic term used to describe officers of Egypt's

General Intelligence Directorate, were colluding with the Sudanese government to deport him back to Sudan for a military trial. "My kidney went to an important figure in the Sudanese government," he said. "I thought this would help me get a pardon. . . . I just thank Allah that I am still alive." I asked him whether the organ trade was still active or whether anything had changed since the new legislation was introduced. "What legislation?" he asked, laughing at the suggestion. "People are being murdered for their kidneys," he said, pointing toward the piles of rubbish surrounding his apartment building. "Look at that garbage out there. How long would it take you to find a body, an African body that no one is interested in?" He had heard stories about entire families from Sudan, Somalia, and Eritrea found dead in apartments with their vital organs missing: heart, lungs, corneas, liver, and kidneys. Zarif claimed that because the organ trade was more dangerous, people no longer viewed it as a viable means to generate an income. Nonetheless, he confided, if he had another kidney to sell, he would have to consider it. There were worse scenarios: "No one wants to sell a kidney anymore, but there are worst things than doing this. I know a guy who pimps out his daughter for food. It is better to sell a kidney." Zarif put his head in his arms, taking some time to compose himself. One of his children, a small boy, sat down beside him and handed him a packet of cigarettes. Zarif smiled at the boy and took several deep breaths before lighting a cigarette with trembling hands. "You must understand, that life is different here. Sometimes we have to do terrible things to survive."

Other people I spoke to at street markets and cafés shared similar stories. Hakim, a market vendor selling *asab* (sugar cane juice), told me about a Sudanese woman who was murdered by a group of men he described as the mafia: "I don't know if this woman was promised anything for her kidney, but days after she had the operation some people came into her house took all her money and killed her. This was only two months ago [August 2017]. This mafia, they don't care what happens to you after they have your kidney." Another common story, repeated in the media, involved patients undergoing medical care and having their kidneys removed in the process (Baraaz 2018). Others recalled reports about smugglers and/or Islamic militants selling children to "the organ mafia," who they claimed were making millions from the bodies of dead migrants. Most of these stories were variations of organ theft narratives that had originated in 2009, concerning migrants kidnapped in the Sinai, with the addendum of Islamic military groups harvesting organs to fund terrorist attacks (see, e.g., Groisman 2016). Three people I interviewed from

Eritrea and Ethiopia who had crossed the Sinai on their way to Egypt were threatened with organ removal by Bedouin tribes demanding a ransom in return for their continued passage (see also van Reisen and Mawere 2017). These accounts, communicated by word of mouth, along with rumors of organ theft reconfigured attitudes toward and perceptions of the organ trade. Although these reports were common, no one that I spoke to could confirm whether or not people had been murdered subsequent to organ removal. Regardless of their veracity, the reports have no doubt affected the way migrant communities perceive the organ trade and the different market players involved (i.e., brokers, medical professionals, and hospitals). In particular, reports of pervasive cheating and deception over payment have damaged the social legitimacy of the trade as an economic activity. This breakdown in trust between brokers and sellers has led to more violent methods of recruitment.

Shifting Dynamics

A loss of legitimacy corresponded with a loosening of informal social controls and an escalation in violence. As discussed in Chapter 3, migrants normally residing in Cairo were the primary targets for brokers who had learned of their circumstances through their shared social networks. These brokers were not career criminals associated with a specific criminal group. They had entered into the organ trade independently as low-level recruiters with direct or indirect links, through another intermediary, to analytic labs located in the Greater Cairo region. Involvement in the organ trade was more of a one-shot opportunity to make easy money as opposed to a career plan. These brokers were known to their respective communities and were held accountable by their shared social relations and ethnic ties. It was not in their interest to deceive organ sellers, who were residing in the same locale, out of their proposed payment. Not only would this affect their reputation to broker organ sales, but it would also impair their position in the community and close off important social networks and potential sources of income. However, as the network expanded and more transient brokers from diverse ethnic backgrounds (e.g., Egyptian, Sudanese, Eritrean, Ethiopian) began targeting incoming migrants with no support network to rely on, these affective social controls began to break down. The objective was to solicit a kidney for the lowest price possible and sell it for the highest price available. Accordingly, there was a noticeable shift in people's perceptions and attitudes toward brokers between 2014 and

2019. In the intervening years since I first visited Cairo (2014), people had become more aware of the negative health outcomes and the level of deception involved. This change in attitude cannot be attributed to the success of new government measures (see Chapter 5)—the people I interviewed were unaware of legislative changes. Rather, it was a result of the shared experience of organ sellers communicated within and among migrant communities.

Throughout my fieldwork I asked the people I interviewed whether, based on their experience, they would recommend selling a kidney. Most responded in the negative, citing a lack of payment as the primary reason. Some people, for example, Dawitt (Chapter 5), suggested that if payment was guaranteed, they would not dissuade others from selling a kidney. Others were more forthright in their condemnation. When I asked Mohamed (Chapter 4) for his opinion, he recalled a conversation he had with a young woman who was considering selling her kidney: "I met a woman in Ataba that I knew from before, in Sudan. She said that she had come here for work and that people promised to give her money in return for her kidney. I told her that this is not work. 'Don't sell your kidney,' I said. I told her about my experience and suggested that she goes to the police to report the broker." After selling his kidney, Mohamed suffered from chronic fatigue and complained of persistent breathing difficulties. He received $3,000, half of what he had been promised. Najla, a respondent from South Sudan who sold her kidney in 2016, gave a similar reply: "I would tell people not to do this, even if they give you money. You cannot sleep well or work well. Your life becomes nothing."

A combination of negative reports, sustained over a period of time, has affected the social legitimacy of the trade, discouraging potential organ sellers from entering into agreements with brokers and disrupting their supply chain. This threatened the income of brokers, particularly brokers who had become established in their positions over time, leading to more violent means of recruitment. With the local supply chain inhibited and an increase in transaction costs, the market in organs became more protected and controlled. The market coalesced around more structured criminal groups composed of intermediaries with established partnerships developed over years of informal trading in the illicit economy. This shift in organizational structure brought about an escalation in violence and redefined the nature of organ trading in Egypt.

Azim (Chapter 5) explained how the trade in organs had become more dangerous. He spoke about one group in particular that recruited people in

Khartoum and coerced them into organ sale when they arrived in Cairo. This group, he said, was operating out of apartments in Alexandria and the urban periphery of the Greater Cairo region.

> Alexandria is now the center of the organ trade [not Cairo]. They moved their operations after the arrests and the media reports. Now people are very afraid. Nobody wants to know about this. This is an organ mafia. It is only mafia who can do this now. It is too risky for other people, but the mafia is not afraid of the police, the UN, or anyone. I know for a long time now there is a group of Egyptians and Sudanese recruiting people from Sudan. They put them into apartments outside of Cairo and make them give their kidney.

The Sudanese brokers I interviewed (see Chapter 3) had arrangements with select officials at the Sudanese embassy in Cairo who provided the requisite consent forms necessary for transplantation between foreign nationals (Sudanese) in Egypt. The forms were retrieved for a nominal fee of $1,000. As a consequence of increased scrutiny of the organ trade, the asking price was doubled, limiting the availability of these forms to more established brokers with long-standing connections in the trade. According to Azim, there had been an internal inquiry at the Sudanese embassy after a military general from the Sudanese Armed Forces who had received a transplant in Cairo died shortly after the surgery. Without preapproved consent forms, operations could no longer be performed on medically licensed premises. In the absence of official documents from the Sudanese embassy preapproving a transplant between Sudanese nationals in Egypt, physicians could no longer avoid culpability by claiming they had no knowledge of a commercial agreement. It was at this juncture that a criminal group emerged that recruited migrants from different nationalities (e.g., Sudanese, Eritrean, Ethiopian, Somali, Syrian) in Khartoum and brought them to Cairo for organ removal.

Organ Extortion

I interviewed 27-year-old Omar in November 2017 at a discreet bar in downtown Cairo. Omar had arrived in Cairo three years earlier. He had been working as a driver in Khartoum for a meager wage that was well below the cost of living required to support a young family. After work he would frequent a local coffee shop to speak with friends and smoke *shisha*. He was asking about job op-

FIGURE 5. An apartment block in Cairo where respondents were taken to recover after surgery. Photo by author.

portunities when he was approached by Malik, a heavy-set man in his late 40s who introduced himself as a recruitment agent with employment opportunities in Cairo: "He told me that he had a job for me in Egypt. He said I would be paid E£7,000 per month as a driver for a prestigious company. That was more than double what I was earning in Khartoum. This guy prepared everything for me. He got me a passport and organized transport for me to come to Cairo."

After arriving in Cairo, Omar was placed in an apartment in Faisal, an impoverished district with a large immigrant community. "When I got to the apartment, he [Malik] asked me to give him back the money for arranging my passport and travel documents. He was asking for much more than was possible. He wanted E£40,000 from me. I told him I could not pay him the money.

'I came here for a job. How can you expect me to pay when you know I have nothing to give?' I said." When Omar refused to pay, Malik made a phone call and left the room. When he returned, he was accompanied by four men, whom Omar identified as Egyptian. "There were four Egyptian guys there who threatened to kill me if I did not pay Malik. Or, they said, I could take another option, 'You can sell us your kidney to repay the debt.' All of this happened when I arrived in Cairo."

Omar explained that he did not want to sell his kidney. He offered to repay the debt as soon as he found work and suffered a beating in response. After receiving several strikes to his head, Omar was offered $12,000 for his kidney. Malik reasoned that this would allow Omar to pay off the debt he owed and to pay for travel to Europe, where he would be better placed to find employment. Omar was asked to sign a consent form confirming his intention to donate a kidney. "They asked me to sign some papers. I can't read or write so I don't know what these papers were for. I used my fingerprint instead. The broker had all of this prepared before my arrival. It was all ready for me when I got to the apartment. I was under pressure to agree to this, but I did not want to sell my kidney."

Omar remained in the apartment for three weeks before the surgery. He was not allowed to leave the apartment or to speak with anyone during this time. Two of the Egyptian men stayed behind to watch over him, as well as two other female occupants whom Omar believed were also waiting to have their kidneys removed. Two days before Omar was taken to a hospital on the periphery of the Greater Cairo region, blood tests were completed in the apartment. "I stayed there for three days. The broker came the first day to make sure I was being operated on. The doctor asked me if I was sure I wanted to do this. He said, 'You know you are about to donate your kidney?' I told him yes. After that it was just me and a nurse, who did not speak to me. The broker came back on the third day with the two guys and brought me back to an apartment." He continued, "They gave me the money I was promised in the apartment and brought me food. There were two girls there also, who were waiting to sell their kidneys. But when I went to sleep, they took everything: my money, passport, and papers from the operation."

The rent for the apartment was paid for a month in advance. With nowhere else to go, Omar remained at the apartment until he recovered enough strength to move on. He asked about the whereabouts of Malik at a coffee shop below the apartment and was informed that Malik was in Alexandria. Omar went to Alexandria in search of Malik and the $12,000 he had been promised for his kidney. He spent several days looking for Malik and/or his accomplices but was unable to find him. Omar believes that Malik used the money to secure passage to Europe, via the port of Alexandria. Since the operation, Omar has found it difficult to find regular employment, explaining that the only work available to him is manual labor. As a consequence of having his kidney removed, he is unable to lift heavy objects for a long period of time. I asked Omar if he would return to his family in Sudan—Omar has a wife and two children. He took several minutes to respond: "I feel too much shame; I cannot go back now. I am finding it difficult to work. I can't lift anything heavy. I am living with a friend who is supporting me. My father told me not to come back to Sudan. 'You have brought shame on the family,' he said. He told me that a man would not give away his kidney. I should have done everything there is to resist. I did not know what to do at the hospital. I should have tried to run away, but my mind stopped working. I was afraid for my life."

Before the interview finished, Omar told me about a woman named Hana whom he had met in Ataba. She told him that she had been promised a large sum of money in return for her kidney. A week later I met Omar along with Hana outside a coffee shop on a quiet street corner near Ataba metro station. It was around 12 noon. We sat in a circle and ordered anise tea. Hana spoke first: "I moved to Cairo in February [2017], age 22. I had been working at a coffee shop in Khartoum where I was paid around E£500 per month." Hana was propositioned by a Sudanese man while working at the coffee shop. She described him as being short and overweight and about 40 years old. He offered to help her find work in Cairo, where he promised she would earn three times what she was making in Khartoum. He suggested that they work together buying clothes from Cairo (where they are much cheaper) and selling them at a market in Khartoum. If the business was going well, and he assured her it would, she could open a shop in Khartoum to sell the merchandise. Her life and her parents' welfare would be guaranteed.

As the only unmarried sibling with no children to care for, Hana felt responsible for her parents' welfare, in particular her mother, who had a serious heart condition and required surgery. The treatment she needed was not available in Sudan. The man offered to buy Hana a passport and arrange travel to Cairo. "I could not even support myself in Sudan. My family needed me to help them, so I took a risk and trusted this man. He had an office in Khartoum and an official looking car, so I thought that he was legitimate.

This was a good opportunity for me. I was thinking I could help my family and then go to college. After this, I could maybe leave here."

When Hana got to Cairo, she was taken to an apartment and handed over to four Egyptian men in their 30s. They told her that before they could buy clothes, she would need to work for them in Alexandria to raise the necessary capital. When Hana questioned the men about the nature of the work, they beat and tortured her. "They tied to me to a chair, burned me with cigarettes and cut my hair. They kept me tied up for days. I could only move when I needed to use the toilet. Even then they followed me, watching me. There were four of them, all Egyptian. They took my passport and clothes. Then they drugged me and when I was awake, I found myself alone in an apartment in Alexandria. I was in pain and there was blood on my side coming from a bandage. I had no idea what was happening."

Hana took the train back to Cairo, where she solicited help from a local NGO run by Sudanese refugees. "They could not help me when I went there. People were afraid of me, but I met a woman who showed me mercy. I am living with her now. This all happened to me last month." She refused to tell her parents what had happened to her, concerned that the news would compromise her mother's health. "I cannot tell them this. It is *haram* to sell a kidney. They would be so disappointed. It would kill my mother to know this. I don't know where to go from here. I need to find work, but I do not feel strong enough. I hate Egypt. People here harass you all the time."

These narratives reveal the existence of a criminal group operating between Sudan and Egypt. The group consisted of five core individuals who recruited Sudanese nationals in Khartoum, offering employment opportunities in Cairo and/or travel to Europe to induce people into their services. A Sudanese *samsar* acting as a recruitment agent identifies potential clients or "donors" and recruits them through false promises of employment in Egypt and Europe. Passports are counterfeited or supplied by corrupt officials in Khartoum. People are transported by *Muharibin* in a private car to Cairo, via the Egyptian border at *Wadi Halfa*. The group has access to various apartments located across Cairo and Alexandria where people are detained and subjected to physical abuse and intimidation to ensure compliance. In contrast to previous accounts, where payment for kidney transactions was negotiated between brokers and sellers, this particular group uses physical violence to extort kidneys from people who have no intention of selling. The Sudanese *samsar* described in the above narratives offered to pay for travel expenses in advance.

The people he recruited could not afford to purchase a passport or pay for transport and were indebted to him for facilitating their entry into Egypt, at a cost of between $300 and $500. They were in no position to negotiate a price for their kidney. This change in network structure marked a shift towards more violent means of recruitment in an attempt to maximize profits and conceal activities. The promise of payment became an unnecessary deception. Instead, organs were taken under threat of force without negotiation or compromise. In this regard, we are no longer talking about organ sales. What is being described here is organ extortion.

Criminal Synergies

I met Asha outside a church in downtown Cairo that was providing information and offering emergency services (e.g., food parcels, temporary accommodation) to asylum seekers and refugees. I visited the church with Solomon to speak with refugees from Sudan, Eritrea, and South Sudan who had recently arrived from Khartoum. We were informed by Omar that some of the refugees asking for assistance had been solicited for organ sale. I also wanted to get a better sense of what support services were available to refugees and how local NGOs working with refugee communities coordinated their activities. There was a woman sitting against a wall outside the church grounds. Asha was visibly upset and appeared to be in pain. I asked her, in rudimentary Arabic, if everything was okay. She said that she had come to the church for food supplies and help finding accommodation. Her request for assistance was refused because she had already been placed in a temporary shelter for a two-month period. Asha winced as she spoke; her voice wavered with the effort. I asked her if she needed to see a doctor. Solomon spoke to Asha for several minutes, his body language signaling that something was wrong. We waved down a taxi and took Asha to the nearest hospital. Blood tests and an ultrasound scan revealed that her kidney had been removed and that the wound had become infected. The hospital staff treated the incision where the kidney had been extracted, and Asha was prescribed a course of antibiotics. We met Asha three weeks later at Solomon's apartment. She said, "I was working at a tea stall in Khartoum. Two men approached me. The leader was very charming and professional. He said that they could find me good [well-paid] work in Cairo. From there, they could take me to Italy. They convinced me I would find a better life for my children." Asha's husband died in a hit-and-run accident in Khartoum in 2016. She had three small children to take care of and felt compelled to consider their offer. "I did not trust these men, but it was impossible for me to stay in Khartoum. My children were sick from not eating. So, I listened to them." The men purchased passports, under false names, for Asha and her children. Asha had not confirmed that she would travel. Nevertheless, her accommodation and transport had already been arranged. "I said to them that I cannot afford it. And they kept telling me, 'Don't worry, don't worry.' They said I could pay them back in Cairo. I was never told how much this would cost."

Asha assumed she would work as a housekeeper to keep up her maintenance costs while further transport to Italy was being organized. When she arrived in Cairo, she was informed that she would not be going to Italy. Instead, she would be "donating" her kidney. Asha was offered $2,000 if she complied. If not, they would take her kidney by force. "They locked me in a room and told me to think of my children." Asha's kidney was removed in October 2017, a week after she had reached Cairo. She was taken by taxi to a nondescript apartment in Alexandria. "I know it was Alexandria. I could see the lights and the ocean from the taxi. I was in a room with medical equipment . . . but this is all I can tell you about that place." I offered Asha a cup of tea. She accepted, taking a moment to compose her thoughts. "I did whatever they told me to do, because my children were still at the apartment [in Cairo]. They could do anything to them," she said.

There were three other people at the apartment: two men (an Ethiopian and a Sudanese) and one woman from Somalia. "I was not allowed to talk to them, but I'm sure they were here to have their kidneys taken." After the surgery was performed, Asha reported one of the brokers to the police. He was arrested for a 30-day period and then released without charge.[3] Asha explained that she felt in constant fear of her life, having been subjected to continued threats and intimidation from the broker and his associates. She was told that if she did not withdraw her statement from the police, her children would bear the consequences. "I need to leave this place. I pray to God every day for help, for my children. If I stay here any longer, I am worried about what will happen to my children. I am worried they will come for their organs also."

I asked Asha if she had informed the UNHCR of her circumstances or spoken to a local NGO. "This is a dead place," she responded. "If I stay here, my situation will be worse. I have tried to get help, but they [NGOs] don't want to listen. They just tell me to register with the UN. I have done that [reg-

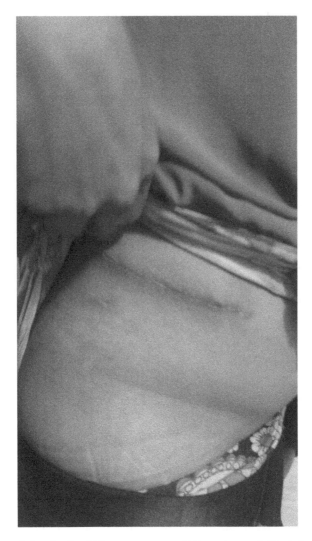

FIGURE 6. Asha after her kidney was removed, November 2018. Photo by author.

istered as an asylum seeker]. The UN tells me to wait for help that I know will never come. If there is an opportunity to leave, I have to take the chance."

Asha's account shares several characteristics with the group described by Omar and Hana, indicating the emergence of a more structured criminal network operating within and between Egypt and Sudan. Contrary to traditional mafia consortiums, the criminal group that they described was not part of a large-scale organization bound by deep kinship ties similar to the Sicilian Mafia or Chinese triads (see, e.g., Gambetta 1993; Wang 2017). Rather, the actors formed a functionally specific group operating within a larger interpersonal network, connecting with other groups (i.e., smuggling organizations) and actors (i.e., medical staff, corrupt officials) through personal communications and common objectives.

Organ brokers regularly come into contact with other intermediaries (e.g. housing brokers, drivers, counterfeiters, translators) in Cairo's informal economy to exchange information and resources. Constrained by local market dynamics, organ brokers enlist the services of *samasira* to incentivize organ sales as a means to pay off debts and/or to fund further travel costs. *Samasira* act as links between smuggling and organ trading networks. This arrangement benefits *samasira* enabling them to extract higher payments from client-migrants they refer for organ sale (see Chapter 5). These criminal synergies developed alongside and subsequent to crime and immigration controls established as part of Egypt's National Coordination Committee for Combating and Preventing Illegal Migration and Human Trafficking. Over time the connections and partnerships that were developed in Cairo's informal economy coalesced around a more structured and coordinated criminal network in response to changing law enforcement priorities and shifting market dynamics. This network is composed of specialized groups of intermediaries sourcing organs from marginalized populations inside and outside of Egypt. The professional and clandestine nature of these groups has coincided with higher levels of violence and exploitation.

Strategic Violence

I spoke to Martha outside the UN International Organization for Migration (IOM) country office in Zamalek, Cairo. She had been sleeping there for a month, sheltering under a concrete overhang adjacent to the main entrance. Martha arrived in Egypt in 2016 intending to register with the UNHCR and apply for resettlement in Canada or the United States. After registering with the UN, Martha was housed temporarily in an apartment in Faisal with five other asylum seekers from Sudan. She found work at a restaurant, where she was paid less than E£1,000 (about $60) per month, well below living standards in Cairo, where prices have escalated since the revolution in 2011. Martha traveled to and from work using one of the many microbuses that link Cairo's disparate districts. One evening on her way home she stepped into a microbus with two male passengers. The door closed abruptly after she entered the vehicle. Martha was restrained by two men and forced to her knees at gunpoint. A third man, the driver, told her that from now on she would work for them. Pointing to the other men, he warned her, "If you do not do what we tell you to do, we will end you." To illustrate his point, he took a cat from the front passenger seat and held it out at arm's length close to Martha. "This cat's life is more valuable than yours," he claimed, before sending a bullet through the cat's head.

Shaking and covered in blood, Martha was taken to an apartment in Nasr City where she was forced into domestic servitude. She shared the apartment with the three men (two Egyptian and one Sudanese) who had abducted her and another woman (Egyptian) working for her captors. "When I got to the apartment, they told me that I would clean and that was all. I was not to ask any questions but to do what they say. If I did this, I would be safe. The first night in the apartment was awful. They brought in a sheep and butchered it before my eyes. They told me that I would have a lot of blood to clean and I was to learn how to do it properly. They watched me clean the sheep's blood and then they locked me in a room for the night."

I asked Martha to describe the apartment: "The apartment had two floors. There were four rooms upstairs. One of these rooms had five beds and silver tools that looked like they were from a hospital. The apartment was in Nasr City." Martha cleaned blood from the floors and walls of the rooms in the upper story, each morning at around 5 a.m. She regularly heard screaming during the night and observed men and women, mainly of African origin (Sudanese, Ethiopian, Somalian, Eritrean) entering the apartment. Fearful about what was happening in the apartment, she asked the Egyptian woman where the blood had come from and what the medical equipment was being used for. The woman slapped her in the face and called for the other men. Martha was beaten and tied to a chair. Two of her fingernails were removed from her right hand and three of her fingers were broken on her left hand. Martha spent a further two weeks in the apartment, until one night she seized her opportunity to escape.

> I know what they were doing there. They were taking the kidneys. They did not pay these people. They were there to be harvested. I was there to be a slave.

I knew I had to leave that place, but it was difficult for me. They would beat me if I screamed, and the other woman was always watching me, reporting my every move. One night, when they were drinking, I had my chance. It was the two Egyptian men. They had been drinking for hours and started arguing—I don't know why. It was violent. One guy hit the other with his beer bottle, and then they were fighting and throwing things. I hit the woman with all my strength and ran to the door. I thought I would never escape but with God's help I was able to.

Martha reported the men to the police and provided them with an address for the apartment. It was close to eight hours before they decided to investigate. When they arrived at the apartment, the men were gone and the medical equipment had been removed. The beds, manufactured for hospital use, remained. Martha was referred to the UNHCR, where she was registered as an asylum seeker. Within months of registering, she found work as a cleaner through a recruitment agency in downtown Cairo. The agent who hired Martha arranged for a taxi to collect her at Taalat Harp and take her to a villa where she would be working as part of the cleaning staff. Martha was working alongside women from Sudan, Eritrea, Ethiopia, and the Philippines for a period of three months. Martha believed that these women were being held for "slave labor" (cleaning and sex) and in some cases "organ harvesting." She claimed that the house was guarded and that they were prevented from leaving. She had tried to leave several times but was prevented from doing so by private security staff. Martha feigned insanity and was eventually let go: "I started acting crazy, always staring at the wall and never responding to orders even when they hit me. After a few months they decided I wasn't worth it and let me go."

Martha reported everything to UNHCR, an international humanitarian organization that delivers emergency medical aid. After months of moving between apartments and receiving anonymous death threats, Martha opted to set up camp outside the IOM office in Zamalek. "I don't care where I go, once it is far away from here. I would rather be in Sudan than Cairo. I know I can be killed here at any time. But I am safer here [outside the IOM building in Zamalek]. They [criminal group] don't want attention, so they cannot take me here. I wish I had never come here. The mafia can control you here."

Martha's account of the women who were drugged for "slave labor" and "organ harvesting" cannot be corroborated. The level of violence that she reported and the nature of her abduction are inconsistent with the accounts of other respondents. However, her description of the apartment does correspond with the narratives presented in this chapter. Seven of the people I interviewed between 2017 and 2019 described the activities of a criminal group consisting of Sudanese and Egyptian nationals who recruited people in Khartoum and took them to Cairo for (involuntary) organ removal. All seven reported having a kidney removed at private residences outside Cairo. Their narratives are indicative of a change in structure and activities organized around a central group of actors. This functionally specific group appears to involve organ brokers and *samasira* with knowledge of local cultures and trade routes, together with medical professionals performing operations in covert locations. Enforcers, acting as aides to the brokers, supply physical violence to collect debts and/or to extort organs from people who are socially and legally marginalized from and by formal spheres of protection.

It is possible that this particular group was looking to build a reputation for violence by advertising their ability to deliver on threats (Reuter 1985; Williams 2002). Peter Reuter has noted how a reputation to wield violence is more effective when the criminals have contacts through a continuous chain of other individuals, with at least one witness to the violent act (Reuter 1985: 21–22; see also Varese 2011). This could explain why high levels of violence were leveled at specific people and why the specter of an "organ mafia" had become so prevalent among migrant communities residing in Cairo. In the absence of legitimacy, a reputation to wield violence is an effective strategy to secure organ transactions and establish market control. More generally, the level of physical violence exhibited by the criminal group(s) described in this chapter reflects the regulatory violence of crime and immigration controls against people who are socially and legally marginalized by state policy, at a national and international level. In this regard, economic desperation and a lack of social constraints regarding the exploitation of foreign bodies disqualified by the state are predictive indicators of societal violence, physical or otherwise (see Naylor 2009).

The Extralegal Service Industry

The UNHCR report *Projected Resettlement Needs 2019* (UNHCR 2019) estimates that resettlement places are available for 1 of every 13 of the 1.2 million refugees identified as in need of resettlement. In 2017 the Trump administration cut refugee referrals to the United States down from the proposed 110,000 places under the Obama administration to 45,000. This translated into a 43% decrease in referrals from the previous year. Accordingly, there is a growing backlog of refugees awaiting resettlement with no definitive timeframe as to when this might happen (Schemm 2018). The decrease in resettlement places is especially acute for refugees from sub-Saharan Africa, with just 18,000 available places for more than half a million refugees. UNHCR Egypt estimates that there are 15,000 refugees in need of resettlement (UNHCR 2018). A resettlement officer working with the UNHCR informed me that "we [Egypt] might get an allocation for about 5% of these cases, and there are many more that we have not identified."

Without formal protection or access to state-provided public services, migrants, regardless of their refugee status, accrue large debts as they await resettlement or seek alternative routes to Europe and beyond (Sanchez 2014). Increased border patrols on the Libyan and Egyptian coastlines has driven up prices related to people smuggling, locking people into relationships of debt bondage as they struggle to keep up payments (see Andersson 2014; Campana 2018). A migrant wanting to go to Italy, for example, may have to wait in Alexandria for several months before a vessel becomes available and an opportunity for departure is presented. Given the covert and uncertain nature of people smuggling, it is not possible to schedule a departure date, nor is there any guarantee of arrival to an agreed-on destination. Often boats are raided before departure, and people are left stranded after having already paid a substantial fee (Brachet 2018). According to Ibrahim (interviewed in the previous chapter), the fee can cost anywhere between $3,000 and $8,000, depending on the level of the service offered, the route taken, and the length of the journey involved. Once the fee is paid, there is no possibility of receiving a refund.

In the meantime, while people wait for another opportunity to travel, they have to find some form of employment. Barred from access to the formal labor market, migrants vie for whatever work they can find in marginal sectors of the informal economy, all the time amassing debts for services due. Illegal entrepreneurs are profiting from these circumstances, providing services (e.g., unregulated housing, loans, passports, transport, employment) that the state does not (see also Skaperdas 2001). People smuggling and the organ trade are key components of this extralegal service industry.

Organized crime is traditionally associated with the illegal production and distribution of goods or services. Examples of illegal production include coca production in Latin America (Zaitch 2002) and heroin production in Burma (Chin and Zhang 2015). Organized crime groups also engage in the exchange of illegal commodities or services, for example, drug trafficking (Paoli and Reuter 2008), the trade in animal parts (Titeca 2019), and people smuggling (Campana 2018). The criminal group described in this chapter developed from the extralegal service industry. That is, it is part of the "service industry" of organized crime that provides services to migrant populations excluded by state policies. In a context devoid of economic opportunity, the organ trade is a recognized source of income for people who are socially and legally excluded from the formal labor market. Organ brokers are key players in the organ trade; they provide a service connecting buyers with sellers. Moreover, they organize and facilitate networks of supply, sourcing organs for transplantation. In the Egyptian context this relationship or pattern of economic exchange has evolved in accordance with changing social and political arrangements. The failure of the state to regulate organ donation through legal means (i.e., altruistic living or deceased donation) led to a dependency on paid living donation. In response to international pressure, the government introduced a new law prohibiting organ sales in 2010, effectively creating an illegal market in organs. The destabilizing effect of the Egyptian revolution in 2011 removed any possibility that the law would be enforced.

Moreover, as a consequence of rampant corruption in the public administration, the illegality of organ transplantation was not clearly established. Despite the prohibition of organ sales, the trade in organs was tacitly accepted as an unregulated market solution to the surplus demand for organs, a demand propelled by the commercial expansion of the transplant industry (see Chapter 2). This demand has largely been met by illegal supply, organized by a network of intermediaries with links to analytic labs and transplant centers (see Chapter 3). To begin with, organ brokers operated independently as informal service providers, coordinating the commercial exchange of organs between hospitals, patient-buyers, and donor-sellers. Key partnerships between brokers, corrupt government officials, and medical staff provided the necessary protection from official and/or public scrutiny, enabling the trade to develop as a relatively open market. However, with the introduction of harsher criminal penalties, including the death penalty, these arrangements have been disrupted, prompting brokers and the transplant surgeons they work with to establish new partnerships, find alternative sources of protection, and reorganize their activities to commit and conceal illegal transactions. Regulatory changes between 2010 and 2020 correlated with a breakdown of trust between brokers and sellers and with the subsequent development of a criminal group(s) that recruits people in Khartoum for the involuntary removal of organs in Cairo.

The view that links migration to organized crime can take simplistic and crude forms. Despite being a signatory to the 1951 United Nations Convention Relating to the Status of Refugees, the Egyptian government has routinely labeled undocumented migrants as illegal, representing them as a criminal threat to the nation's security. This language and the rhetorical imagery personified in the criminalized migrant gives way to draconian migration policies and border controls, which are justified as a means to prevent organized crime. In fact, these exclusionary policies produce the very environment and circumstances that enable organized crime to develop. Without a supply of migrants compelled to sell a kidney, because of a lack of legal options to otherwise generate an income, the organ trade would not have developed in Egypt the way that it has. Continued conflict across the Middle East and North Africa and the forced displacement of large populations cast aside as "illegal" facilitate the wholesale exploitation of people for their organs, sex, and labor, among other things. Political indifference sustained by an insidious alliance of political, economic, and criminal interests to exploit cheap labor from migrant populations will ensure that this process continues (see Chapter 4). In practice, the dissemination of counter-trafficking measures is in stark contradiction to the welfare of the vulnerable people that such policies claim to protect. In the Egyptian context a combination of crime and immigration controls has pushed the trade in organs further underground, increasing the level of exploitation that organ sellers are exposed to. Punitive policies have done nothing to limit the demand for organs procured through payment or coercion. Rather, the introduction of criminal sanctions has shifted the nature of criminality toward more violent means of control. The incidental crackdown on existing networks of informal exchange has created a space for organized crime groups to enter the market, resulting in increased violence and exploitation. Taking this into consideration, in the following chapter I consider how to regulate the organ trade.

REGULATING THE ORGAN TRADE

Law enforcers are at the frontline concerning the identification of both trafficking victims and traffickers. Police officers, customs, immigration and border officials should be provided with training that equips them to identify potential and actual victims as well as perpetrators of trafficking in persons for the purpose of organ removal. (UNODC 2015a)

To combat the transnational nature of organ harvesting and trafficking, international partnerships and collaboration among governments, law enforcement, including immigration, customs, and border officials; health organizations; legal entities; nongovernment organizations; community groups and leaders; public health; human services; and the private sector are essential. International partnerships and collaboration will increase knowledge and awareness of illegal organ harvesting and trafficking and help identify modus operandi, participants, illegal or fraudulent document use, funding sources and movement, and corruption. (FBI 2017)

Countless acts of generosity by organ donors and their families, as well as the many important scientific and clinical advances achieved by dedicated health professionals, have made transplantation not only a life-saving therapy but a symbol of human solidarity. Yet these accomplishments have been tarnished by numerous instances of organ trafficking, of trafficking in persons for the purpose of organ removal, and of patients who travel abroad to purchase organs from poor and vulnerable people. In 2007 it was estimated that up to 10%

of transplants worldwide involved such practices. (DICG [Declaration of Istanbul Custodian Group] 2018)

WHEN THE PRACTICE of buying kidneys from impoverished sellers was first brought to public attention, it generated shock and horror in equal measure, bringing the transplant industry into disrepute. Professional medical associations quickly denounced the trade, calling on political leaders to criminalize the sale and purchase of organs. There was, and remains, a clear professional and political consensus that the organ trade is an intolerable practice that warrants criminal prohibition. An outright ban on organ sales was viewed as a necessary measure to protect impoverished sellers against exploitation (WHO 2004; 2010). Poor organ sellers, it was argued, are invariably uneducated and do not understand the risks involved in organ donation (Rothman et al. 1997; Delmonico 2009). They are coerced because of their economic circumstances. Therefore their consent cannot be genuine. They have been "trafficked" even if they do not know it. Women and children, it is alleged, are particularly vulnerable to organ trafficking and require urgent protection (Council of Europe and United Nations 2009; UNODC 2015a). Despite the promise of financial reward, paid donors are unlikely to spend the money wisely, because of their inexperience and lack of education (Goyal et al. 2002). Moreover, poor postoperative health could prevent them from reentering the labor market, informal or otherwise (Budiani-Saberi and Delmonico 2008). Accordingly, prohibitionist lobbies, following the lead of the Declaration of Istanbul Custodian Group, have insisted that organ donation must be altruistic in order to be acceptable (DICG 2018). Paying a donor would not just be exploitative; it would also undermine confidence in the medical profession by associating doctors with profiteering (Caplan 2014). Commodifying donation would undercut efforts to establish deceased donor programs and increase demand for illegal transplants (Delmonico and Scheper-Hughes 2003; DICG 2018). These objections expressed on behalf of organ sellers have influenced policy making along punitive lines, conceptualizing the organ trade as a form of human trafficking. As I have shown throughout this book, these objections have had negative consequences for organ sellers in Egypt.

A focus on criminal behavior defined in terms of trafficking portrays an unambiguous representation of the organ trade that serves distinct political and commercial ends. This discursive framing has diverted critical attention away from the transplant industry and the role it has played in producing the economic rationale for organ markets. At the same time, the threat of organ trafficking has been used to create an urgency around organ donation. In Egypt the organ trade has been co-opted into the anti-trafficking framework. This has strengthened a law enforcement agenda that is less concerned with regulating the organ trade than with managing migration (see FBI 2017). The anti-trafficking framework enables the state to contain migrant populations who are categorized as illegal and thus disqualified from state protection. Linking the organ trade to transnational organized crime has played on public opinion, leveraging support for crime control measures and security protocols (e.g., militarized border patrols, arbitrary arrest, indefinite detention, and deportation) that would otherwise be unacceptable outside a declared state of emergency. In the Egyptian context the introduction of criminal sanctions prohibiting organ sales has pushed the trade further underground. This has reduced the bargaining position of organ sellers and increased the role of intermediaries. As discussed in Chapter 6, the perceived threat of criminal sanction has changed the dynamic of informal market relations, increasing transaction costs, the need for secrecy, and the level of violence. To maintain profits, organ trading networks have adapted their modus operandi, recruiting people outside Egypt, withholding payment, and/or taking organs by force. The militarization of borders along the Central Mediterranean Route has stimulated criminal synergies between smuggling and organ trading networks. With the majority of migrants, asylum seekers, and refugees unable to find paid labor, *samasira* and their agents refer their (potential) clients to organ brokers to raise the requisite capital to fund travel overseas. Organ brokers, on the other hand, incentivize organ sale with the (false) promise of secure passage to Europe.

The cumulative effects of crime and immigration controls coincided with progressively higher levels of physical harm, deception, and negative health outcomes reported by respondents over the course of my fieldwork. Most of the people I interviewed during my final research visit to Cairo (e.g., Asha, Dawitt, Petros, Hana, and Omar) were operated on in poorly equipped premises located in residential settlements outside Alexandria and on the periphery of the Greater Cairo region. The adverse effects of these policies suggest that more far-reaching legal reform is needed with regard to the organ trade, as well as other forms of exploitation nominally defined as trafficking offenses. In this chapter I explore alternative regulatory approaches beyond criminal sanction.

The Ethical Dilemma of Organ Sales

Ethical claims and concerns regarding the organ trade have combined to form a moral consensus condemning the purchase or sale of organs as a criminal act. In general, the case for legal prohibition rests on the assumption that paying a commercial donor is inherently harmful and exploitative. It is assumed that organ sales take advantage of the most vulnerable members of society, commodifying their bodies and exposing them to harm (Scheper-Hughes 2000; Delmonico 2009; Caplan 2014). Yet the actual risk of harm following a kidney donation performed under the appropriate medical conditions is minimal (Nicholson and Bradley 1999). The medical outcomes for organ recipients and donors are comparatively worse when performed by physicians operating illegally (Canales et al. 2006). Cameron and Hoffenberg (1999) argue that if the ethical objection to the sale of organs is premised on the risk of harm to donors and/or recipients, then banning organ sales is the last thing we should be doing. The lack of medical oversight, preoperative screening, and postoperative care demonstrated by the narratives in this book would support this assertion. Many forms of paid manual labor (e.g., mining) and some recreational activities (e.g., free diving) are arguably more dangerous than donating a kidney. Payment alone does not compromise the safety of an organ donation. Conversely, it could be argued that impoverished donors benefit from a payment they would not otherwise receive (Wilkinson 2004). Dawitt (Chapter 5) sold his kidney to send money home to his family and to raise the necessary capital to cover smuggling fees across the Mediterranean. He received $2,000 out of the $5,000 he had been promised. When I asked him what he would do next, he responded, "If I had another kidney, I would sell it. The problem is they did not pay me what I was promised. This guy, he took my kidney and my money. Now I have nothing." For Dawitt, along with many of the other people I interviewed who sold a kidney, the harm he associated with organ sale was attributed to unfair payment.

Taking an outcome-orientated approach to exploitation, scholars have argued that organ markets need not be exploitative, assuming the price of a kidney is sufficiently generous in value and/or proportionate to the health risks involved (Dworkin 1994; Radcliffe-Richards 2003; I. G. Cohen 2014). Indeed, several people I interviewed suggested that if they were guaranteed a fair price for their kidney, they would not be opposed to paid donation, despite their concerns over the possible health implications. Making the case for organ sales, Gerald Dworkin reasons that "another objection based on the fact of income inequality is that because of unequal bargaining power, the price paid to the poor will not be a fair one. They will not get the full market value of their organs. If there were evidence that this was true, the solution would be to regulate the market, not forbid the sale. One could establish minimum prices analogous to minimum wage laws" (Dworkin 1994: 157). Glenn Cohen agrees: "If the problem is that a seller of a kidney is being exploited by being offered the opportunity to sell at a given price, there likely exists a hypothetical higher price at which he will not be exploited" (I. G. Cohen 2014: 18).

The charge against organ sales is not, however, that paid donation is in and of itself particularly harmful. Organ sales are condemned and prohibited because they take unfair advantage of the poor. The moral objection is against the wrongful use of a person in poor financial circumstances, as opposed to the level of payment a donor receives. What makes organ sales objectionable and nonconsensual is the process, which can involve assault, coercion, murder, and/or theft. Forcing the point that paid donation is immoral and unconscionable, some claim that organ sales inevitably lead to organ trafficking. Organ sellers are coerced and/or deceived into selling their organs because of their poor economic status, regardless of whether or not consent has been provided (Delmonico et al. 2015). Prohibition is therefore a fundamental necessity required to safeguard the body's integrity and to protect the vulnerable from exploitation (DICG 2018). Altruism, narrowly conceived of as a selfless act, is equivocated with free donation and the "gift of life," a distinct counterpoint to the immorality of organ sales. However, there are occasions when selling a kidney could be considered altruistic. Kamal, discussed in Chapter 4, sold his kidney to pay for his mother's medical care. He was acting out of concern for the well-being of his mother. Although he received $5,000 in return for his kidney, this was nonetheless a compassionate and selfless act. Donating his kidney to an unspecified recipient without payment would have denied him the opportunity to support his mother. Accordingly, many of the transplant professionals I interviewed (see Chapter 2) considered it unethical not to pay a donor.

There is nothing particularly wrongful or dangerous about organ sales per se, assuming there has been no undue influence (e.g., assault, coercion, murder, theft) or trafficking. Hence there is considerable merit to the argument that a minimum fee in exchange for a kidney would prevent or at least minimize the risk of unfair payment. Making a case for a legal market in organs,

Erin and Harris (2003) outlined their proposals for a single-purchaser system operating within a confined marketplace, for example, a nation-state. A government agency similar to the National Health Service in the United Kingdom would act as the sole purchaser and distributor of organs, allocated to citizen-patients according to medical priority. Only organs received from residing citizens would be accepted for transplantation, presumably ruling out the exploitation of impoverished foreign nationals. Further proposals from the Working Group on Incentives for Living Donation (2012) envision a "regulated incentive system" whereby states would have specific guidelines to evaluate and select fully informed donors, with clearly defined policies for "follow up, outcome determination and detection and correction of irregularities." Organs would be allocated according to one's position on a state approved waiting list and donors would receive a fixed incentive determined by the state. Theoretically this system would benefit both donors and patients, increasing the supply of organs and saving lives while providing donors with adequate compensation.

> Patients who desperately need organs would obviously benefit if more were available and there is no reason to doubt that many donors would benefit from receiving an incentive under properly controlled circumstances. Permitting incentives would allow competent, properly informed adults to make their own judgments about their own best interests—widely regarded as an essential feature of respect for human dignity. (Working Group on Incentives for Living Donation 2012)

The problem with these proposals is that they are transaction specific and fundamentally dismissive of global inequalities. Erin and Harris (2003) suggest that a free market price could be approximated by setting the payment to organ sellers at the minimum value required to ensure a reliable supply. Following the rationale of neoliberal market dynamics, it is assumed that fair terms of exchange reflective of the broader social and economic context will emerge. However, in practice this could lead to a situation in which, in a context of relative poverty (e.g., Egypt), the exploitation of an economic underclass is taken for granted. For example, although it is exploitative to pay a worker in the United States $5 a day, it may not be considered exploitative to pay a worker situated in the global South (e.g., India) the same amount. Similarly, what is considered an unfair market price for a kidney in the United Kingdom might be considered fair in Egypt. Patients would arguably continue to travel overseas to receive transplants—supplied by relatively poor donors—at a lower cost, despite an increased domestic supply. When we take global inequalities into consideration, the argument for outcome-orientated approaches to exploitation becomes so diluted that the result does not, by any account, justify the means. Moreover, the presumed benefits of a regulated market, as described, are restricted to citizens, further excluding migrant populations. Notwithstanding the ethical objections and concerns over the bounded rationality of organ sellers to consent to organ sale, logistically the kind of regulatory oversight required for a regulated market would be costly and difficult to implement and audit, particularly in low-income countries. A legally regulated market could nonetheless afford a level of transparency that would enable, at the very least, transplant professionals to be held accountable for poor medical treatment and organ sellers to be given full information on the risks of surgery. Further, it would help ensure that sellers are medically screened and that they receive proper surgical and postoperative care.

Decriminalization

In discussing the ethical parameters of organ sale, professional associations, campaigners, and policymakers tend to overlook the types of environments and circumstances that predispose people to selling a kidney. Thus far, the question of regulation has been demarcated along moral fault lines of right and wrong, without due consideration of the social, political, and economic conditions that shape people's lives. The potential for law reform has therefore been limited to polarizing debates as to whether or not organ sales should be legalized and regulated. An alternative regulatory approach that has received considerably less attention is decriminalization.[1] There are different models and forms of decriminalization to consider, and they can have contrasting benefits and outcomes for the people involved. With regard to organ trading, *partial decriminalization* would, for example, decriminalize the activities of organ sellers but criminalize the organ recipient, organ brokers, and other third parties (e.g., transplant professionals, medical staff, hospitals). *Complete decriminalization* would involve the repeal of any specific criminal legislation dealing with organ sales, albeit related activities (e.g., fraud, kidnapping, theft, smuggling) could still be prosecuted as a criminal offense under generally applicable laws. This is not to be confused with *legalization*, which would involve complete decriminalization coupled with positive legal provisions, that is, a regulated market. These different approaches to decriminalization have been applied to variable effect against other illicit markets. The decriminalization of illicit drugs and sex work, in particular, offer important insights for the organ trade.

Evidence-based studies on drug markets demonstrate that increased law enforcement has no significant impact on rates of drug use (see Dorn and South 1990; Reuter and Stevens 2007; and Mostyn et al. 2012). Nevertheless, decriminalization has been widely resisted by government authorities. In the United Kingdom, policymakers have warned that the removal of criminal sanctions for "gateway" drugs (e.g., cannabis) could lead to more harmful drug use (e.g., heroin) and addiction (see Home Affairs Committee Inquiry into Drug Policy 2002, par. 74). In the United States the Office of National Drug Control Policy (2019) envisions a drug-free society. The National Drug Control Strategy for 2019 emphasizes the need for bold and decisive national security and law enforcement efforts to eradicate illegal supply chains. However, data collected from the United States (Colorado and Washington), Australia, Italy, and Spain suggest that the removal of criminal penalties for the possession of cannabis has had largely positive results (MacCoun and Reuter 2001). The burden and cost on the criminal justice system has been reduced, as has the level of black market transactions. Furthermore, drug users from less privileged backgrounds, who were disproportionately targeted by criminal measures, have been subjected to less harassment from law enforcement officials. The overall impact on cannabis use has been negligible, however.[2] In states and regions where cannabis has been legalized for recreational purposes, studies suggest that commercial access is associated with growth in the drug-using population (see Pacula et al. 2005; and Palamar et al. 2014). There is, however, no evidence to suggest that there has been a concomitant rise in the use of other illegal drugs (Kim and Monte 2016). On the contrary, in the United States the legalization of cannabis use in Colorado was associated with a decline in opioid-related deaths (Livingston et al. 2016).[3]

In 2001 the Portuguese government decriminalized the possession of all drugs for personal use. Contrary to predictions that decriminalization would inevitably lead to a rise in problematic drug use, there has been no evidence of increased drug taking in Portugal. Rather, the removal of criminal sanctions together with an emphasis on health and welfare has correlated with a reduction in drug-related harms (Hughes and Stevens 2010; 2015). Further studies demonstrate how misconceived law enforcement strategies can increase the level of violence in the illicit drug trade (see Goldstein 1985; Reuter 2009; Shirk 2010; and Werb et al. 2011). Intensified enforcement campaigns against Mexican drug cartels have resulted in high levels of violence and civilian casualties (see Shirk 2010; Reuter 2009). The much maligned "war on drugs" in the United States has cost U.S. taxpayers billions of dollars without having had any tangible impact on the level of drug-related harms (see Bobo and Thompson 2006; Babor et al. 2010; Stevens 2010; and Bourgois 2015). The comparatively negative consequences of criminalization illustrated by evidence-based studies on the drug trade support an argument for further decriminalization with regard to other illicit markets.

Over the past decade international reform of prostitution laws has trended toward a more liberal approach to sex work. Several countries have removed criminal sanctions (e.g., Sweden, Germany, New Zealand) for the sale and purchase of sex. However, decriminalization regimes do not serve universal interests. The same legislation can have highly disparate consequences for different sex workers (Bernstein 2007; Kotiswaran 2011). The decriminalization of brothel-based sex work can lead to more harassment and extortion of street workers where loitering laws that criminalize the soliciting of sex are still in effect (Davidson 2006). In Sweden, where the sex trade is partly decriminalized, sex workers are "protected" from prosecution, but other actors, including customers, can be charged for criminal conduct, for example, purchasing sex (Raymond 2003; Ekberg 2004). Although the "Swedish model" was intended to protect sex workers from violence, in practice the law has focused exclusively on visible forms of sex work. After the policy change in 1999, Swedish law enforcement began targeting potential customers who were found soliciting or purchasing the services of street-based sex workers. This led to the displacement of street-level sex workers into underground brothels, where they were exposed to higher levels of physical harm and a loss of earnings from regular clientele (Levy and Jackobsson 2014).

Similarly, complete decriminalization or regulation can further entrench social divisions, for example, between migrant and nonmigrant workers (Agustín 2007: 73). In Germany, where sex work is legalized, regulatory controls (taxation, supervision, registration) have limited the autonomy that sex workers have to choose where and how they want to work. Although sex work is recognized as a form of labor, sex workers have not been afforded the same rights and entitlements (e.g., health insurance, pension schemes) as other workers (Pates 2012). Comparatively, the health and well-being of sex workers has been well supported by the decriminalization model adopted in New Zealand (Armstrong 2017). However, the benefits of decriminalization are not extended to disenfranchised migrant workers, who remain subject to prosecution for the illegal supply of sex. In effect, migrant sex workers are no better off than when the sex trade was prohibited, the negative effects of which are well documented in the literature on sex work (see Weitzer 2011; and Ellison 2015).

Ostensibly different regulatory approaches (prohibition, partial decriminalization, complete decriminalization, legalization) can produce decidedly similar results. The recurring limitations of alternative regulatory models has led some scholars to conclude that the law does not matter (Scoular 2010; Agustín 2007). Sexual exploitation, it is argued, has little to do with the law. Rather, it is located in and subsequent to a deeper sociopolitical malaise. The narratives presented in this book would appear to further this analysis. Decriminalization, partial or complete, would not change the legal or material reality of organ sellers, particularly those categorized as illegal migrants. Nor would it eradicate organ markets and the networks that supply them. However, the experiences and perspectives of the people in this book suggest that the way we perceive illicit markets, as legitimate or not, has wider import in the social domain. The significance of decriminalization, I argue, is in the potential for the formal recognition it would provide to persons normatively defined as illegal and marked out as expendable.

In her book *Precarious Life*, Judith Butler discusses how the public sphere is constituted in part by what can appear as credible and what cannot: "To decide what views will count as reasonable within the public domain, however, is to decide what will and will not count as the public sphere of debate.... The regulation of the sphere of appearance is one way to establish what will count as reality and what will not. It is also a way of establishing whose lives can be marked as lives, and whose deaths can count as deaths" (Butler 2006: 20–21). Criminalizing organ sales in the Egyptian context has served to further invalidate the claim of immigrant populations to corporeal sanctity and equal status before the law. This is evident in the political and social indifference to the welfare of a subclass of organ sellers recruited from an "illegal" demographic of migrants. If we are to prevent corporal violence against an illegal underclass, then recognizing the precarious underbelly of organ sales is an important first step.

To be clear, I am not suggesting that decriminalization is a panacea. Nor am I suggesting that we implement a regulated market established around neoliberal principles of supply and demand. I am suggesting that we reset the normative frame through which we perceive and recognize the precarious lives of others. The criminal stigma attached to organ sales forecloses the possibility of a credible claim to abuse, caused by direct physical violence or by structural forces such as poverty, marginalization, and exploitation (see Kohler and Alcock 1976).[4] Although decriminalization may not change the conditions that underpin the organ trade, it would, at a minimum, increase access to nonviolent means of dispute resolution and open up the potential for dialogue and legal reform beyond criminal law.

Decriminalization is often represented as a singular concept. However, as the examples presented here demonstrate, the selective removal of criminal sanctions can take variable forms and advance different interests. As discussed, a legal or regulated market in organs might include a standardized payment in exchange for a kidney as well as state-mandated medical postoperative care (Erin and Harris 2003; Working Group on Incentives for Living Donation 2012). This would almost certainly increase organ supply. However, as evidenced by the Iranian system, a regulated market could also reproduce social inequalities and close off the possibility for more progressive reforms (see, e.g., Zargooshi 2001; and Bagheri 2006). Following the Swedish model, the partial decriminalization of organ sales could further displace organ sellers and organ recipients into poorly equipped medical clinics, increasing the risk of negative health outcomes. Complete decriminalization, however, could encourage transparency by enabling organs sellers and recipients to come forward and report abuse, physical or otherwise, without the threat of sanction. This would, in turn, encourage people to seek out assistance and information from medical professionals before and after organ sale. A more informed decision-making process would enhance the bargaining power of organ sellers and promote transparency between organ recipients and their acting physicians in their country of origin. This information could be used to support law enforcement investigations into the activities of intermediaries and hospital personnel, who would remain subject to criminal prosecution. Because organ sellers are no longer potential criminals, they would, arguably, be more willing to report financial and physical abuse to the police. Assuming their claims to exploitation are formally recognized by legal authorities, the normative violence against organ sellers would likely be reduced. Reducing the social stigma attached to organ sales might also promote and strengthen informal social controls and support networks within communities disproportionately affected by the organ trade. However, the potential impact of any such policy change would require further research to understand variations in how changes to the law are interpreted and enforced by police and prosecutors, how different levels of understanding influence arrest patterns, and how the removal of criminal charges would be perceived by the wider public.

Beyond Sanction

The failure of policymakers to protect organ sellers from criminal sanction has contributed to their legal and social marginalization. In Egypt the introduction of criminal penalties prohibiting organ sales has served to further conceal the nature and extent of organ trading, obscuring the level of harm that organ sellers are subjected to. The threat of sanction has (unintentionally) increased the importance of organ brokers, who are in greater demand as medical facilities attempt to distance themselves from criminal activity. The increased role of brokers has further reduced the bargaining power of organ sellers, leaving them more vulnerable to exploitation. Meanwhile, law enforcement crackdowns have had a negligible effect on the level of organ trading taking place. The brokers I interviewed between 2017 and 2020 explained how the network members they worked with had adapted their modus operandi to respond to law enforcement efforts. Operations were, in some cases, relocated from public and private hospitals to apartments to avoid police detection (although illegal transplants also continued to take place in licensed medical facilities). The move away from medically licensed premises dispensed with the need for official documentation (e.g., consent forms, passports) and professional oversight, thus lowering the standard of care provided to both organ sellers and recipients. The displacement of transplant operations to poorly medically equipped apartments correlated with the emergence of an organized crime group. This group was composed of Egyptian doctors and Sudanese middlemen who recruited people in Khartoum, Sudan, and transported them to Cairo with the assistance of *samasira* for organ removal (see Chapter 6). This organizational change coincided with a higher incidence of reports describing physical abuse, forced labor, and sexual violence. Some of the people I interviewed, for example, Talia, Martha, and Asha, reported the brokers and their associates to the Egyptian authorities (see Chapters 3 and 6). However, despite the grave nature of their reports, they were not taken seriously. Others, for example, Dawitt, Petros, Patrick, and Mohamed, were threatened with deportation for their alleged complicity in criminal acts: illegal entry and selling a kidney (see Chapters 4 and 5).

The Convention Against Trafficking in Human Organs (Council of Europe 2014a), discussed in Chapter 1, represents a missed opportunity to formally protect organ sellers from criminal liability. Instead, by disregarding the potential liability of organ sellers, in Article 4, the Convention has contributed to the perceived "bio-availability" of people who consent to organ sale. As expressed in Articles 4(a) and 4(b), criminalization is contingent on (1) the lack of informed consent and (2) the exchange of money. This is problematic for a number of reasons. Consent is generally taken to denote a voluntary agreement to another's proposition. This involves having the capacity, intention, and knowledge to make an informed decision. Accordingly, most transplant laws require that voluntary and informed consent is obtained before a transplant can be approved. Here, however, the notion of consent is fixed to a particular construction of illegality and used as a standard bearer for criminality.

The reliance on "financial gain or comparable advantage" under Article 4 obviates the personal circumstances of a person who, out of economic necessity, is compelled to sell a kidney. On this basis the act of exchanging an organ is rendered criminal by way of material advantage, regardless of the conditions involved. This means that a person who consents to sell an organ for financial reasons is potentially liable for a criminal offense. Although the stated purpose of the Convention is to prevent trafficking and protect victims, according to paragraph 29 of the explanatory report to the Convention, an organ seller can "also be considered as having participated in, or even instigated, the trafficking in human organs" (Council of Europe 2014b).

Selling a kidney is far from an ideal choice, but in an environment devoid of social or economic opportunity it might not be regarded as a particularly bad decision. Contrary to the fervent proclamations of commentators such as Delmonico and Scheper-Hughes, who claim the organ trade is responsible for "the formation of an economic underclass . . . to serve the wealthy" (2003: 694), organ markets have not produced an economic underclass; they are a condition of it. Although the removal of criminal sanctions is at odds with the altruistic ideal of transplantation, the moral paralysis that has occasioned a narrow criminal response to this issue is clearly failing to prevent the exploitation of people compelled by force of circumstance to sell an organ. Although criminal prosecution is important, insofar as it represents society's intolerance for particular crimes and may act as a deterrent for future offenses, punishment does little to alleviate the conditions that produce crime. Rather, an emphasis on prosecution and crime control may serve a distinct ideological and political function. The periodic assessment of "kidney scandals" and high-profile cases defers a more sustained inquiry into the local politics that underpin the everyday dealings that negotiate the terms and conditions of the organ trade (see Chapter 2). An emphasis on limiting the level of exploitation that organ sellers are exposed to would seem a more pragmatic approach than persisting with damaging punitive measures, particularly in countries where a culture of organ sales persists. The critical question is not whether we should or should not sell our organs, but what measures we might take to limit the risk of exploitation.

The decriminalization models adopted by Portugal and New Zealand suggest that the removal of criminal sanctions alone would have a limited impact on people's lives. Effective decriminalization policies require public support and political commitment to social welfare. With regard to organ sales, stronger (international) commitments are needed to reduce demand for organ transplants and to increase access to primary health care for citizens and noncitizens (see Kierans 2019). The much-vaunted life-saving capacity of organ transplantation represents an undeniable medical achievement. Nevertheless, the fact that the global incidence of renal disease is increasing to epidemic proportions is a serious cause for concern, which calls for a reassessment of how we structure our national health systems. In a number of states identified as being hot spots of organ trafficking, such as Egypt, India, Pakistan, and the Philippines, where large sections of the population do not have access to basic sanitation and/or clean water, it seems counterproductive to invest limited resources in expensive transplantation programs that are inaccessible to the general public. In such states where access to transplantation is limited, legal restrictions may be necessary to reserve treatment for the most serious cases—that is, where transplantation is the only feasible option—while resources are made available to promote the early identification of diseases associated with organ failure. Early intervention is pivotal in responding to patients' needs before transplantation becomes necessary (see Luyckx et al. 2013). Hence, rather than prioritizing the investment of resources in a technology that attends to the consequences of organ failure, resources could be invested in public health schemes to improve waste management, sanitation, environmental degradation, and food security (see Hamdy

2013). Essentially, if policymakers are serious about reducing the commercial demand for organs, transplantation needs to be uncoupled from economic incentives and restructured to accommodate domestic needs.

As a social group, migrants, asylum seekers, and refugees are structurally positioned as organ sellers because of their precarious legal status and the insecurity this brings. Migrant populations disenfranchised and relegated to marginal spaces of the informal economy have limited or no access to housing, education, health care, or employment. In the Egyptian context it seems clear that more services and support for housing, health, childcare, and education are needed, for the general population as well as people seeking refuge. The €11.5 million that the EU provided to the Egyptian government to enhance its border security could have been put to much better use in this regard (see Chapter 5). More generally, increased labor informalization and the precarious working conditions that leave people exposed to exploitation of various kinds need to be addressed. Existing attention to immigration and criminal offenses limits the existential scope of exploitation and reorients critical attention away from the social and economic arrangements that perpetuate patterns of social exclusion. If the law is to have any impact on organ trading, it must first address the structural asymmetries that compel people to submit to the will of others. It may prove impossible to eradicate organ markets, but the legal barriers and policy decisions that predispose people to organ sale can be addressed.

Protective Limits

In accordance with the Trafficking Protocol, Egyptian Law 64/2010 asserts that victims of trafficking will not be held criminally or civilly liable for any illegal activity they may have been involved in "as long as the crime occurred or was directly related to being a victim." Furthermore, it guarantees repatriation "in an expeditious and safe manner" (Articles 21 and 22). "Illegal" migrants, however, are not recognized within the framework of regulatory protection. On the contrary, they are subject to criminal prosecution. Mohamed, Patrick, and Tariq (see Chapters 4 and 5) were arrested and detained for not having up-to-date identification documents, resident permits, or valid visas. Although the government did not press legal charges for illegal immigration or unauthorized employment, they were held in administrative detention and/or deported. Despite the abundance of government reports and media statements alluding to victim identification and protection for victims of trafficking, undocumented migrants in Egypt (and elsewhere) are often punished for unlawful acts committed as a direct result of their own exploitation. For many of the people interviewed in this book the police were the main perpetrators of racial and gendered violence (see Chapters 4 and 5). Unsurprisingly, organ sellers were reluctant to report instances of abuse, fraud, or deception to state authorities.

Most of the people I spoke with did not conform to a trafficking profile, despite having experienced variable levels of abuse over a sustained period of time. For many, the organ trade was viewed as an economic lifeline in a context with limited opportunities to produce an income. Their kidneys were not removed by force, nor were they explicitly coerced into selling. They were compelled to consent to organ sale as a consequence of their social and economic exclusion in both formal and informal spheres of the economy. The different life trajectories of the people I interviewed reveal a history of difficult choices, from leaving family members behind and working under precarious conditions in foreign countries, to selling a kidney. Yet the routine exploitation they experienced was not and is not recognized under current anti-trafficking legislation at the national or international level. On the contrary, their bodies are rendered expendable as a consequence of their "illegal" status, constructed vis-á-vis anti-trafficking policies. For people who experienced the kind of violence typified in the pages of governmental reports and media exposés on human trafficking, no meaningful protection was provided. Egypt's anti-trafficking law guarantees protection of victims and witnesses of trafficking crimes. Yet there is neither a formal witness protection program nor any established witness protection procedure. Without tangible safeguards to protect people from reprisal and/or pressure from criminal groups, any criminal charges that might be filed are unlikely to proceed to court.

The protection provided by the UNHCR and its partner organizations for "victims of trafficking" or "survivors of sexual and gendered based violence" consists of inane services that have little to do with actual protection. Under the heading "Protection," the UNHCR fact sheet for Egypt lists registration by means of the collection of biometric information, special assistance, and psychosocial support, as well as legal remedies for refugee and asylum seekers arrested at sea (UNHCR 2016). In a meeting with a UNHCR representative, I asked what protection was provided to refugees under serious and immediate threat of harm. In response, the aforementioned services were listed verbatim, repeating a tired humanitarian vernacular suggestive of a wider level of "compassion fatigue" that has worked its way through the political system and into civil society (see Fassin 2010).

Official indifference and the deferral of responsibility was a constant theme during interviews with people who sought assistance from law enforcement, UN agencies, and/or NGOs. Asha, whose narrative appears in Chapter 6, was forced to withdraw a statement made against a broker because of a lack of credible safeguards over the safety of her children. Asha, who had her kidney removed under threat of violence (see Chapter 6) filed a report against the broker who recruited her in Khartoum. She explained her circumstances to the police, who referred her to the UNHCR to seek protection. After waiting nervously for a meeting with a UN representative, she was referred to PSTIC (Psycho-Social Services and Training Institute in Cairo), a UNHCR partner agency that provides "special assistance and psychosocial support for persons of concern who have been exposed to trauma." Asha withdrew her statement, fearing for the lives of her children. In April 2018 Asha's case was accepted by the United Kingdom for resettlement. As I am writing, March 2020, Asha remains in Cairo awaiting her actual resettlement.

Identifying people based on their ethnicity, police officials referred African nationals to the UNHCR as asylum seekers or refugees, regardless of their legal status. Aside from being admitted into life skills programs and/or referred for psychosocial support, no other tangible assistance was forthcoming. The limited assistance that the UNHCR provides extends to registered refugees only. To maintain refugee status and avoid deportation, refugees are required by the Egyptian government to apply for residency every 6 months. Failure to do so means that refugee status can be revoked, and residency becomes irregular (see Chapter 4). Refugees designated as "irregular" or "illegal" no longer qualify as "people of concern." They are beyond the protective limits of humanitarian government and can be deported back to their country of origin, where the process of irregular migration repeats itself.

Impressions of Justice

The capacity of NGOs to assist refugees, undocumented migrants, and/or Egyptian nationals has been significantly impaired by Egypt's Law on Non-Governmental Organizations (Human Rights Watch 2017a). The law requires centers of all types, charitable or otherwise, to register as NGOs with the Ministry of Social Affairs. Foreign NGOs are required to pay $16,500 for registration, which is subject to renewal on a biannual basis. Only NGOs that meet the government's (unspecified) criteria for work that contributes to the state's developmental needs are approved. According to the strict provisions of the law, any organization found to represent a threat to national security, public order, or public morals is refused a permit and/or ordered to cease activities with immediate effect (Article 88). The National Authority for the Regulation of Non-Governmental Foreign Organizations was established under Article 77 with a mandate to monitor and verify that funding received from international sources is allocated only for preapproved services and/or activities. Organizations found to be in breach of regulatory provisions are subject to penalties ranging from a fine between E£50,000 and E£1 million to a prison term of up to five years. This includes organizations that conduct or participate in field research or opinion polls without prior approval. During my fieldwork in Cairo, the Nadeem Center for Rehabilitation of Victims of Violence was closed for noncompliance. The Center, which had been providing medical care to victims of torture, including Egyptian nationals, was accused of encouraging seditious behavior and damaging national security.

When I returned to Cairo in 2017–2020, many of the NGO representatives that I consulted with during my field research in 2014 were no longer open to talking about the organ trade or related activities (e.g., people smuggling). One aid worker, working with an international organization in Cairo, who did agree to speak to me (June 2018) explained that the organ trade was a source of contention for the Egyptian state. Fearing the acrimony of a public inquiry into the activities of state representatives, the organ trade is not an issue that the incumbent regime wants reported. Accordingly, NGOs have not received approval to work on this issue. According to a representative working with a local NGO in Cairo, "If any NGO were to release a report indicating that the organ trade was active and/or was critical of the government's response, the organization and the researchers responsible would almost certainly be persecuted." This would explain why many NGO workers denied knowledge of the organ trade, despite several people having informed me that they had sought support from different civil society organizations. At the same time, journalists were being deported from Egypt for taking a critical stance against the Sisi regime and the litany of human rights abuses carried out under the premise of social security (Michaelson 2018). The impending sense of political oppression and social control was not something that was lost on my respondents. One Eritrean refugee commented, "How can we find protection here when the state does not protect its own people?"

Increased state control of Egyptian NGOs and the media has led to further opacity surrounding organ markets and the networks that supply them. On July 12, 2018, various media outlets reported that 37 people had been found guilty by an Egyptian court on charges related to illicit trading in human organs. According to these reports, the convicted were sentenced to prison terms ranging from 3 to 15 years and fined between E£200,000 and E£500,000 (H. Ahmed and Aboudi 2018). The story originated in the state-owned newspaper *Al-Ahram*. In 2016 the same newspaper ran a story claiming that police had raided a series of private hospitals and health centers where "illegal organ harvesting, and organ trafficking had taken place" (Ahram Online 2016). A government spokesperson from the Ministry of Health who was quoted in the article claimed that millions of dollars had been recovered and that several people, including doctors, nurses, and middlemen, had been arrested in connection with the crime. There was no mention of victims. The court documents from the case have not been made public. Nor have I been able to retrieve any information regarding the case from the Egyptian authorities. When asked to comment on the case, a spokesman from the Egyptian Ministry of Foreign Affairs sent the following statement: "Egyptian authorities continue to vigilantly pursue, investigate and bring to justice any such crimes of organ trade in accordance with the stringent provisions of the criminal law. Furthermore, this hideous illegal trade has never been condoned by the Egyptian government and law enforcement authorities. We will continue to combat such crimes and bring those engaged in the organ trade to justice, while protecting Egyptian citizens as well as our host refugee and migrant community."[5] During a visit to Beirut, Lebanon, in 2018 I spoke with a law enforcement official who claimed to have made inquiries into the case as part of an investigation into people smuggling operations on the Central Mediterranean Route. His interest in the case had come from intelligence he received in 2016, from Dutch, German and Italian intelligence agencies, that asylum seekers were selling kidneys to reach Europe (see Chapter 5). He claimed that, according to a reliable source, the names of the surgeons that were "leaked" to the media belonged to unidentified decedents. He dismissed the case as part of a wider public relations strategy to demonstrate the strength of Egypt's anti-trafficking framework.

Regardless of the veracity of a given case, the impression of justice that a conviction conveys allows policymakers to claim success for legal measures and policy frameworks that in practice cause more harm than good. High-profile prosecutions give the appearance that positive action has been taken, without challenging the broader political framework that produces victimization. Nevertheless, cases that receive media attention ingrain a particular interpretation of criminal phenomena into the social consciousness. The hyperbole surrounding criminal cases communicates a narrow sense of justice at odds with the social context of crime, giving form and substance to provisional and often contradictory legislative proposals with no tangible importance for the people they ostensibly protect. The capacity of the judiciary to impart a fair ruling or the implications that a criminal sentence might have on victims is rarely considered. Nine of the people I interviewed during my fieldwork in Cairo sold or arranged for the sale of an organ between 2017 and 2020. While the alleged raids on transplant clinics were being reported in the media, they were navigating the contours of economic survival. In contrast to the moral victory presented by the state media in light of the arrests, the immigration and crime controls established under the National Coordination Committee for Preventing and Combating Illegal Migration and Human Trafficking (2018) limited the economic options of my respondents, further embedding their social exclusion and rendering them expendable to the extremes of exploitation.

As I have demonstrated, prohibitory legislation has had a negative effect on the most socially marginalized individuals in Egyptian society, who are targeted for organ sale. Increasing raids and arrests of human traffickers and people smugglers has translated into the indiscriminate arrest and deportation of "illegal" migrants. Further, a combination of increased penalties and limited enforcement efforts has led to the displacement of organ sellers into more hidden spheres of the informal economy, increasing the hold criminal groups have over their lives. Several organ sellers named well-known private and public hospitals in Cairo that they claimed were hosting illegal transplants. Organ brokers were clear that high ranking government officials were not only turning a blind eye to illegal procedures, but actively profiting from them. Okot, introduced in chapter 6, claimed that criminal groups working in the organ trade do not fear arrest because they are paying protection money to police and government officials. From a law enforcement perspective, resources would be better served by combating corruption and investigating the organ laundering process described in Chapter 3. Reviewing transplant waiting times, I suggest, would be a good place to start. The waiting time is likely to be much shorter for someone receiving a commercial transplant as opposed to someone on a public register awaiting an altruistic donation. The number of immunosuppressant drugs being used by any given hospital would be a further indicator of the level of transplant activity taking place, legitimate or not.

Lessons from Egypt

Current responses to the organ trade and human trafficking more generally adopt a narrow criminal paradigm that requires the criminalization of perpetrators responsible for trafficking people for the purposes of exploitation. Linking organ sales with human trafficking or modern slavery neglects more subtle forms of abuse, which can involve elements of trafficking or develop into them. Legal reform is needed to address the structural vulnerability behind the organ trade, lowering the normative baseline from which people are exploited. An emphasis on preventing or at least limiting the extent of exploitative relations manifest in more explicit forms of violence (e.g., human trafficking) would be a start. The imposition of draconian migrant controls on the Central Mediterranean Route has created opportunities for states (e.g., authoritarian regimes in Egypt, Libya, and Sudan) and nonstate actors (e.g., organ brokers and smugglers) to benefit at the expense of migrant populations. Claims for asylum are being routinely ignored, and funding for punitive measures to prevent migration is being increased. If the host environment were less hostile, then it would fall to reason that refugees would be less likely to enter into exploitative relations where selling body parts to fund hazardous journeys over land and sea is a realistic consideration. Internationally recognized labor standards and protections, including but not limited to a minimum wage, statutory periods of rest, and occupational safety and health, need to be extended to migrant populations, including asylum seekers, refugees, and those without legal status (see Shamir 2012; Chuang 2014). This would involve mandating work permits and making access to work meaningful features of refugee protection. At the same time, more legal avenues for refugees and economic migrants need to be created. The current UNHCR resettlement process is critically underfunded and mismanaged, leading people into exploitative relations of power and dependency. The vast majority of the world's asylum seekers and refugees are concentrated in marginalized enclaves in the global South (Trilling 2018; Andersson 2016). More resettlement places are required to prevent the development of smuggling economies along migrant routes and the systematic abuse of entire communities disregarded by the international community. World leaders exhorting "the misery of exploitation" as "a crime against humanity" would do well to reconsider exploitation as a legal concept by addressing the legal barriers and policy decisions that leave people vulnerable to exploitation by state and nonstate actors.

The exploitation that people experience is implicated in and contingent on particular environments and circumstances mediated by legal rules and political conditions. States, through the policies they implement, are key players that determine the extent of exploitative practices which people are exposed to. Governments mediate territorial borders and determine labor and employment laws and business practices, which can both stimulate and constrain demand for clandestine trading activities, such as the organ trade. As a consequence of their "illegal" status, the people I interviewed during my fieldwork in Cairo were invariably employed in informal sectors of the economy where they worked long hours for insufficient wages. The commercial expansion of the transplant industry created a demand for organ sales that could not be satisfied by legal or formal channels. Organ markets emerged as an economic activity for impoverished Egyptians and migrants, asylum seekers, and refugees who were socially and economically marginalized from formal income-generating activities. News coverage of "organ scandals" followed and brought the Egyptian government and the National Health Ministry into disrepute. In response, criminal penalties prohibiting organ sales were introduced. Meanwhile, stories of organ theft and trafficking continued, prompting the government to double up on penalties and co-opt the organ trade into a wider punitive strategy to counter illegal migration and human trafficking. This approach pushed the trade further underground, and undocumented migrants in particular became the preferred choice of organ supply. Prohibition combined with misconceived law enforcement measures has led to the development of organized crime and a concurrent rise in victimization and violence in organ markets. On this evidence, decriminalization together with an emphasis on work-related and structural exploitation would represent a better approach. Disentangling humanitarian concerns from law enforcement objectives would facilitate the development of solutions that speak to our shared humanity rather than reproducing social divisions. This might involve prioritizing investment in communities that are the most vulnerable to exploitation, expanding access to education and health care, providing safe and affordable accommodation, and creating jobs. Perhaps then the narrative would change from trading life to sharing it.

The existing commentary on the organ trade is dominated by expert opinions, most notably from professional practitioners in the field of transplant medicine. In contrast, the experiences of organ sellers and organ brokers have largely been discounted or bypassed by a narrow bioethical debate contesting the pros and cons of a regulated market in organs. To go beyond conventional theorizing, often construed from an external perspective or grounded in a particular ideology or tradition, I found it necessary to engage with individuals who are directly affected by the existence of organ markets. In writing this book, I have endeavored to present and communicate the perspectives of the people who are involved in various aspects of organ trading; to reconstruct described scenes and situated contexts, locating the narratives of my respondents within their own frame of apprehension; and to explain and render intelligible the social and political forces played out in the corporal violence against their bodies. This book is for them and of them.

NOTES

CHAPTER 1

1. I use the term *organ seller* as opposed to *donor* to clearly differentiate being different acts and motivations that are often conflated. Organ sales are not donations.

2. This is a relatively low number, compared with the 225,000 victims of trafficking in persons for all other purposes reported by the United Nations Office of Drugs and Crime (UNODC 2018).

3. Article 3(a) of the Trafficking Protocol defines trafficking in persons as "the recruitment, transportation, transfer, harbouring or receipt of persons, by means of the threat or use of force or other forms of coercion, of abduction, of fraud, of deception, of the abuse of power or of a position of vulnerability or of the giving or receiving of payments or benefits to achieve the consent of a person having control over another person, for the purpose of exploitation. Exploitation shall include, at a minimum, the exploitation or the prostitution of others or other forms of sexual exploitation, forced labour or services, slavery or practices similar to slavery, servitude or the removal of organs."

4. The Trafficking Victims Protection Act (TVPA) in the United States does not directly recognize organ trafficking or the removal of organ(s) as a form of exploitation. See Pugliese (2007: 181).

5. This is assuming that the resource in question is put to good use, which is a debate in and of itself—for example, natural resource extraction.

6. These NGOs are not named to protect the anonymity of the informants. In 2015 the Egyptian government introduced a new law governing NGOs. Any NGO found to be working against the national interest is subject to criminal penalties, up to life imprisonment. See Human Rights Watch (2017a).

7. It was not possible to gather demographic information on all the respondents. For example, organ brokers did not respond well to questions regarding their demographic profile. The information I list includes the demographic data I gathered.

CHAPTER 2

1. This estimate has been repeated on an annual basis (2007–2019), despite there being more than 160,000 kidney transplants in 2019.

2. At the time of writing this was the most up-to-date statistical record at an international level.

3. Although the accuracy of these statistics is questionable, they do provide a general sense of the discrepancy between those who need a transplant and those who receive one.

4. This is not an indictment of the transplant profession or a dismissal of the therapeutic benefits that successful transplantation can provide. In referring to the transplant industry, I am referring to the various parties (e.g., pharmaceutical companies, insurance companies, private transplant clinics, organ-sharing organizations, medical professionals) that have a commercial stake in transplantation.

5. According to Mahoney (2000), in the United States 70% of the organ procurement agencies regulated by the federal government sold body parts directly to for-profit firms.

6. Again, this is not an indictment of the transplant profession or a dismissal of the therapeutic benefits that successful transplantation can provide.

7. Nevertheless, patients do use their relative economic privilege to purchase organs from less privileged sellers.

8. Polluted water has been linked to many illnesses in Egypt, including organ failure. See Barnes (2014).

9. The law was amended in 2015, further increasing criminal sanctions. See Egyptian Medical Syndicate, http://www.ems.org.eg/, updated in 2017. The law appears in the Egypt penal code as Law 5/2010. This was updated in 2017, introducing harsher penalties. The copy of the law that I received was translated from the original Arabic.

10. According to the United Nations Declaration of Basic Principles of Justice for Victims of Crime and Abuse of Power (1985), "victims of crime" are defined in the broad sense as "persons who, individually or collectively, have suffered harm, including physical or mental injury, emotional suffering, economic loss or substantial impairment of their fundamental rights, through acts or omissions that are violations of national criminal laws or of internationally recognized norms relating to human rights." However, used in this broad sense the term *victim* has no specific legal status. Not all individuals who sell an organ can be considered a victim of trafficking. I use the term *organ seller* to make this distinction. With regard to organ trafficking, the term *victim* assumes that an individual has been trafficked. For legal purposes this can be established only after a judicial process. Unless the three elements of human trafficking (action, means, purpose) are satisfied, an individual who may indeed be a victim, at least in the broader sense of the word, cannot be considered a victim of trafficking. Moreover, as I indicate, the term *victim* is routinely used to convey a particular perspective or metanarrative of trafficking that does not reflect the diverse experiences of trafficked persons, not least for their organs.

11. All the organ sellers who participated in the research for this book sold a kidney after the Transplantation of Human Organs and Tissues Act was passed in 2010.

CHAPTER 3

1. The organization in question is not named for confidentiality reasons.
2. Two years later an Italian student, Giulio Regeni, was killed, a murder later linked to his research into Egypt's labor unions (see Tondo and Michaelson 2018).
3. Article 2 of the Law of Trafficking in Persons specifically refers to "the removal of human organs, tissues or parts thereof" as a form of exploitation. Similar to the Trafficking Protocol, trafficking in persons is defined as an act (including selling, exposing for sale, buying, promising to sell or buy, using, transporting, handing over, harboring or receiving a person, either inside the country or across its borders) committed by a certain means (using force or violence or threats thereof, or by abduction or fraud or deception, or the exploitation of a position of power or the exploitation of a state of weakness or need, or the promise of financial compensation or benefits in exchange for the consent of a person to the trafficking of another person he/she has control over) for the purposes of exploitation (exploitation in prostitution and all other forms of sexual exploitation, sexual exploitation of children or exploitation of children for pornography, forced labor or services, slavery and slavery-like practices, begging and the removal of organs or human tissue or parts thereof).
4. Tissue typing is a procedure in which the tissues of a prospective donor and recipient are tested for compatibility before a transplant. This usually takes place in analytic labs, where clients undergo blood and urine tests to screen for underlying health complications (e.g., HIV infection).
5. Currency rates have fluctuated significantly between 2014 and 2020, generally reflecting a depreciation of the Egyptian pound.
6. The term *organ laundering* has also been used by Manzano et al. (2014).
7. It is not illegal to pay for a transplant procedure. It is only illegal to purchase a kidney. Furthermore, organ transplantation in a foreign country is legal, whereas the purchase of an organ is illicit.
8. Egyptian Medical Syndicate, http://www.ems.org.eg/, updated 2017.

CHAPTER 4

1. In the absence of a functioning and impartial judiciary, it is unlikely that Fatimah's case would have advanced through the courts, regardless of her legal status. In Egypt migrants of African ethnicity are invariably treated as illegal, whether or not they possess the necessary documentation confirming proof of residence.
2. There are no official figures on the number of undocumented migrants and displaced individuals in Egypt.
3. Owing to the historical ties between Sudan and Egypt and as a consequence of the widespread displacement of the Sudanese population, the two countries signed the Wadi El Nil Treaty in 1976, which allowed Sudanese migrants to enter Egypt and obtain residency without needing to file for asylum. See Y. Ahmed (2009).
4. The Four Freedoms Agreement was made after a series of border disputes and negotiations over oil transportation between Sudan and Egypt. Journalists have sug-

gested that this agreement was introduced as a bargaining chip during the negotiations. See "Sudan-Egypt relations hit speed bump over Four Freedoms accord," *Sudan Tribune*, February 25, 2013, http://www.sudantribune.com/spip.php?article45646 (accessed March 1, 2016).

5. In July 2013, after a few Syrians were accused of participating in protests in Egypt, the Egyptian government announced that Syrians from then on would need a visa and a security clearance before being allowed into the country.

6. Other nationalities are required to pay significantly more. The cost for Eritreans is E£4,530 ($681).

7. In 2004, after the ceasefire between Sudan and South Sudan, the UNHCR suspended all RSD interviews for Sudanese migrants. This led to protests outside the United Nations headquarters in Cairo. Civil disobedience was brutally and abruptly brought to a halt. At least 28 protesters were killed. See Moulin and Nyers (2007).

8. Egypt is also a signatory to the 1969 Organization of African Unity Convention.

9. Charities are set up to help women find work as housekeepers. This work falls short of most migrant women's aspirations. A number of respondents commented on their dissatisfaction with the type of work available.

10. Housekeepers are in high demand in Egypt. Therefore the average wage for females is higher than that for males.

11. Mohamed passed away during the writing of this book, in 2016.

12. Yea (2015) has noted how nervous medical staff in the Philippines discharged patients "suspected" of organ sales as quickly as possible, without providing sufficient postoperative care.

CHAPTER 5

1. "Vessel" means any type of watercraft, including nondisplacement craft and seaplanes, that are used or capable of being used as a means of transportation on water, except a warship, naval auxiliary, or other vessel owned or operated by a government and used, for the time being, only on government noncommercial service.

2. Plans to "externalize" Europe's borders were already in place long before the so-called migrant crisis. The "crisis" provided the necessary level of urgency to push these security measures through with public opinion firmly onside. Essentially, the suffering of migrants lost at sea was exploited by political leaders to justify the very measures that had caused, or at least contributed to, their suffering to begin with.

3. Egyptian Law 82/2016, Combating Illegal Migration and Smuggling of Migrants, can be found at https://www.refworld.org/pdfid/58b68e734.pdf.

4. It also fulfills requirements set out in Section 108 of the U.S. Department of State "Trafficking in Persons Report" (2016) to comply with the "minimum standards for the elimination of trafficking."

5. Article 3(a) of the Protocol Against the Smuggling of Migrants by Land, Sea, and Air, supplementing the United Nations Convention Against Transnational Organized Crime (UNODC 2000a), states that the "'smuggling of migrants' shall mean the procurement, in order to obtain, directly or indirectly, a financial or other mate-

rial benefit, of the illegal entry of a person into a State Party of which the person is not a national or a permanent resident."

6. In October 2015 the UN Security Council adopted Resolution 2240, which authorized member states to enforce exceptional powers on vessels allegedly involved in smuggling and human trafficking in international waters off the Libyan coast (United Nations Security Council 2015). In June 2015 The European Union launched the European Union Naval Force Mediterranean (EUNAVFOR), a military operation also known as Operation Sophia, with the aim of neutralizing the Central Mediterranean Route.

7. For more information on European agreements with Libya, see "Memorandum of Understanding on Cooperation in the Fields of Development, the Fight Against Illegal Immigration, Human Trafficking, and Fuel Smuggling and on Reinforcing the Security of Borders Between the State of Libya and the Italian Republic" (2017), https://eumigrationlawblog.eu/wp-content/uploads/2017/10/MEMORANDUM_translation_finalversion.doc.pdf (accessed December 4, 2019).

8. See, for example, "Agreements Between Germany and Egypt/Tunisia Concerning Cooperation in the Field of Security," https://www.bundestag.de/dokumente/textarchiv/2017/kw17-de-aegyptentunesien/501784 (accessed December 4, 2019).

9. According to Law 82, an organized criminal group is a group of at least three people formed as a specific organization that works continuously or for a specific period of time with the purpose of committing one or more specific crimes, including the crime of smuggling migrants, or committing other crimes in order to directly or indirectly obtain material for moral gain or for any other purpose, without its members taking on certain roles or maintaining continuous membership. This follows the definition of an organized criminal group set out under Article 2(a) of the United Nations Convention Against Transnational Organized Crime.

10. The people I spoke with viewed *samasira* as guides, service providers, and occasional allies who facilitated travel to otherwise inaccessible territories. This role was distinguished from people-smugglers, who transported people overseas, in contravention of the law. *Samasira* and their activities were not considered criminal but rather part of an established system of cross-border movement, existing long before border management became a feature of diplomatic relations and foreign policy in North Africa. The role of the *samsar* is to provide advice and guidance along migrant routes, navigate pathways through vast desert terrain, and facilitate travel across national boundaries. Essentially, the *samsar* acts as informal travel agent connecting client-migrants to smugglers (*Muharib*) at different points of departure. This role became more ambiguous when irregular migration became a political objective for Egyptian and Libyan authorities.

CHAPTER 6

1. There is no single definition of organized crime, which can involve different forms, structures, networks, activities, and actors. For a detailed discussed about the definitions of organized crime, see Varese (2010).

2. According to Article 2(a) of the United Nations Convention Against Transnational Organized Crime, an "'organized criminal group' shall mean a structured group of three or more persons, existing for a period of time and acting in concert with the aim of committing one or more serious crimes or offences established in accordance with this Convention, in order to obtain, directly or indirectly, a financial or other material benefit."

3. In Egypt a criminal suspect can be held for a 30-day period without charge.

CHAPTER 7

1. Decriminalization involves the removal of criminal status for a particular activity, behavior, or service. This is distinct from depenalization, which involves a reduction in criminal penalties.

2. These findings are based on the partial decriminalization of cannabis possession only. The sale of cannabis remained a criminal offense, and civil fines for the possession of small quantities were retained in the United States and Australia. The authors also noted variations in how laws were interpreted and enforced in different countries and jurisdiction within those countries.

3. For a more detailed analysis of drug use and policy, see A. Stevens (2010) and Babor et al. (2010).

4. Kohler and Alcock use the term *structural violence* to describe the effects of indirect violence caused by structural forces such as poverty and social exclusion.

5. This quotation also appeared in an article I wrote for the *Guardian* in February 2019. See Columb (2019).

REFERENCES

CASE LAW

Medicus Clinic case, District Court of Priština, KA 278/10, P 309/10, and KA 309/10, P 340/10, March 2011.

The State v. Netcare Kwa-Zulu (Pty.) Ltd., [2010], South Africa, Agreement in Terms of S.105A (1) of Act 51 of 1977; 41/1804/2010 (Commercial Crime Court, Regional Court of Kwa-Zulu Natal, Durban, South Africa, November 2010).

U.S. v. Rosenbaum, 11-cr-00741, U.S. District Court, District of New Jersey (Trenton), 2012.

SOURCES

Adham, Khaled. 2005. "Globalization, neoliberalism, and new spaces of capital in Cairo." *Traditional Dwellings and Settlements Review* 17(1): 19–32.

Agustín, Laura María. 2007. *Sex at the margins: Migration, labour, and the rescue industry.* London: Zed Books.

Ahmed, Haitham, and Sami Aboudi. 2018. "Egypt court finds 37 guilty at illegal organ trading trial." Reuters, July 12. https://uk.reuters.com/article/uk-egypt-trial-trafficking/egypt-court-finds-37-guilty-at-illegal-organ-trading-trial-idUKKBN1K22PO?il=0 (accessed May 12, 2019).

Ahmed, Y. 2009. *The prospects of assisted voluntary return among the Sudanese population in greater Cairo.* Cairo: International Organization for Migration.

Ahram Online. 2016. "Egypt arrests organ trafficking ring," December 6. http://english.ahram.org.eg/NewsContent/1/64/251476/Egypt/Politics-/Egypt-arrests-organ-trafficking-ring.aspx (accessed May 15, 2019).

———. 2017. "Egypt's attorney general refers 41 suspects in organ trafficking network to criminal court." *Al-Ahram*, July 4. http://english.ahram.org.eg/NewsContent/1/64/273015/Egypt/Politics-/Egypts-Attorney-General-refers—suspects-in-organ-.aspx (accessed May 15, 2019).

Al-Bugami, Meteb M., Fahad E. al-Otaibe, Abdulnaser M. Alabadi, Khaled Hamawi, and Khalid Bel'eed-Akkari. 2018. "Transplant tourism following the Declaration of Istanbul: Poor outcomes and nephrologist dilemma." *Nephrology* 23(12): 1139–44.

Al Jazeera. 2014. "Egypt court sentences Al Jazeera journalists." *Al Jazeera*, June 23. https://www.aljazeera.com/news/middleeast/2014/06/egypt-finds-al-jazeera-journalists-guilty-201462373539293797.html (accessed February 28, 2018).

———. 2019. "Al Jazeera decries Mahmoud Hussein's extended detention in Egypt." *Al Jazeera*, May 23. https://www.aljazeera.com/news/2019/05/al-jazeera-decries-mahmoud-hussein-extended-detention-egypt-190529161130389.html (accessed June 1, 2019).

Allain, John. 2011. "Trafficking of persons for the removal of organs and the admission of guilt of a South African hospital: *The State v. Netcare Kwa-Zulu (Pty) Limited*." *Medical Law Review* 19(1): 117–22.

Amar, Paul. 2013. *The security archipelago: Human security states, sexuality politics, and the end of neoliberalism*. Durham, NC: Duke University Press.

Ambagtsheer, Frederike, Damian Zaitch, and Willem Weimar. 2013. "The battle for human organs: Organ trafficking and transplant tourism in a global context." *Global Crime* 14(1): 1–26.

Amnesty International. 2017. "Libya's dark web of collusion: Abuses against Europe bound refugees and migrants." https://www.amnesty.org/download/Documents/MDE1975612017ENGLISH.PDF (accessed October 7, 2019).

Anderson, Bridget. 2012. "Where's the harm in that? Immigration enforcement, trafficking, and the protection of migrants' rights." *American Behavioral Scientist* 56(9): 1241–57.

———. 2013. *Us and them? The dangerous politics of immigration control*. Oxford, UK: Oxford University Press.

———. 2017. "Towards a new politics of migration?" *Ethnic and Racial Studies* 40(9): 1527–37.

Anderson, Bridget, and Ben Rogaly. 2005. *Forced labour and migration to the UK*. Report prepared by COMPAS and the Trade Union Congress. Oxford, UK: COMPAS, School of Anthropology, University of Oxford.

Anderson, Bridget, and Martin Ruhs. 2010. "Researching illegality and labour migration." *Population, Space, and Place* 16(3): 175–79.

Andersson, Ruben. 2014. *Illegality Inc.: Clandestine migration and the business of bordering Europe*. Berkeley: University of California Press.

———. 2016. "Europe's failed 'fight' against irregular migration: Ethnographic notes on a counterproductive industry." *Journal of Ethnic and Migration Studies* 42(7): 1055–75.

Arab Republic of Egypt. 2010. "Law No. 64 Regarding Combating Human Trafficking." http://www.protectionproject.org/wp-content/uploads/2010/09/Egypt_TIP-Law_2010-Ar+En.pdf (accessed June 19, 2019).

Armstrong, Lynzi. 2017. "Decriminalization and the rights of migrant sex workers in Aotearoa/New Zealand: Making a case for change." *Women's Studies Journal* 31(2): 69–76.

Aronowitz, Alexis A. 2001. "Smuggling and trafficking in human beings: The phenomenon, the markets that drive it, and the organisations that promote it." *European Journal on Criminal Policy and Research* 9(2): 163–95.

Aziz, Mahmoud. 2017. "Egypt's State Council approves law to increase penalties for illegal transplants." Ahram Online, March 15. http://english.ahram.org.eg/News ContentP/1/261005/Egypt/Egypts-State-Council-approves-law-to-increase-pena.aspx (accessed January 20, 2019).

Babor, Thomas F., Jonathan P. Caulkins, Griffith Edwards, Benedikt Fischer, David R. Foxcroft, Keith Humphreys, Isidore S. Obot, Jürgen Rehm, and Peter Reuter. 2010. *Drug policy and the public good.* Oxford, UK: Oxford University Press.

Bagheri, Alireza. 2006. "Compensated kidney donation: An ethical review of the Iranian model." *Kennedy Institute of Ethics Journal* 16(3): 269–82.

Baraaz, Tamara. 2018. "Illegal organ harvesting is rampant in Egypt and refugees are the main target." *Haaretz*, September 22. https://www.haaretz.com/middle-east-news/egypt/.premium.MAGAZINE-illegal-organ-harvesting-is-rampant-in-egypt-and-refugees-are-the-main-target-1.6492013 (accessed March 17, 2018).

Barnes, Jessica. 2014. *Cultivating the Nile: The everyday politics of water in Egypt.* Durham, NC: Duke University Press.

Barsoum, Rashad S. 2008. "Trends in unrelated-donor kidney transplantation in the developing world." *Pediatric Nephrology* 23(11): 1925–29.

———. 2013. "Burden of chronic kidney disease: North Africa." *Kidney International Supplements* 3(2): 164–66.

———. 2016. "Burden of end-stage kidney disease: North Africa." *Clinical Nephrology* 86(7): 14–17.

———. 2017. "End stage renal disease (ESKD) in Egypt and North Africa." In *Chronic Kidney Disease in Disadvantaged Populations*, ed. Guillermo Garcia-Garcia, Lawrence Agodoa, and Keith Norris, 113–23. Cambridge, MA: Academic Press.

Bayat, Asef. 1997. "Un-civil society: The politics of the 'informal people.'" *Third World Quarterly* 18(1): 53–72.

BBC. 2016. "Egypt arrests 'organ trafficking ring.'" BBC, December 6, http://www.bbc.co.uk/news/world-middle-east-38224836 (accessed May 23, 2019).

BBC News. 2017. "Egypt convicts 56 over migrant boat sinking that killed 200." *BBC News*, March 26. http://www.bbc.com/news/world-middle-east-39399941 (accessed June 3, 2019).

Bernstein, Elizabeth. 2007. "Sex work for the middle classes." *Sexualities* 10(4): 473–88.

Bilger, Veronika, Martin Hofmann, and Michael Jandl. 2006. "Human smuggling as a transnational service industry: Evidence from Austria." *International Migration* 44(4): 59–93.

Bloch, Alice, and Sonia McKay. 2016. *Living on the margins: Undocumented migrants in a global city.* Bristol, UK: Policy Press.

Block, Alice, and W. J. Chambliss. 1981. *Organizing crime.* New York: Elsevier North Holland.

Bobo, Lawrence D., and Victor Thompson. 2006. "Unfair by design: The war on drugs,

race, and the legitimacy of the criminal justice system." *Social Research: An International Quarterly* 73(2): 445–72.
Boffey, Daniel. 2019. "Migrants detained in Libya for profit, leaked EU report reveals." *The Guardian*, November 20. https://www.theguardian.com/uk-news/2019/nov/20/migrants-detained-in-libya-for-profit-leaked-eu-report-reveals (accessed November 20, 2019).
Boltanski, Luc, and Eve Chiapello. 2005. "The new spirit of capitalism." *International Journal of Politics, Culture, and Society* 18(3–4): 161–88.
Bosworth, Mary, Katja Franko, and Sharon Pickering. 2018. "Punishment, globalization, and migration control: 'Get them the hell out of here.'" *Punishment and Society* 20(1): 34–53.
Bourgois, Philippe. 2015. "Insecurity, the war on drugs, and crimes of the state: Symbolic violence in the Americas." In *Violence at the urban margins*, ed. Javier Auyero, Philippe Bourgois, and Nancy Scheper-Hughes, 305–21. Oxford, UK: Oxford University Press.
Brachet, Julien. 2016. "Policing the desert: The IOM in Libya beyond war and peace." *Antipode* 48(2): 272–92.
———. 2018. "Manufacturing smugglers: From irregular to clandestine mobility in the Sahara." *Annals of the American Academy of Political and Social Science* 676(1): 16–35.
Bruinsma, Gerban, and Wim Bernasco. 2004. "Criminal groups and transnational illegal markets." *Crime, Law, and Social Change* 41(1): 79–94.
Budiani-Saberi, Debra A., and Francis L. Delmonico. 2008. "Organ trafficking and transplant tourism: A commentary on the global realities." *American Journal of Transplantation* 8(5): 925–29.
Buehn, Andreas, and Frederich Schneider. 2012. "Shadow economies around the world: Novel insights, accepted knowledge, and new estimates." *International Tax and Public Finance* 19(1): 139–71.
Butler, Judith. 2006. *Precarious life: The powers of mourning and violence*. London: Verso.
Cameron, J. Stewart, and Raymond Hoffenberg. 1999. "The ethics of organ transplantation reconsidered: Paid organ donation and the use of executed prisoners as donors." *Kidney International* 55(2): 724–32.
Campana, Paolo. 2018. "Out of Africa: The organization of migrant smuggling across the Mediterranean." *European Journal of Criminology* 15(4): 481–502.
Campana, Paolo, and Federico Varese. 2016. "Exploitation in human trafficking and smuggling." *European Journal on Criminal Policy and Research* 22(1): 89–105.
Canales, Muna T., Bertram L. Kasiske, and Mark E. Rosenberg. 2006. "Transplant tourism: Outcomes of United States residents who undergo kidney transplantation overseas." *Transplantation* 82(12): 1658–61.
Caplan, Arthur L. 2014. "Trafficking and markets in kidneys: Two poor solutions to a pressing problem." In *The future of bioethics: International dialogues*, ed. Akira Akabayashi, 407–16. Oxford, UK: Oxford University Press.

Castells, Manuel. 2011. *The information age: Economy, society, and culture*, vol. 1, *The rise of the network society*. West Sussex, UK: Wiley.

Castells, Manuel, Alejandro Portes, and Lauren Benton, eds. 1989. *The informal economy: Studies in advanced and less developed countries*. Baltimore: Johns Hopkins University Press.

Chacón, Jennifer M., and Susan Bibler Coutin. 2018. "Racialization through enforcement." In *Race, criminal justice, and migration control: Enforcing the boundaries of belonging*, ed. Mary Bosworth, Alpa Parmar, and Yolanda Vázquez, 159–78. Oxford, UK: Oxford University Press.

Chin, Ko-Lin, and Sheldon X. Zhang. 2015. *The Chinese heroin trade: Cross-border drug trafficking in Southeast Asia and beyond*. New York: NYU Press.

Christys, Patrick. 2017. "Revealed: People smugglers making millions selling child migrants' organs on black market." *Daily Express*, January 5. https://www.express.co.uk/news/world/750681/Child-migrants-people-smuggling-organs-mafia-gangs-Africa-European-Union-refugee-asylum (accessed December 12, 2018).

Chuang, J. A. 2010. "Rescuing trafficking from ideological capture." *University of Pennsylvania Law Review* 1655–1728.

———. 2014. "Exploitation creep and the unmaking of human trafficking law." *American Journal of International Law* 108(4): 609–49.

COFS (Coalition of Organ Failure Solutions). 2011. "Sudanese victims of organ trafficking in Egypt." http://cofs.org/home/wp-content/uploads/2012/06/REPORT-Sud-Victims-of-OT-in-Egypt-NEW-COVER-16-Jan-20124.pdf (accessed June 19, 2019).

Cohen, Gerald A. 1979. "The labor theory of value and the concept of exploitation." *Philosophy and Public Affairs* 8(4): 338–60.

Cohen, I. Glenn. 2013. "Transplant tourism: The ethics and regulation of international markets for organs." *Journal of Law, Medicine, and Ethics* 41(1): 269–85.

———. 2014. *Patients with passports: Medical tourism, law, and ethics*. Oxford, UK: Oxford University Press.

Cohen, Lawrence. 2001. "The other kidney: Biopolitics beyond recognition." *Body and Society* 7(2–3): 9–29.

Cohen, Stanley. 2011 [1972]. *Folk devils and moral panics*. Abingdon, UK: Routledge.

Columb, Seán. 2019. "Organ trafficking in Egypt: 'They locked me in and took my kidney.'" *The Guardian*, February 19. https://www.theguardian.com/global-development/2019/feb/09/trafficking-people-smugglers-organs-egypt-mediterranean-refugees-migrants (accessed December 5, 2019).

Council of Europe. 2014a. *Convention Against Trafficking in Human Organs*. Strasbourg: Council of Europe. www.coe.int/en/web/conventions/full-list/-/conventions/treaty/216 (accessed June 19, 2019).

———. 2014b. "Convention Against Trafficking in Human Organs: Explanatory report." https://wcd.coe.int/ViewDoc.jsp?Ref=CM(2013)79&Language=lanEnglish&Ver=addfinal&Site=COE&BackColorInternet=DBDCF2&BackColorIntranet=FDC864&BackColorLogged=FDC864 (accessed September 30, 2018).

Council of Europe and United Nations. 2009. "Trafficking in organs tissues and cells and trafficking in human beings for the purpose of the removal of organ." http://www.coe.int/t/dghl/monitoring/trafficking/docs/news/OrganTrafficking_study.pdf (accessed June 19, 2019).

Coutin, Susan Bibler. 2005. "Contesting criminality: Illegal immigration and the spatialization of legality." *Theoretical Criminology* 9(1): 5–33.

Crawley, Heaven, and Dimitris Skleparis. 2018. "Refugees, migrants, neither, both: Categorical fetishism and the politics of bounding in Europe's 'migration crisis.'" *Journal of Ethnic and Migration Studies* 44(1): 48–64.

Daniels, Peter W. 2004. "Urban challenges: The formal and informal economies in mega-cities." *Cities* 21(6): 501–11.

Danovitch, Gabriel M., and Alan B. Leichtman. 2006. "Kidney vending: The 'Trojan horse' of organ transplantation." *Clinical Journal of the American Society of Nephrology* 1(6): 1133–35.

Danovitch, G. M., J. Chapman, A. M. Capron, A. Levin, M. Abbud-Filho, M. Al Mousawi, W. D. Budiani-Saberi, W. Couser, I. Dittmer, V. Jha, J. Lavee, D. Martin, M. Masri, S. Naicker, S. Takahara, A. Tibell, F. Shaheen, V. Anantharaman, and F. L. Delmonico. 2013. "Organ trafficking and transplant tourism: The role of global professional ethical standards—The 2008 Declaration of Istanbul." *Transplantation* 95(11): 1306–12.

Dauvergne, Catherine. 2008. *Making people illegal: What globalization means for migration and law.* Cambridge, UK: Cambridge University Press.

Davidson, Julia O'Connell. 2006. *Prostitution, power, and freedom*, 2nd ed. Ann Arbor: University of Michigan Press.

De Haas, Hein. 2008. "The myth of invasion: The inconvenient realities of African migration to Europe." *Third World Quarterly* 29(7): 1305–22.

Dehghan, Saeed Kamali. 2017. "Migrant sea route to Italy is world's most lethal." *The Guardian*, September 11. https://www.theguardian.com/world/2017/sep/11/migrant-death-toll-rises-after-clampdown-on-east-european-borders (accessed April 6, 2019).

Delmonico, Francis L. 2009. "The implications of Istanbul Declaration on organ trafficking and transplant tourism." *Current Opinion in Organ Transplantation* 14(2): 116–19.

Delmonico, Francis L., and Nancy L. Ascher. 2017. "Opposition to irresponsible global kidney exchange." *American Journal of Transplantation* 17(10): 2745–46.

Delmonico, Francis, and Nancy Scheper-Hughes. 2003. "Why we should not pay for human organs." *Zygon: Journal of Religion and Science* 38(3): 689–98.

Delmonico, Francis, D. Martin, B. Domínguez-Gil, E. Muller, V. Jha, A. Levin, G. M. Danovitch, and A. M. Capron. 2015. "Living and deceased organ donation should be financially neutral acts." *American Journal of Transplantation* 15(5): 1187–91.

De Vries, Leonie Ansems, and Elspeth Guild. 2018. "Seeking refuge in Europe: Spaces of transit and the violence of migration management." *Journal of Ethnic and Migration Studies*, 11 pp. doi: 10.1080/1369183X.2018.1468308, https://warwick.ac.uk

/fac/soc/mmrp/outputs/seeking_refuge_in_europe_spaces_of_transit_and_the _violence_of_migration_management.pdf (accessed September 25, 2019).

Diaz, Lizbeth. 2008. "Mexico's death industry thrives on drug war killings." *Washington Post*, November 1.

DICG (Declaration of Istanbul Custodian Group). 2018. "The Declaration of Istanbul on organ trafficking and transplant tourism (2018 edition)." https://www.decla rationofistanbul.org/images/Policy_Documents/2018_Ed_Do/2018_Edition_of _the_Declaration_of_Istanbul_Final.pdf (accessed November 7, 2019).

Dorn, Nicholas, and Nigel South. 1990. "Drug markets and law enforcement." *British Journal of Criminology* 30(2): 171–88.

Dutton, Peter. 2017. "Opinion: Operation Sovereign Borders milestone." July 27. http://minister.homeaffairs.gov.au/peterdutton/Pages/opinion-operation-sovereign-borders-milestone.aspx (accessed December 23, 2019).

Dworkin, Gerald. 1994. "The Market and morals: The case for organ sales." In *Morality, Harm, and the Law*, ed. G. Dworkin, 155–61. Boulder, CO: Westview Press.

Edelstein, Ludwig. 1943. *The Hippocratic oath: Text, translation, and interpretation*. Baltimore: Johns Hopkins University Press.

Egyptian Initiative of Personal Rights and International Federation for Human Rights. 2007. *Egypt: Protection of the rights of all migrants workers and members of their families*. NGO Alternative Report to the UN Committee on the Rights of All Migrant Workers and Members of their Families. http://www2.ohchr.org/english/bodies/cmw/docs/eipr_fidh.pdf (accessed June 19, 2019).

EIPR (Egyptian Initiative for Personal Rights). 2009. *Challenges face health expenditure in Egypt: Report on the proceedings of a roundtable discussion*. https://eipr.org/sites/default/files/reports/pdf/Health_Expenditure_in_Egypt.pdf (accessed June 19, 2019).

———. 2010. "Organ transplant legislation: From trade to donation." https://eipr.org/sites/default/files/reports/pdf/Organ_Transplant_Legislation_En.pdf (accessed June 19, 2019).

Ekberg, Gunilla. 2004. "The Swedish law that prohibits the purchase of sexual services." *Violence Against Women* 10(10): 1187–1218.

El-Agroudy, Amgad E., Alaa A. Sabry, Ehab W. Wafa, Ahmed H. Neamatalla, Amani M. Ismail, Tarek Mohsen, Abd Allah Khalil, Ahmed A. Shokeir, and Mohamed A. Ghoneim. 2007. "Long-term follow-up of living kidney donors: A longitudinal study." *BJU International* 100(6): 1351–55.

Ellison, Graham. 2015. "Criminalizing the payment for sex in Northern Ireland: Sketching the contours of a moral panic." *British Journal of Criminology*, doi: 10.1093/bjc/azv107.

Erin, Charles A., and John Harris. 2003. "An ethical market in human organs." *Journal of Medical Ethics* 29(3): 137–38.

European Commission. 2015. "EU Emergency Trust Fund for Africa (EUTF)." https://ec.europa.eu/europeaid/sites/devco/files/eu-emergency-trust-fund-africa-20171218_en.pdf (accessed September 17, 2019).

———. 2017. "Enhancing the response to migration challenges in Egypt." https://ec.europa.eu/trustfundforafrica/sites/euetfa/files/action_document_egypt_action_fiche_20170523_en.pdf (accessed November 21, 2019).

———. 2018a. "EU-Turkey statement, two years on." April. https://ec.europa.eu/home-affairs/sites/homeaffairs/files/what-we-do/policies/european-agenda-migration/20180314_eu-turkey-two-years-on_en.pdf (accessed June 28, 2019).

———. 2018b. "Managing Migrations." December 4. https://ec.europa.eu/commission/news/managing-migration-2018-dec-04_en (accessed November 18, 2019)

European Council. 2015a. "Council decision (CFSP) 2015/778 of 18 May 2015 on a European Union military operation in the Southern Central Mediterranean (EUNAVFOR MED operation SOPHIA)." May 18. https://eur-lex.europa.eu/legal-content/EN/TXT/PDF/?uri=CELEX:02015D0778-20151026&from=en (accessed November 25, 2019).

———. 2015b. "Valletta summit: Political declaration." November 11–12. https://www.consilium.europa.eu/media/21841/political_decl_en.pdf (accessed November 22, 2019).

———. 2015c. "Valletta summit on migration: Action plan." November 11–12. https://www.consilium.europa.eu/media/21839/action_plan_en.pdf (accessed July 4, 2019).

———. 2016. "EU-Turkey statement." March 18. http://www.consilium.europa.eu/en/press/press-releases/2016/03/18/eu-turkey-statement/ (accessed November 25, 2019).

Europol. 2018. "Joint investigation teams JITS." European Agency for Law Enforcement Cooperation, European Union. https://www.europol.europa.eu/activities-services/joint-investigation-teams (accessed June 28, 2019).

Farrell, Amy, Colleen Owens, and Jack McDevitt. 2014. "New laws but few cases: Understanding the challenges to the investigation and prosecution of human trafficking cases." *Crime, Law, and Social Change* 61(2): 139–68.

Fassin, Didier. 2010. "Inequality of lives, hierarchies of humanity: Moral commitments and ethical dilemmas in humanitarianism." In *In the name of humanity: The government of threat and care*, ed. Ilana Feldman and Miriam Iris Ticktin, 238–55. Durham, NC: Duke University Press.

FBI (Federal Bureau of Investigation). 2017. "International partnerships among public health, private sector, and law enforcement necessary to mitigate ISIS's organ harvesting for terrorist funding." May 11. https://www.dni.gov/files/NCTC/documents/jcat/firstresponderstoolbox/First-Responders-Toolbox---International-Partnerships-Among-Public-Health-Private-Sector-and-Law.pdf (accessed November 7, 2019).

Fiske, Gavriel. 2013. "Netanyahu: Egypt border fence halted flow of migrants." *Times of Israel*, July 7. https://www.timesofisrael.com/netanyahu-egypt-border-fence-halted-flow-of-migrants/ (accessed March 13, 2019).

Flynn, Michael. 2017. "Kidnapped, trafficked, detained? The implications of non-state actor involvement in immigration detention." *Journal on Migration and Human Security* 5(3): 593–613.

Ford, Richard. 2019. "Priti Patel vows tougher action to stop Channel migrant gangs." *The Times*, August 30. https://www.thetimes.co.uk/article/priti-patel-vows-tougher-action-to-stop-channel-migrant-gangs-v2q8f8hgt (accessed November 16, 2019).

Fox, R. C., and J. P. Swazey. 1992. *Spare parts: Organ replacement in American society.* New York: Oxford University Press.

Freedman, Jane. 2016. "Engendering security at the borders of Europe: Women migrants and the Mediterranean 'crisis.'" *Journal of Refugee Studies* 29(4): 568–82.

Frelick, Bill, Ian M. Kysel, and Jennifer Podkul. 2016. "The impact of externalization of migration controls on the rights of asylum seekers and other migrants." *Journal on Migration and Human Security* 4(4): 190–220.

Frontex. 2015. "Annual risk analysis." https://frontex.europa.eu/assets/Publications/Risk_Analysis/Annual_Risk_Analysis_2015.pdf (accessed November 24, 2019).

Galeotti, Mark. 2014. *Global crime today: The changing face of organized crime.* Oxon, UK: Routledge.

Gambetta, Diego. 1993. *The Sicilian Mafia.* Cambridge, MA: Harvard University Press.

Garland, David. 2001. *Culture of control.* Oxford, UK: Oxford University Press.

Gill, Jagbir, Bhaskara R. Madhira, David Gjertson, Gerald Lipshutz, J. Michael Cecka, Phuong-Thu Pham, Alan Wilkinson, Suphamai Bunnapradist, and Gabriel M. Danovitch. 2008. "Transplant tourism in the United States: A single-center experience." *Clinical Journal of the American Society of Nephrology* 3(6): 1820–28.

GODT (Global Observatory on Donation and Transplantation). 2016. "Organ donation and transplantation activities." http://www.transplant-observatory.org/download/2016-activity-data-report/ (accessed October 19, 2019).

Goldstein, Paul J. 1985. "The drugs/violence nexus: A tripartite conceptual framework." *Journal of Drug Issues* 15(4): 493–506.

Goyal, Madhav, Ravindra L. Mehta, Lawrence J. Schneiderman, and Ashwini R. Sehgal. 2002. "Economic and health consequences of selling a kidney in India." *JAMA* 288(13): 1589–93.

Grabska, Katarzyna. 2006. "Marginalization in urban spaces of the global south: Urban refugees in Cairo." *Journal of Refugee Studies* 19(3): 287–307.

Grey, Stephanie, and Amina Ismali. 2016. "The forgotten shipwreck." Reuters, December 6. https://www.reuters.com/investigates/special-report/migration/#story/60 (accessed May 16, 2019).

Groisman, Maayan. 2016. "Egypt's Islamist Authority blasts ISIS organ harvesting." May 8. https://www.jpost.com/Middle-East/ISIS-Threat/Egypts-Islamist-Authority-blasts-ISIS-organ-harvesting-453421 (accessed June 1, 2019).

Gutmann, Ethan. 2014. *The slaughter: Mass killings, organ harvesting, and China's secret solution to its dissident problem.* New York: Prometheus.

Hamdy, Sherine. 2012. *Our bodies belong to God: Organ transplants, Islam, and the struggle for human dignity in Egypt.* Berkeley: University of California Press.

———. 2013. "Political challenges to biomedical universalism: Kidney failure among Egypt's poor." *Medical Anthropology* 32(4): 374–92.

———. 2016. "All eyes on Egypt: Islam and the medical use of dead bodies amidst Cairo's political unrest." *Medical Anthropology* 35(3): 220–35.

Hamlin, Rebecca. 2014. *Let me be a refugee: Administrative justice and the politics of asylum in the United States, Canada, and Australia.* Oxford, UK: Oxford University Press.

He, Ming, and John Taylor. 2014. "Renal transplantation." *British Medical Journal* 348. doi: https://doi.org/10.1136/bmj.g68.

Hedges, Chris. 1992. "Egyptian doctors limit kidney transplants." *New York Times*, January 23, A5.

Hobbs, Dick. 1998. "Going down the local: The local context of organized crime." *Howard Journal of Criminal Justice* 37(4): 407–22.

Holmes, Simon. 2016. "Isis harvesting organs from dead." *Daily Mail*, September 19. http://www.dailymail.co.uk/news/article-3796719/Cash-strapped-ISIS-trades-23-stolen-human-organs-northern-Iraq-oil-reserves-dry-up.html (accessed June 19, 2019).

Home Affairs Committee Inquiry into Drug Policy. 2002. "Home Affairs: Third report." https://publications.parliament.uk/pa/cm200102/cmselect/cmhaff/318/31802.htm (accessed November 11, 2019).

Home Office. 2016. "Tackling exploitation in the labour market." https://assets.publishing.service.gov.uk/government/uploads/system/uploads/attachment_data/file/471048/BIS-15–549-tackling-exploitation-in-the-labour-market.pdf (accessed June 6, 2018).

Horowitz, Jason. 2019. "Salvini's Standoff at Sea Highlights Italy's War on Rescue Ships." New York Times, August 16. https://www.nytimes.com/2019/08/16/world/europe/salvini-italy-migrants-open-arms.html (accessed December 4, 2019).

Hughes, Caitlin Elizabeth, and Alex Stevens. 2010. "What can we learn from the Portuguese decriminalization of illicit drugs?" *British Journal of Criminology* 50(6): 999–1022.

———. 2015. "A resounding success or a disastrous failure: Re-examining the interpretation of evidence on the Portuguese decriminalization of illicit drugs." In *New Approaches to Drug Policies*, ed. Marten W. Brienen and Jonathan D. Rosen, 137–62. London: Palgrave Macmillan.

Human Rights Watch. 2016. "Q&A: Why the EU-Turkey migration deal is no blueprint." November 14. https://www.hrw.org/news/2016/11/14/qa-why-eu-turkey-migration-deal-no-blueprint (accessed August 1, 2019).

———. 2017a. "Egypt: New law will crush civil society." Human Rights Watch, Beirut, June 2. https://www.hrw.org/news/2017/06/02/egypt-new-law-will-crush-civil-society (accessed September 10, 2019).

———. 2017b. "Germany/Egypt: Agreement risks complicity in abuses." April 24. https://www.hrw.org/news/2017/04/24/germany/egypt-agreement-risks-complicity-abuses (accessed November 21, 2019).

Hüsken, Thomas. 2017. "The practice and culture of smuggling in the borderland of Egypt and Libya." *International Affairs* 93(4): 897–915.

ILO (International Labor Organization). 2012. "Statistical update on men and women in the informal economy." http://laborsta.ilo.org/applv8/data/INFORMAL_ECONOMY/2012-06-Statistical%20update%20-%20v2.pdf (accessed June 19, 2019).

International Summit on Transplant Tourism and Organ Trafficking. 2008. "The Declaration of Istanbul on Organ Trafficking and Transplant Tourism." *Clinical Journal of the American Society of Nephrology* 3(5): 1227–31. doi: 10.2215/CJN.03320708. https://www.ncbi.nlm.nih.gov/pubmed/18701611 (accessed November 12, 2019).

IOM (International Organization for Migration). 2011. *Glossary on migration*. International Migration Law Series, no. 25. Geneva: IOM. https://publications.iom.int/system/files/pdf/iml25_1.pdf (accessed June 19, 2019).

———. 2017a. *Fatal journeys*, Vol. 3, Pt. 1, *Improving data on missing migrants*. Geneva: International Organisation for Migration. https://publications.iom.int/books/fatal-journeys-volume-3-part-1-improving-data-missing-migrants (accessed June 19, 2019).

———. 2017b. "Key Migration Terms." http://www.iom.int/key-migration-terms (accessed July 16, 2019).

Isin, Engin F., and Greg M. Nielsen, eds. 2008. *Acts of citizenship*. London: Zed Books.

Jacobsen, Karen, Maysa Ayoub, and Alice Johnson. 2014. "Sudanese refugees in Cairo: Remittances and livelihoods." *Journal of Refugee Studies* 27(1): 149–59.

Jefferson, Tony. 2002. "Subordinating hegemonic masculinity." *Theoretical Criminology* 6(1): 63–88.

Jones-Correa, Michael, and Els de Graauw. 2013. "The illegality trap: The politics of immigration and the lens of illegality." *Daedalus* 142(3): 185–98.

Joya, Angela. 2011. "The Egyptian revolution: Crisis of neoliberalism and the potential for democratic politics." *Review of African Political Economy* 38(129): 367–86.

Kagan, Michael. 2011. *"We live in a country of UNHCR": The UN surrogate state and refugee policy in the Middle East*. UNHCR Research Paper 201. https://www.unhcr.org/en-us/research/working/4d5a8cde9/live-country-unhcr-un-surrogate-state-refugee-policy-middle-east-michael.html (accessed December 5, 2019).

Ketchley, Neil. 2017. *Egypt in a time of revolution*. Cambridge, UK: Cambridge University Press.

Kierans, Ciara. 2019. *Chronic failures: Kidneys, regimes of care, and the Mexican state*. New Brunswick, NJ: Rutgers University Press.

Kim, Howard S., and Andrew A. Monte. 2016. "Colorado cannabis legalization and its effect on emergency care." *Annals of Emergency Medicine* 68(1): 71–75.

Kingsley, Patrick. 2016. "Death toll in migrant shipwreck off Egypt rises to 300." *The Guardian*, September 23. https://www.theguardian.com/world/2016/sep/23/death-toll-in-migrant-shipwreck-off-egypt-rises-to-300 (accessed November 11, 2019).

Kirchgaessnerr, Stephanie, Ian Traynor, and Patrick Kingsley. 2015. "Two more migrant boats issue distress calls in Mediterranean." *The Guardian*, April 20. https://www.theguardian.com/world/2015/apr/20/two-more-mediterranean-migrant-boats-issue-distress-calls-as-eu-ministers-meet (accessed June 6, 2019).

Kishore, Raghav. 2004. "Human organs, scarcities, and sale: Morality revisited." *Journal of Medical Ethics* 31(6): 362–65.
Kleemans, Edward R. 2009. "Human smuggling and human trafficking." In *The Oxford handbook of crime and public policy*, ed. Michael Tonry, 409–27. Oxford, UK: Oxford University Press.
Kleemans, Edward R., and Hank G. van de Bunt. 1999. "The social embeddedness of organized crime." *Transnational Organized Crime* 5(1): 19–36.
Klerks, Peter. 2001. "The network paradigm applied to criminal organizations: Theoretical nitpicking or a relevant doctrine for investigators? Recent developments in the Netherlands." *Connections* 24(3): 53–65.
Koenig, Barbara A. 2003. "Dead donors and the 'shortage' of human organs: Are we missing the point?" *American Journal of Bioethics* 3(1): 26–27.
Kohler, Gernot, and Norman Alcock. 1976. "An empirical table of structural violence." *Journal of Peace Research* 13(4): 343–56.
Koser, Khalid. 2010. "Dimensions and dynamics of irregular migration." *Population, Space, and Place* 16(3): 181–93.
Kotiswaran, Prahba. 2008. "Born unto brothels: Toward a legal ethnography of sex work in an Indian red-light area." *Law and Social Inquiry* 33(3): 579–629.
———. 2011. *Dangerous sex, invisible labor: Sex work and the law in India*. Princeton, NJ: Princeton University Press.
Kroet, Cynthia. 2019. "Viktor Orbán: Migrants are a poison." *Politico*, July 27. https://www.politico.eu/article/viktor-orban-migrants-are-a-poison-hungarian-prime-minister-europe-refugee-crisis/ (accessed November 24, 2019).
Kumar, Sanjay. 2003. "Police uncover large-scale organ trafficking in Punjab." *British Medical Journal* 326(7382): 180.
Levy, Jay, and Pye Jakobsson. 2014. "Sweden's abolitionist discourse and law: Effects on the dynamics of Swedish sex work and on the lives of Sweden's sex workers." *Criminology and Criminal Justice* 14(5): 593–607.
Livingston, Melvin D., Tracey E. Barnett, Chris Delcher, and Alexander C. Wagenaar. 2017. "Recreational cannabis legalization and opioid-related deaths in Colorado, 2000–2015." *American Journal of Public Health* 107(11): 1827–29.
Lock, Margaret M. 2002. *Twice dead: Organ transplants and the reinvention of death*, Vol. 1. Berkeley: University of California Press.
López-Navidad, Antonio, and Francisco Caballero. 2003. "Extended criteria for organ acceptance: Strategies for achieving organ safety and for increasing organ pool." *Clinical Transplantation* 17(4): 308–24.
Luyckx, Valerie A., Saraladevi Naicker, and Martin McKee. 2013. "Equity and economics of kidney disease in sub-Saharan Africa." *The Lancet* 382(9887): 103–4.
MacCoun, Robert J., and Peter Reuter. 2001. *Drug war heresies: Learning from other vices, times, and places*. Cambridge, UK: Cambridge University Press.
Macklin, Audrey. 2005. "Disappearing refugees: Reflections on the Canada-U.S. safe third country agreement." *Columbia Human Rights Law Review* 36: 365–426.

———. 2007. "Who is the citizen's other? Considering the heft of citizenship." *Theoretical Inquiries in Law* 8(2): 333–66.

———. 2014. "Citizenship revocation, the privilege to have rights, and the production of the alien." *Queen's Law Journal* 40(1): 1–54.

Mada Masr. 2017. "Health Ministry asserts report on organ trafficking in Egypt harms national security." August 20. https://madamasr.com/en/2017/08/20/news/u/health-ministry-asserts-report-on-organ-trafficking-in-egypt-harms-national-security/ (accessed June 12, 2019).

Mahoney, Julia D. 2000. "The market for human tissue." *Virginia Law Review* 86(2): 163–223.

Mannocchi, Francesca. 2017. "Trapped: Inside Libya's detention centers." UNICEF blog, February 22. https://blogs.unicef.org/blog/libyan-detention-centres/ (accessed June 28, 2019).

Mantouvalou, Virginia. 2018. "Legal construction of structures of exploitation." In *Philosophical Foundations of Labour Law*, ed. Hugh Collins, Gillian Lester, and Virginia Mantouvalou, 188–204. Oxford, UK: Oxford University Press.

Manzano, A., M. Monaghan, B. Potrata, and M. Clayton. 2014. "The invisible issue of organ laundering." *Transplantation* 98(6): 600–603.

Marks, Susan, ed. 2008. *International law on the left: Re-examining Marxist legacies*. Cambridge, UK: Cambridge University Press.

Martin, Philip L. 2017a. "Election of Donald Trump and migration." *Migration Letters* 14(1): 161–71.

Martin, Philip L. 2017b. "Trump and US immigration policy." *California Agriculture* 71(1): 15–17.

Mayntz, Renate. 2017. "Illegal markets." In *The architecture of illegal markets: Towards an economic sociology of illegality in the economy*, ed. Jens Beckert and Matías Dewey, 37–48. Oxford, UK: Oxford University Press.

McGrath, Cam. 2009. "Egypt: Move to end organ trafficking." InterPress Service, May 18. http://www.ipsnews.net/2009/05/egypt-move-to-end-organ-trafficking/ (accessed May 7, 2019).

McKernan, Bethan. 2017. "Turkish soldiers arrested after video shows horrific beatings and abuse of Syrian refugees." *The Independent*, August 4. https://www.independent.co.uk/news/world/middle-east/turkey-soldiers-syria-refugees-video-beatings-abuse-turkish-army-a7876306.html (accessed May 6, 2019).

Meagher, Kate. 2010. *Identity economics: Social networks and the informal economy in Nigeria*. Woodbridge, UK: Boydell & Brewer.

Mendoza, Roger Lee. 2011. "Price deflation and the underground organ economy in the Philippines." *Journal of Public Health* 33(1): 101–7.

Michaelson, Ruth. 2018. "Egypt expels British journalist, raising fears for press ahead of election." *The Guardian*, March 23. https://www.theguardian.com/world/2018/mar/23/bel-trew-egypt-british-journalist-expelled-the-times (accessed April 6, 2019).

Le Monde and AFP. 2016. "Niger: Trente-quatre migrants retrouvés morts dans le désert." *Le Monde*, June 16. https://www.lemonde.fr/afrique/article/2016/06/16/niger-trente-quatre-migrants-retrouves-morts-dans-le-desert_4951479_3212.html (accessed November 18, 2018).

Mostyn, Ben, Helen Gibbon, and Nicholas Cowdery. 2012. "The criminalisation of drugs and the search for alternative approaches." *Current Issues in Criminal Justice* 24(2): 261–72.

Moulin, Carolina, and Peter Nyers. 2007. "'We live in a country of UNHCR': Refugee protests and global political society." *International Political Sociology* 1(4): 356–72.

Mourad, Mahmoud, and Lin Noueihed. 2016. "Egypt busts organ trading racket." Reuters, June 19. https://www.reuters.com/article/us-egypt-crime-organs/egypt-busts-organ-trading-racket-arrests-45-people-idUSKBN13V1IZ (accessed January 16, 2019).

Muller, E. 2016. "Transplantation in Africa: An overview." *Clinical Nephrology* 86(7): 90–95.

Munro, Vanessa E. 2008. "Of rights and rhetoric: Discourses of degradation and exploitation in the context of sex trafficking." *Journal of Law and Society* 35(2): 240–64.

Mussi, Francesca. 2018. "Countering migrant smuggling in the Mediterranean Sea under the mandate of the UN Security Council: What protection for the fundamental rights of migrants?" *International Journal of Human Rights* 22(4): 488–502.

Naylor, R. Thomas. 2009. "Violence and illegal economic activity: A deconstruction." *Crime, Law, and Social Change* 52(3): 231–42.

NBC/Associated Press. 2009. "Black market organ trade still thrives in Egypt." *NBC News*, March 17. http://www.nbcnews.com/id/29740869/ns/health-health_care/t/black-market-organ-trade-still-thrives-egypt/#.VpuTiJOLRE5 (accessed June 19, 2019).

The New Humanitarian (formerly IRIN News). 2011. "New law targets illegal organ transplants." *The New Humanitarian*, July 5. http://www.irinnews.org/news/2011/07/05/new-law-targets-illegal-organ-transplants (accessed June 21, 2019).

NHS (National Health Service). 2019. "Organ donation and transplantation activity report 2018/19." https://nhsbtdbe.blob.core.windows.net/umbraco-assets-corp/16537/organ-donation-and-transplantation-activity-report-2018-2019.pdf (accessed April 7, 2019).

Nicaso, Antonio, and Lee Lamothe. 1995. *Global mafia: The new world order of organized crime*. Toronto: Macmillan Canada.

Nicholson, Michael L., and Andrew Bradley. 1999. "Renal transplantation from living donors should be seriously considered to help overcome the shortfall in organs." *British Medical Journal* 318(7181): 409–10.

Nordstrom, Carolyn. 2000. "Shadows and sovereigns." *Theory, Culture, and Society* 17(4): 35–54.

Office of National Drug Control Policy. 2019. "National Drug Control Strategy." January. https://www.whitehouse.gov/wp-content/uploads/2019/01/NDCS-Final.pdf (accessed December 5, 2019).

OHCHR (Office of the High Commissioner of Human Rights). 2013. "Trafficking in persons, especially women and children." http://www.ohchr.org/Documents/Issues/Trafficking/A-68-256-English.pdf (accessed June 19, 2019).

Oliver Michael, Aimun Ahmed, and Alexander Woywodt. 2012. "Donating in good faith or getting into trouble? Religion and organ donation revisited." *World Journal of Transplantation* 2(5): 69–73.

Oliver, Michael, Alexander Woywodt, Aimun Ahmed, and Imran Saif. 2010. "Organ donation, transplantation, and religion." *Nephrology, Dialysis, Transplantation* 26(2): 437–44.

OSCE (Organization for Security and Cooperation in Europe). 2013. "Trafficking in human beings for the purpose of organ removal in the OSCE region: Analysis and findings." http://www.osce.org/cthb/103393 (accessed June 19, 2019).

Pacula, Rosalie L., Robert MacCoun, Peter Reuter, Jamie Chriqui, Beau Kilmer, Katherine Harris, Letizia Paoli, and Carsten Schäfer. 2005. "What does it mean to decriminalize marijuana? A cross-national empirical examination." In *Substance use: Individual behaviour, social interactions, markets, and politics*, ed. Björn Lindgren and Michael Grossman, 347–69. Bingley, UK: Emerald Publishing.

Palamar, Joseph J., Danielle C. Ompad, and Eva Petkova. 2014. "Correlates of intentions to use cannabis among US high school seniors in the case of cannabis legalization." *International Journal of Drug Policy* 25(3): 424–35.

Paoli, Letizia. 2002. "The paradoxes of organized crime." *Crime, Law, and Social Change* 37(1): 51–97.

Paoli, Letizia, and Peter Reuter. 2008. "Drug trafficking and ethnic minorities in Western Europe." *European Journal of Criminology* 5(1): 13–37.

Paris, Wayne, and Bakr Nour. 2010. "Organ transplantation in Egypt." *Progress in Transplantation* 20(3): 274–78.

Parsons, Talcott, Renee C. Fox, and Victor M. Lidz. 1972. "The 'gift of life' and its reciprocation." *Social Research* 39(3): 367–415.

Pastore, Ferruccio, Paola Monzini, and Giuseppe Sciortino. 2006. "Schengen's soft underbelly? Irregular migration and human smuggling across land and sea borders to Italy." *International Migration* 44(4): 95–119.

Pates, Rebecca. 2012. "Liberal laws juxtaposed with rigid control: An analysis of the logics of governing sex work in Germany." *Sexuality Research and Social Policy* 9(3): 212–22.

Pitel, Laura. 2016. "Refugee crisis: Turkish coast guard 'attacks boat packed with migrants.'" *The Independent*, March 18. https://www.independent.co.uk/news/world/europe/refugee-crisis-turkish-coastguard-attacks-boat-packed-with-migrants-a6939936.html (accessed April 2018).

Pokharel, Sugam. 2015. "Nepal's organ trail: How traffickers steal kidneys." CNN, July 15. http://edition.cnn.com/2014/06/26/world/asia/freedom-project-nepals-organ-trail/ (accessed June 19, 2019).

Prasad, G. V. Ramesh, Ashutosh Shukla, Michael Huang, R. John d'A. Honey, and Jeffrey S. Zaltzman. 2006. "Outcomes of commercial renal transplantation: A Canadian experience." *Transplantation* 82(9): 1130–35.

Pugliese, E. 2007. "Organ trafficking and the TVPA: Why one word makes a difference in international enforcement efforts." *Journal of Contemporary Health Law and Policy* 24(1): 181–208.

Radcliffe-Richards, Janet. 2003. "Commentary: An ethical market in human organs." *Journal of Medical Ethics* 29(3): 139–40.

Raymond, Janice. 2003. "Ten reasons for not legalizing prostitution and a legal response to the demand to prostitution." In *Prostitution, trafficking, and traumatic stress*, ed. Melissa Farley, 326–27. Abington, UK: Routledge.

Reuter, Peter. 1985. *The organization of illegal markets: An economic analysis*. National Institute of Justice Research Report, vol. 84, no. 9. Washington, DC: U.S. Department of Justice.

———. 2009. "Systemic violence in drug markets." *Crime, Law, and Social Change* 52(3): 275–84.

Reuter, Peter, and Mark A. R. Kleiman. 1986. "Risks and prices: An economic analysis of drug enforcement." *Crime and Justice* 7: 289–340.

Reuter, Peter, and Alex Stevens. 2007. *An analysis of UK drug policy: A monograph prepared for the U.K. Drug Policy Commission*. London: U.K. Drug Policy Commission.

Rios, Lorena. 2015. "Egypt's ailing health care system." *Al Monitor*, July 23. http://www.al-monitor.com/pulse/originals/2015/07/egypt-health-care-hospitals-poor-illness-ministry.html# (accessed June 19, 2019).

Roemer, John E. 1989. "What is exploitation? Reply to Jeffrey Reiman." *Philosophy and Public Affairs* 18(1): 90–97.

Rothman, D. J., E. Rose, T. Awaya, B. Cohen, A. Daar, S. L. Dzemeshkevich, C. J. Lee, R. Munro, H. Reyes, S. M. Rothman, K. F. Schoen, N. Scheper-Hughes, Z. Shapira, and H. Smit. 1997. "The Bellagio Task Force report on transplantation, bodily integrity, and the international traffic in organs." *Transplantation Proceedings* 29(6): 2739–45.

Roushdy, Rania, and Irène Selwaness. 2017. *Who is covered and who underreports: An empirical analysis of access to social insurance on the Egyptian labor market*. GLO Discussion Paper, no. 29. Global Labor Organization.

Ruggiero, Vincenzo. 2000. "Transnational crime: Official and alternative fears." *International Journal of the Sociology of Law* 28(3): 187–99.

———. 2001. *Crime and markets: Essays in anti-criminology*. Oxford, UK: Oxford University Press.

Rutherford, Bruce K., and Jeannie Sowers. 2018. *Modern Egypt: What everyone needs to know*. Oxford, UK: Oxford University Press.

Salahudeen, A. K., H. F. Woods, A. Pingle, M. Nur-El-Huda Suleyman, K. Shakuntala, M. Nandakumar, T. M. Yahya, and A. S. Daar. 1990. "High mortality among recipients of bought living-unrelated donor kidneys." *The Lancet* 336(8717): 725–28.

Salt, John. 2000. "Trafficking and human smuggling: A European perspective." *International Migration* 38(3): 31–56.

Sanchez, Gabriella. 2014. *Human smuggling and border crossings*. Abington, UK: Routledge.

Satz, Debra. 2015. *Why some things should not be for sale*. Oxford, UK: Oxford University Press.

Schemm, Paul. 2018. "A widening budget gap is forcing the UN to slash food aid to refugees." *Washington Post*, January 1. https://www.washingtonpost.com/world/africa/a-widening-budget-gap-is-forcing-the-un-to-slash-food-aid-to-refugees/2017/12/27/b34cfd40-e5b1-11e7-927a-e72eac1e73b6_story.html?utm_term=.39ca960a892f (accessed November 17, 2018).

Scheper-Hughes, Nancy. 2000. "The global traffic in human organs." *Current Anthropology* 41(2): 191–224.

———. 2001. "Bodies for sale—whole or in parts." *Body and Society* 7(2–3): 1–8.

Scoular, Jane. 2010. "What's law got to do with it? How and why law matters in the regulation of sex work." *Journal of Law and Society* 37(1): 12–39.

Sea-Watch. 2017. "Turkish coast guards attack refugees." *Sea-Watch*, November 11. https://sea-watch.org/en/breaking-turkish-coast-guards-attack-refugees/ (accessed October 7, 2019).

Shaheen, Faissal A. M. 2017. "End-stage renal disease in the Middle East." In *Chronic kidney disease in disadvantaged populations*, ed. Guillermo Garcia-Garcia, Lawrence Agodoa, and Keith Norris, 107–11. Cambridge, MA: Academic Press.

Shamir, Hila. 2012. "A labor paradigm for human trafficking." *UCLA Law Review* 60(1): 76–135.

Sharif, Adnan. 2012. "Organ donation and Islam: Challenges and opportunities." *Transplantation* 94(5): 442–46.

Sharp, Lesley A. 2006. *Strange harvest: Organ transplants, denatured bodies, and the transformed self*. Berkeley: University of California Press.

Shelley, Louise I. 1995. "Transnational organized crime: An imminent threat to the nation-state?" *Journal of International Affairs* 48(2): 463–89.

Shimazono, Yosuke. 2007. "The state of the international organ trade: A provisional picture based on integration of available information." *Bulletin of the World Health Organization* 85: 955–62.

Shirk, David A. 2010. "Drug violence in Mexico: Data and analysis from 2001–2009." *Trends in Organized Crime* 13(2–3): 167–74.

Skaperdas, Stergios. 2001. "The political economy of organized crime: Providing protection when the state does not." *Economics of Governance* 2(3): 173–202.

Snajdr, Edward. 2013. "Beneath the master narrative: Human trafficking, myths of sexual slavery, and ethnographic realities." *Dialectical Anthropology* 37: 229–56.

Standing, Guy. 2011. *The precariat: The new dangerous class*. London: Bloomsbury Press.

Statewatch. 2019a. "The 'temporary solidarity mechanism' on relocation of people rescued at sea—what does it say?" 27 September. http://www.statewatch.org/news/2019/sep/eu-relocation-deal.htm (accessed December 23, 2019).

Statewatch. 2019b. "EuroMed Rights: EU-Egypt migration cooperation: at the expense of human rights." July. https://statewatch.org/news/2019/jul/Report-on-EU-Egypt-cooperation-on-migration%20.pdf (accessed December 26, 2019).

Steinfatt, Thomas. 2011. "Sex trafficking in Cambodia: Fabricated numbers versus empirical evidence." *Crime, Law, and Social Change* 56(5): 443–62.

Sterling, Claire. 1994. *Thieves' world: The threat of the new global network of organized crime*. New York: Simon & Schuster.

Stevens, Alex. 2010. *Drugs, crime, and public health: The political economy of drug policy*. Abingdon-on-Thames, UK: Routledge-Cavendish.

Stevens, Dallal, and Angeliki Dimitriadi. 2018. "Crossing the Eastern Mediterranean Sea in search of 'protection.'" *Journal of Immigrant and Refugee Studies* 17(3): 261–78.

Stumpf, Juliet. 2006. "The crimmigration crisis: Immigrants, crime, and sovereign power." *American University Law Review* 56(2): 367–419.

Tataryn, Anastasia. 2016. "Reconceptualizing labor law in an era of migration and precarity." *Law, Culture, and the Humanities*. doi: https://doi.org/10.1177/1743872116683381.

Thiruchelvam, Paul, M. Willicombe, N. Hakim, D. Taube, and V. Papalois. 2011. "Renal transplantation." *British Medical Journal* 343. doi: https://doi.org/10.1136/bmj.d7300.

Thomas, Chantal. 2010. "Migrant domestic workers in Egypt: A case study of the economic family in global context." *American Journal of Comparative Law* 58(4): 987–1022.

Titeca, Kristof. 2019. "Illegal ivory trade as transnational organized crime? An empirical study into ivory traders in Uganda." *The British Journal of Criminology* 59(1): 24–44.

Tondo, Lorenzo, and Ruth Michaelson. 2018. "Giulio Regeni: Italy names Egyptian agents as murder suspects." *The Guardian*, November 29. https://www.theguardian.com/world/2018/nov/29/giulio-regeni-murder-italy-names-egyptian-national-security-agents-suspects (accessed March 15, 2019).

Tondo, Lorenzo, and Rosie Scammell. 2016. "Italian police arrest 23 over alleged people-smuggling ring." *The Guardian*, July 4. https://www.theguardian.com/world/2016/jul/04/italian-police-arrest-23-over-alleged-people-smuggling-ring (accessed April 16, 2019).

Traynor, Ian. 2015. "EU to launch military operations against migrant-smugglers in Libya." *The Guardian*, April 20. https://www.theguardian.com/world/2015/apr/20/eu-launch-military-operations-libya-migrant-smugglers-mediterranean (accessed March 23, 2019).

Trilling, Daniel. 2018. *Lights in the distance: Exile and refuge at the borders of Europe*. London: Picador.

Turner, C. 1995. "Egypt's leader survives assassination attempt." *Los Angeles Times*, June 27. http://articles.latimes.com/1995-06-27/news/mn-17703_1_president-mu barak (accessed September 2, 2018).

UN (United Nations). 1951. *Convention Relating to the Status of Refugees*. United Nations General Assembly resolution 429(V), December 14, 1950. http://www.unhcr .org/refworld/docid/3b00f08a27.html (accessed October 19, 2018).

UNHCR (United Nations High Commissioner for Refugees). 2016. "Egypt factsheet." February. http://www.unhcr.org/uk/protection/operations/53cd1f429/egypt-fact -sheet.html (accessed October 4, 2019).

———. 2018. "Match resettlement commitments with action: UN refugee chief." http://www.unhcr.org/afr/news/press/2017/6/593e5c364/match-resettlement-com mitments-action-un-refugee-chief.html (accessed June 19, 2019).

———. 2019. *Projected resettlement needs 2019*. June 26, 2018. https://reliefweb.int /sites/reliefweb.int/files/resources/5b28a7df4.pdf (accessed November 7, 2019).

United Nations Security Council. 2012. "Statement by the president of the Security Council." S/PRST/2012/16, April 25.

———. 2015. Resolution 2240 (2015), adopted by the Security Council at its 7531st meeting, on October 9, 2015. https://digitallibrary.un.org/record/806095/files/S _RES_2240%282015%29-EN.pdf (accessed November 7, 2019).

UNODC (United Nations Office of Drugs and Crime). 2000a. *Protocol Against the Smuggling of Migrants by Land, Sea and Air, Supplementing the United Nations Convention Against Transnational Organized Crime*. https://www.unodc.org/doc uments/middleeastandnorthafrica/smuggling-migrants/SoM_Protocol_English .pdf (accessed June 19, 2009).

———. 2000b. *Protocol to Prevent, Suppress, and Punish Trafficking in Persons, Especially Women and Children, Supplementing the United Nations Convention Against Transnational Organized Crime*. http://www.uncjin.org/Documents/Conventions /dcatoc/final_documents_2/convention_%20traff_eng.pdf (accessed June 19, 2019).

———. 2000c. *United Nations Convention Against Transnational Organised Crime*. General Assembly Resolution 55/25, November 15.

———. 2015a. *Assessment toolkit: Trafficking in persons for the purpose of organ removal*. https://www.unodc.org/documents/human-trafficking/2015/UNODC_As sessment_Toolkit_TIP_for_the_Purpose_of_Organ_Removal.pdf (accessed November 1, 2018).

———. 2015b. "Transnational organised crime: The globalised illegal economy." http://www.unodc.org/toc/en/crimes/organized-crime.html (accessed June 19, 2019).

———. 2018. *Global report on trafficking in persons*. https://www.unodc.org/docu ments/data-and analysis/glotip/2018/GLOTiP_2018_BOOK_web_small.pdf (accessed June 19, 2019).

UNOS (United Network for Organ Sharing). 2007. "UNOS board further addresses transplant tourism." June 26. https://optn.transplant.hrsa.gov/news/board-op poses-transplant-tourism/ (accessed May 24, 2019).

———. 2019. "Organ transplantation in United States set sixth consecutive record in 2018." https://unos.org/news/organ-transplants-in-united-states-set-sixth-consecutive-record-in-2018/ (accessed November 2, 2019).

U. S. Department of State. 2016. "Trafficking in persons report." https://2009-2017.state.gov/documents/organization/258876.pdf (accessed October 28, 2019).

Van Balen, L. J., Frederike Ambagtsheer, Ninoslav Ivanovski, and Willem Weimar. 2016. "Interviews with patients who traveled from Macedonia/Kosovo, The Netherlands, and Sweden for paid kidney transplantations." *Progress in Transplantation* 26(4): 328–34.

Van Reisen, Mirjam, and Munyaradzi Mawere. 2017. *Human trafficking and trauma in the digital era*. Bamenda, Cameroon: Langaa RPCIG.

Varese, Federico, ed. 2010. *Organized crime*. London: Routledge.

———. 2011. *Mafias on the move: How organized crime conquers new territories*. Princeton, NJ: Princeton University Press.

Walker, Peter. 2014. "Migrant boat was 'deliberately sunk' in the Mediterranean sea, killing 500." *The Guardian*, September 15. https://www.theguardian.com/world/2014/sep/15/migrant-boat-capsizes-egypt-malta-traffickers (accessed December 8, 2018).

Walker, Shaun. 2018. "Hungarian leader says Europe in now 'under invasion' by migrants." *The Guardian*, March 15. https://www.theguardian.com/world/2018/mar/15/hungarian-leader-says-europe-is-now-under-invasion-by-migrants (accessed November 17, 2019).

Wang, Peng. 2017. *The Chinese mafia: Organized crime, corruption, and extra-legal protection*. Oxford, UK: Oxford University Press.

Weitzer, Ronald. 2011. "Sex trafficking and the sex industry: The need for evidence-based theory and legislation." *Journal of Criminal Law and Criminology* 101(4): 1337–69.

Werb, Dan, Greg Rowell, Gordon Guyatt, Thomas Kerr, Julio Montaner, and Evan Wood. 2011. "Effect of drug law enforcement on drug market violence: A systematic review." *International Journal of Drug Policy* 22(2): 87–94.

WHA (World Health Assembly). 2004. World Health Assembly Resolution 57.18. http://apps.who.int/gb/ebwha/pdf_files/WHA57/A57_R18-en.pdf (accessed April 1, 2018).

The White House. 2019. "President Donald Trump's border security victory." White House Press Briefings, February 15. https://www.whitehouse.gov/briefings-statements/president-donald-j-trumps-border-security-victory/ (accessed June 16, 2019).

WHO (World Health Organization). 2004. *Organ trafficking and transplantation pose new challenges*. http://www.who.int/bulletin/volumes/82/9/feature0904/en/index.html (accessed June 19, 2019).

———. 2010. *World Health Organisation (WHO) guiding principles on human cell, tissue, and organ transplantation*. http://www.who.int/transplantation/Guiding_PrinciplesTransplantation_WHA63.22en.pdf (accessed June 19, 2019).

———. 2016. "Egypt: Health profile." http://applications.emro.who.int/dsaf/EMRO PUB_2016_EN_19264.pdf?ua=1 (accessed October 2, 2019).

Wilkinson, Stephen. 2004. *Bodies for sale: Ethics and exploitation in the human body trade*. Abington, UK: Routledge.

Williams, Phil. 2002. "Cooperation among criminal organizations." In *Transnational organized crime and international security: Business as usual*, ed. Mats R. Berdal and Monica Serrano, 67–80. Boulder, CO: Lynne Rienner.

Winickoff, David E. 2003. "Governing population genomics: Law, bioethics, and biopolitics in three case studies." *Jurimetrics* 43(2): 187–228.

Witsman, Katherine (U.S. Department of Homeland Security). 2019. "Immigration Enforcement Actions: 2017, Annual Report, U.S. Department of Homeland Security." https://www.dhs.gov/sites/default/files/publications/enforcement_actions _2017.pdf (accessed December 19, 2019).

Working Group on Incentives for Living Donation (A. J. Matas et al.). 2012. "Incentives for organ donation: Proposed standards for an internationally acceptable system." *American Journal of Transplantation* 12(2): 306–12.

World Bank. 2018. "Transforming Egypt's healthcare system project." June 6. http://documents.worldbank.org/curated/en/796381530329773770/pdf/Egypt-PAD-0608 2018.pdf (accessed January 2, 2019).

World Food Program. 2013. *The status of poverty and food security in Egypt: Analysis and recommendations*. https://documents.wfp.org/stellent/groups/public/documents/ena/wfp257467.pdf (accessed April 27, 2019).

Wright, L., J. S. Zaltzman, J. Gill, and G. V. R. Prasad. 2013. "Kidney transplant tourism: Cases from Canada." *Medicine, Health Care, and Philosophy* 16(4): 921–24.

Yea, Sallie. 2010. "Trafficking in part(s): The commercial kidney market in a Manila slum, Philippines." *Global Social Policy* 10(3): 358–76.

———. 2015. "Masculinity under the knife: Filipino men, trafficking, and the black organ market in Manila, the Philippines." *Gender, Place, and Culture* 22(1): 123–42.

Zaitch, Damián. 2002. *Trafficking cocaine: Colombian drug entrepreneurs in the Netherlands*, vol. 1. New York: Springer Science & Business Media.

Zargooshi, Javaad. 2001. "Quality of life of Iranian kidney 'donors.'" *Journal of Urology* 166(5): 1790–99.

INDEX

Page numbers in italic indicate figures.

Abaza, Hamid, 29
Abdal (organ seller), 75
Abido (migrant), 67, 70, 72
action element of trafficking, 41
age minimum for organ donation, 102
agency of organ sellers, 12, 34, 72
Ahmed (Cairo transplant clinic physician), 26–27, 51
Al-Ahram story on police raids, 151
al-Bashir, Omar, 98, 114–15
Alexandria: Asha in, 123–25, *125*, 144, 149; as center of organ trade, 118, 135; Hana in, 121–22, 135; Malik in, 75, 121; Omar in, 121; as smuggling hub, xv, *90*, 99, 103, 130
Ali (organ broker), 14, 56, 103–4
"alien conspiracy" mentality, 40
altruistic organ donation: DICG insisting on, 134; failure to regulate, 131; Islamic religious concerns over, 18; and medical tourism, 22–23; need to increase, 3, 5, 21–22, 31–32; sale of kidney as, 137; as unethical, 35
Amir (broker), 20
Amirah (organ seller), 79
Amnesty International, 95–96
analytic labs, 14, 48; as nodal points, 14, 60, 116; tissue typing in, 20, 22, 48–50, 52, 54–58, 159n4; use of physical violence, 112–13
animal parts trade, 131
Anisha (organ seller), 105–7

Anita (organ seller), 73
"approval of kinship" forms, 102
Arab Development Index (2016), 34
Arab League, 103
Arab Spring effect on budget, 32, 88
Ard El-Lewa neighborhood, 12, 14, 47, 66, 109
Article 3. *See* Trafficking Protocol
Article 16 (Law 5/2010) definition of victim, 30
Articles 77, 88 (of law on NGOs), 150
Asha (organ seller), 123–25, *125*, 135, 144, 149
Ash-Sha'arâwî (Shaykh), 25
asylum seekers in Egypt, 11; denials of, 153–54; falling into poverty, 66; fearing deportation, 72, 93; ignorant of organ value, 52; in informal economy, 70; versus labor migrants, 68; little protection for, 76, 83; number of, 65; status of, 68; Sudanese, 50, 68–69, 74; treated as illegals, 35, 83–84; Turkish denials of, 92. *See also* Fatimah
Atta, Nuredin Wehabrebi, 93–95
Azim (organ seller), 45, *46*, 108–9, 117

Bashir, Omar al-, 98, 114–15
Bedouin tribes threatening organ removal, 115–16
"bio-availability" of people, 145
bioethics, 43, 154–55
black migrant donors, 8
blue card (refugee status), 69, 71–72

186   INDEX

body belonging to God, 25
Boltanski, Luc, 108
Bombay, India, 21
border security: Australian, 89; civil war and border conflicts, 15; Egyptian, 130, 135; European Union, 88, 91, 147; Libyan, 95–96, 130; migration crisis and, 15, 88–90, 90; organ trade as issue for, 2, 38–39; smuggling networks evading, 99; United States, 89
brain death issues, 24–25
brokers. *See* organ brokers
brothel-based sex work, 141
Burma, 130–31
Butler, Judith, 89, 142

cadaveric donations, 24, 29
Cairo, Egypt: anti-UN protests in, 160n7; author in, 9, 114; Criminal Court, 110; housing shortage, 74; involuntary organ removals in, 16; lack of employment in, 107; as organ market, 28, 113–14; refugees, asylum seekers in, 65–72; Yusef's experience in, 20–21; Zamalek neighborhood, xv, 126, 128. *See also* Egypt; Sudanese in Egypt
Cameron, J. Stewart, 136
capitalism, 27, 47, 73
captive labor, 74–75
Caritas, xv, 62, 78, 106
Castells, Manuel, 47, 74
Central Mediterranean Route: migrants selling kidneys to pay for passage, 151; militarizing of borders along, 91, 135, 153, 161n6; sea crossings, migrant deaths along, 15, 87–88; smuggling monopoly along, 95
Chad, 65
Chiapello, Eve, 108
children: as leverage over parents, 149; parents selling organ to support, 51, 62–64, 79–81, 83–84, 115; reports of organ trafficking, 41, 111, 114–15, 124, 134; sexual exploitation of, 159n3 (ch3)
China, 4
Chinese Triads, 42, 126
chronic kidney disease, 22

circumstantial criminality, 79
"citizen" status in Egypt, 68
clinics. *See* transplant centers, clinics
coca production in Latin America, 130
Cohen, Glenn, 137
Cohen, Stanley, 18
collaboration needed to prevent organ trade, 133
"commuting" between illegality and legality, 47
"compassion fatigue," 149
competition among urban poor, 66
complete decriminalization versus legalization, 139–40
conflict organs, 65–67
consent for kidney removal: assumed by government, 1; and "bio-availability," 145; coerced, 134, 137, 139; compelled by circumstance, 84, 148; crackdown after general's death, 118; criminal liability for, 145; in Egypt, 29–30, 32, 59; by illiterate donors, 20, 120; lack of, xvii, 144; leading to prosecution, 4–5; and meaning of "informed," 145; not reversible, 55; and organ laundering, 57–59; under Trafficking Protocol, 157n3
consequentialism, 43
construction of deviance, 17
Convention Against Trafficking in Human Organs (Council of Europe), 4, 64, 145
Convention Against Transnational Crime (UN), 43
Convention Relating to the Status of Refugees (UN), 71, 97, 132
corporeal sanctity violated, 33, 142
Cosa Nostra (Italian), 42
cost of kidney transplant surgery, 23, 26
Council of Europe Convention Against Trafficking in Organs, 4, 64, 145
criminalizing of migrants and mobility: Egypt, 15, 95, 97–98, 108, 132; results of, 15, 60, 89–90; United States, 7
criminalizing of organ market: advocacy for, 134; Articles 4(a), (b), 145; Cairo organ extortion ring, 9, 122–23; in Egypt, 1, 5, 15, 111, 142, 152–53; failure to shut down market, 111; increasing violence,

coercion, 132, 135; network in Egypt, Sudan, 125–26; pushing trade underground, 84; and sellers, 4, 64, 84, 134
criminalizing of sex work, 141
crony capitalism, 27
"cross-border" rhetoric, 40–41, 90–91, 98–99, 161n10
cyclosporine, 22

Darfur, 49, 98, 106
Dawitt, ix–xvii, 101–4 (102f), 117, 135–36, 144
DCIM (Department for Combating Illegal Migration), Libya, 96
death, legal definition of, 24
death penalty for organ trafficking, 131
debt bondage, 130
deceased organ donation, 4, 21, 24–25, 29, 131, 134
Declaration of Istanbul: Custodian Group, 133–34; International Summit on Transplant Tourism and Organ Trafficking, 18
decriminalization models, 139–44, 146, 154–55, 162n1
Delmonico, Francis L., 145
demand for organs: altruistic donation answer to, 3, 21; by foreign patients, 24, 146; increase in, 4, 22, 24; leading to targeting of migrants, 100–101; market solution to, 19, 31, 44–46, 60, 131, 143, 147; not affected by criminalization, 2; outweighing legal supply, 19, 21–22, 28, 44, 46, 154; political climate affecting, 8, 15; survival needs driving, 5; "transplant tourism" driving, 20
depenalization, 162n1
deportation: of asylum seekers, 72, 93; of journalists, 150; of kidney sellers, 144–45; of refugees, 70, 147, 149; of victims, 104, 114, 152
deregulation trend, 73
detention centers, 91–92, 96, 100
diagnostic testing of organ sellers, 54, 56
dialysis, 20, 26–28
DICG. See Declaration of Istanbul
Djibouti, xvii

doctors, xvii, 112; arrests of, 151; DICG on profiteering, 134; in "high quality" lab, 20–21; part of organized crime group, xvii, 31, 56–58, 110, 120, 144; prison terms for, 29; and privilege of non-disclosure, 59; removing kidneys, 63, 82–83, 135
Doctors Without Borders, 128
donors. See organ sellers
drugs use and trafficking, 42, 113, 131, 140
Dworkin, Gerald, 137

EACA (Egyptian Administrative Control Authority), 110
Eastern Promises (film), 42
economic marginalization and exploitation, 15, 64. See also informal economy
education for refugees, 66, 69–71, 73, 81, 83, 147
Egypt, 4; Article 60, 2014 constitution, 111; cost of kidney transplant surgery, 23, 26; cost of law enforcement, 2; criminalizing organ sales, 1, 5, 15, 110–13; deceased donor program, 29; domestic poor, 76; downplaying organ trade, 150–51; early intervention model, 146; economic decline in, 15; family dynamics in donations, 26–27; foreign national transplants illegal, 76; foreign purchase of organs a scandal, 28–29; increased penalties for trafficking, 108, 111; "irregular" travel to/from, 98; lack of altruistic organ donation, 27; Law 64/2010 Trafficking in Persons, 8, 44, 147; Law 82/2016 Combating Illegal Migration and Smuggling of Migrants, 15, 87, 97, 161n9; lax law enforcement in, 8–9; legal organ transplantation in, 24–26; as main refugee destination, 65–66; media reports on black market, 28; media reports on prosecutions, 151–52; Memorandum of Understanding with UNHCR, 66; National Health Ministry, 154; outcome of prohibition, 35; people smuggling by boats, 66, 86–87; Petros' experience in, x–xvii; poor diet leading to poor health, 26; public health budget in, 32, 146; pub-

Egypt (*continued*)
   lic opinion on organ trade, 28–29, 31; revolution and aftermath, 8, 45, 47; significance of mummification, 25; smuggling routes in, 90; Society of Nephrology, 25, 28–29; statistics on kidney transplants, 25, 150; temporary transplant ban, 28; Transplantation of Human Organs and Tissues Act (2010), 8, 28–30, 102, 142; treatment of refugees, 67–72; urban poor considered expendable, 27; Wadi El Nil Treaty, 67–68, 159n3 (ch4); Yusef receiving organ in, 20–21. *See also* Cairo, Egypt; Eritrean refugees in Egypt; Ethiopian refugees in Egypt; Somali refugees in Egypt; Sudanese in Egypt
Egyptian Initiative for Personal Rights (EIPR), 26, 44, 75
Egyptian Medical Syndicate, 28, 48, 58–59
EIPR (Egyptian Initiative for Personal Rights), 26
Ellison, Graham, 41
El Sawra [displaced persons camp], x
Emergency Trust Fund for Africa (EU), 90–93
end-stage renal failure, 23
enforcement. *See* law enforcement
"enforcers" for brokers, 114, 126, 129
"Enhancing the Response to Migration Challenges in Egypt," 92
Erin, Charles A., 138
Eritrean refugees in Egypt, 65, 115–16, 160n6; arrests of smugglers, 94; blackmailed by Bedouins, 115–16; Dawitt, ix–xvii, 101–4 (102f), 117, 135–36, 144; intercepted by border patrols, 91; kidnapped for organs, 127–28; lost at sea, 86–87; murdered for organs, 115; Petros, ix–xvii, 1, 104, 135, 144; smuggling routes, 90, 101; and UNHCR, 68; Yasmin, 37–38, 51
"essential skills" workshops (UNHCR), 69
Ethiopian refugees in Egypt: arrests of smugglers, 94; fleeing conflict, 65, 87–88, 101; kidnapped for organs, 96, 124, 127–28; as organ traffickers, 94; threatened by Bedouins, 115–16; and UNHCR, 68
EU (European Union), 91; agreements with Egypt, 15, 85, 87; Emergency Trust Fund for Africa, 90–93; EUNAVFOR (Operation Sophia), 161n6; EUROSUR system, 91; EUTF for Africa, 91–92, 95; "externalizing" borders, 160n2; Joint Action Plan with Turkey, 92; migration partnership framework, 108; unintentional for-profit detention, 88, 91, 93, 100. *See also* NCCPIM
European Commission, 86–87, 91–92
exploitation, 6–7, 9; as action, means, purpose, 41; economic marginalization and, 15, 64; hierarchy of, 33; of "illegal" population, 74, 108, 132; Marxism on, 7; of mobility, 108; remedies for, 153–54; sexual, 6, 159n3 (ch3); social exclusion enabling, 15, 64, 108; by states, 153–54; structural, 65
extralegal service industry, 126, 129–32

Faisal neighborhood, 12, 47, 49, 66, 119, 126
family dynamics in organ sales/trade, 26–27, 80–81, 84, 102, 121–22
Fatimah (organ seller), 62–63, 84, 159n1 (ch4)
fatwa overruling *Shari'a* law, 25
FBI (Federal Bureau of Investigation, US), 133
female migrants: forced into marriage, 73; girls used as sex servants, x; lack of good work for, 107; lack of safety for, 76–77; single mothers as donors, 62, 79; vulnerable to organ trafficking, 105–7, 134
forced migration versus labor migration, 68
forced organ removal, 33, 118–29
Four Freedoms Agreement, 68–69, 83, 159–60n4 (ch4)
Frontex, 92

Gaddafi, Muammar al-, 66, 95
"gateway" drugs, 140
Germany, 92, 141

Gezairy, Hussein A., 29
gift exchange, organ donation as, 18
"gift of life" rhetoric, 22, 27, 137
global competition for jobs, 73
Global Financial Integrity, 3
global inequality, 138–39
global mafia, 40
Global Observatory on Donation and Transplantation, 22
Grace (organ seller), 82–83
Greece, 86, 92
Guiding Principles on Human Cell, Tissue, and Organ Transplantation (WHO), 4

hairstylist work, 76
Hakim (doctor at tissue-typing lab), 56
Hakim (market vendor), 115
harâm practice: donation ban overruled by *fatwa*, 25; selling a kidney as, 12, 122
Harris, John, 138
Hana (organ seller), 121–22, 125, 135
Hasim (broker), xii
Hassam, Dr., 30–32
heroin production in Burma, 130–31
Hiba (organ seller), 51, 56–57, 60, 79
hierarchy of exploitation, 33
Hippocratic Oath and confidentiality, 59
HIV infection, 21, 159n4 (ch3)
Hoffenberg, Raymond, 136
homeless migrants, 2, 63, 77–78
housekeepers, 75, 160nn9–10; Anisha, 105–7; Fatimah, 62–63, 84; Hiba, 51, 56–57, 60, 79; insufficient wages for, 76, 79; Joyce, 75, 79; Nasrin, 72–73
human trafficking. *See* trafficking/traffickers
human value dividend, 33

Ibrahim *(samsar)*, 98–100, 105–7, 130
idealized victims, 41
"illegal" migrants, 1, 72–74; "commuting" between illegality and legality, 47; criminocentric response to, 88; determined by skin color, ethnicity, 83, 159n1 (ch4); as expendable, exploitable, 74, 76, 108, 132, 148; in informal economy, 154–55; unable to report victimization, 1, 76–78; as UNHCR interpreters, 70; versus "vulnerable" people, 132, 133. *See also* informal economy
India, 4, 21, 146
infants, claims of organs sold, 111
informal economy, 2, 16; capitalism in, 47; in Egypt, 27, 39, 73–75, 109; and extralegal service industry, 126, 129–32; "illegal" migrants in, 154; informalization of labor, 72–74, 147; no legal access to transplants, 23; and organized crime, 48, 60, 117–18, 152–53; organ trade as part of, 5, 9, 27, 39, 61; vulnerability of workers in, 34, 74
informed consent: affidavit of, 57–58; Articles 4(a) and 4(b), 4, 145
informed decision-making, need for, 143, 145
insurance companies, 19, 23, 158n4
internally displaced people, 65–66
international criminal order narration, 40
internationally recognized guidelines, 3–5, 58, 83
International Organization for Migration (IOM), 15, 86, 88, 97, 126, 128
international organ trafficking ring, 110
international peace, trafficking a threat to, 90–91
international response to human trafficking, 43
International Society of Nephrology, 4, 19
International Summit on Transplant Tourism and Organ Trafficking, 4, 18–19, 90–91
interviews: author affective bias issue, 14; follow-up visits, 15–16; subjects, methods, 10–13
intra-familial donations, 26–27
IOM (International Organization for Migration), 15, 86, 88, 97, 126, 128
Iran, 1, 41, 143
Iraqi refugees, 65
"irregular" status, 11, 89, 98, 149
Isaac (people smuggler), 103–4
Islam: and bodily sanctity of dead, 18, 24–25; Egyptian insurgency, 8; and organ

Islam (*continued*)
  donations, sales, 12, 18, 25; and "organ mafia" stories, 115
Israel, 38, 91
Italy: Atta's testimony on smuggling networks, 93–95; capsizing of boats headed to, 86–87; decriminalizing cannabis, 140; Ibrahim on smuggling networks, 99; murder of Giulio Regeni, 159n2; paying Egypt to take back nationals, 92; as promised destination, 96, 123–24, 130; Salvini's anti-immigrant policies, 88; "voluntary" return of Libyan migrants, 95

job security, lack of, 75
journalism, suppression of, x, 37, 150
Joyce (organ seller), 75, 79

Kalib (organ seller), 50, 54, 79
Kamal (organ seller), 56–57, 80–81, 137
Kariem (organ broker), 13, 53–54
Khartoum, Sudan, 16, 90, 144; Anita in, 73; Dawitt in, 101; Fatimah in, 62–63; Khartoum/Cairo organ network, 118–29, 132, 144, 149; Petros in, x–xi; recruitment of organ donors in, 117–18; street demonstrations in, 98
kidneys for sale: ethics of, 9, 31, 34, 136–37, 146; initial approach regarding, xi–xii; monetary value of, 52; as most valuable resource, 79; to pay for better life, 100–102; price of, xii, 138, 143; shame, embarrassment over, xvii; as survival strategy, 75. *See also* organ brokers
kidney transplant surgery: development of, 22; harm to donors, 136; performed in homes, apartments, 113, 126

labor migration versus forced migration, 68
"Lakha" documentary character, 17
Lancet medical study, 21
Latin America, 130
laundering of donation process, 57–60
law enforcement, 9–10; driving operations underground, 144, 152, 154; driving violence and cost, 112–13; increasingly violent, 112–13, 140–41; judging illegality by skin color, 83; lack of, 2, 131; lack of public documents regarding, 151–52; Law 82 (Combating Illegal Migration and Smuggling of Migrants), 15, 87, 97, 161n9; Law of Trafficking in Persons (Egypt), 8, 44, 159n3 (ch3); Law on Non-Governmental Organizations (Egypt), 149–50; and mob boss model, 42–43; need for training, 133; no effect on drug use, 140; not providing safety to victims, 149; organ trade and human trafficking, 60, 76, 84, 135; over morality, 6; participating in organ trade, 77; and people smuggling, 151; of religious views on organ donation, 18; "Swedish model," 141, 143; trafficking versus smuggling, 89; as transnational, 40. *See also* criminalizing of migrants and mobility; United Nations
law reform, 135, 139, 141–43, 153–54
legal donation, case for, 136–38
legalization versus decriminalization, 139–40
legal marginalization, 9, 34, 83, 108, 129, 143–44
legitimate businesses involved in organ trade, 60
Libya: EU sanctions against irregular migration, 100; migrants detained for profit, 93; migrants paying for passage with kidneys, 94; people smuggling and debt bondage, 130; post-Gaddafi, 66, 95, 97; as refugee destination, xv; smuggling routes in, 90; Tariq detained in, 96–97; traffic into, out of Egypt, 98–99; "voluntary" return of migrants from Italy, 95
live donations: Muslim preference for, 25, 44; versus organ donation systems, 24; relative safety of, 26, 136
local integration, 69–70
local knowledge economy, 53

Mahmoud (Sudanese community leader), 57, 84

INDEX

Mahoney, Julia D., 158n5
Malik (broker), 119–21
Malta, capsized migrant boats near, 86
Mandela, Nelson, 103
market-related violence, 112–13
market solution to organ demand, 19, 31–32, 44–47, 131, 137–39
Marks, Susan, 108
Martha (involuntary worker for organ dealers), 126–29, 144
Marxism on labor exploitation, 7
Masr, Mada, 111
May, Theresa, 6
means element of trafficking, 41
media portrayal of traffickers, 17, 42
medical tourism, 23–24, 111
Medicare, Medicaid (US), 23
Mediterranean Sea crossings, 15–16, 84–88
Mexico, 112–13, 141
migrants: abandoned, traded for ransom, 100; apprehension and return of, 91–92; asylum seekers, 68–69, 83–85; and closure of Egypt sea border, 66; from conflict zones, 15, 65, 132; considered expendable, 76; crackdown increasing danger, 100; cultural detachment from, 76; defined, 11; definition of smuggling of, 160–61n5 (ch5); EU deterrence measures against, 91–93, 100; framed as national security crisis, 85, 88–89, 107; as illegal regardless of status, 159n1; job insecurity of, 75–76; labeling of, 149; labor protections needed for, 153–54; lost at sea, 15, 86–88; as organ brokers, 116–17; as organ sellers, 34–35, 48, 94; racism regarding donors, 8; resourcefulness of, 72; smuggling routes, 90, 97; turned down for asylum, 85, 159n1 (ch4); UNHCR figures on, 130; violence against, 92. *See also* criminalizing of migrants and mobility; Libya; Mediterranean Sea crossings; *samsara* (people smugglers); Sudanese in Egypt
Ministry of Foreign Affairs, Egyptian, 72, 151
Ministry of Health, Egyptian, 26, 32, 58, 110, 113, 151

mob boss model, 42
mobility: exploitation of, 108; obstruction, criminalization of, 15, 40, 87, 89, 91–93, 97; privilege of, 108; social, 66, 76, 84
modern slavery, organ trafficking as, 5, 34, 152
Mogamma administrative complex, 71–72, 71, 98, 104
Mohamed (organ seller), 52, 77–78, 117, 145, 147, 160n11
money lenders, 45, 107
morality and organ trade, 136; decriminalization model, 139–44, 146, 154–55, 162n1; as gray zone, 19; moral outrage, 31–33, 40, 104; moral panic and paralysis, 18, 107, 145; practical solutions, 31, 33–35, 136–37
Morsi, Mohamed, 8, 29–30
Mubarak, Hosni, 8, 29–30, 68
Mukhabarat (secret police), 114
mummification, 25
Musa (organ seller), 80
Muslim Brotherhood, 8, 25, 29–30

Nadeem Center for Rehabilitation of Victims of Violence, 150
Najla (organ seller), 81–82, 117
narcotics trade, 19, 38, 112–13
narration of organized crime, 40–42
Nasrin (Sudanese migrant), 72–73
National Authority for the Regulation of Non-Governmental Foreign Organizations (Egypt), 150
National Drug Control Strategy (U.S.), 140
National Geographic documentary, 17
NCCPIM (National Coordination Committee for Combating and Preventing Illegal Migration), 15, 93, 97, 126, 152
negotiating fees for organs, 20, 38 (38), 48, 52–54, 57, 107–9, 111
neoliberalism, 138, 143
Netanyahu, Binyamin, 91
New Zealand, 141–42, 146
NGOs: in Egypt, 10, 37, 53, 122–24; Egyptian law hindering, 149–51, 157n6
nondisclosure privilege, 59
nonrefoulment principle, 92, 97

Obama administration, 130
occupational safety and health standards, 153
Office of National Drug Control Policy (US), 140
Oman, 21
Omar (organ seller), 118–21, 123, 135
Operation Sophia, 92, 161n6
operations to receive kidneys, 20–21
operations to remove kidneys, xvii; in apartments, xiii–xiv, 127–29; complications from, xv, 121; deaths and complications from, 110, 118, 121; in detention centers, 96–97; in hospitals, transplant centers, 22, 45, 56–57, 82–83, 103; without consent, 82–83, 127–29
opioid-related deaths (U.S.), 140
Orbán, Victor, 88
organ brokers: aided by Sudanese scouts, officials, 51, 102–3; breakdown of social controls over, 116; bribing government officials, 113; commissions for, 54; dealing with medical personnel, 63; deducting money from payments, 104; financing travel of donors, 16; functions performed by, 48; increasing violence by, 109, 111–13, 116–17, 120–29; interview subjects, 11, 13; intimidation, extortion by, 50–51, 55–57, 76, 120–23; lack of enforcement against, 144–45; Law 82 regarding, 87; migrants as, 116–17; and Ministry of Health, 58, 113; moving donors to private dwellings, 104, 144; networks of, 49–50; not honoring promised payments, 64, 117; not organized trafficking rings, 79; and police, 124; price negotiations with, 48, 52–54, 57, 109, 118; public turning against, 116–17; response of to legal ban, 131; and *samsara*, 126, 129; as "service" providers, 2, 14, 35, 50, 116; Sudanese embassy, 118; working with people smugglers, 93–95, 103. *See also* kidneys for sale; Solomon (organ broker)
organ buyers, 53–54
organ donation, involuntary, 82–83, 126–29
organ donation, voluntary, 18, 21, 102, 133, 145
"organ exporting countries," 4
organized crime: defined, 161n1; increasing, 48, 97, 112–13, 115, 131–32, 144, 154
organ laundering, 57–61, 159n6
"organ mafia," 96, 109, 111, 113–14, 115, 118, 129
organ recipients, 114, 118
organ sales/trade, 3, 146; as act of poverty, 27; ban on, 134; as criminal by Council of Europe, 145; death of military general, 118; decriminalization models, 146–47; demand outweighing supply, 19, 21–22, 28, 44, 46, 154; economic underclass and, 145; Egyptian death penalty for, 15; ethical dilemma of, 35, 136–39; and ethnicity, 8; financial scale of, 3; financing people smuggling, 93; framing of as altruism, 31–32; to help family members, 80–81, 84; as human trafficking, 2–3, 18; as informal economic activity, 39; linked to undocumented migration, 135; as market solution, 32; as more ethical than unpaid donation, 35; as mutually beneficial, 33; news coverage of, 154; as option of last resort, 12, 34; prison sentences for, 151; push for prohibition of, 4; recruitment of customers, 48–50; social determinants of, 78–83; usually done knowingly, 84. *See also* morality and organ trade
organ sellers, 158n10; as both criminals and victims, 1, 4–5, 33, 41, 60, 144–45; coercion, violence against, 54–56, 111–12, 115–16, 120, 126–28; driven by shame, guilt, 51–52; due to illness, 81; health effects from, 82, 117, 121, 134; hiding truth from family, 102, 121–22; interview subjects, 11–12; little bargaining power, 52, 143, 144; medically unfit, 63; mostly migrants, 48; motivations of, 5, 80, 84, 119–21; murders of, 115; no ability to back out, 54–57; no commercial agreement, 32; not paid promised amount, 81–82; paid, 19, 64, 137; public unsympathetic toward, 33, 134; recovery period, 53; re-

duced bargaining power of, 144; self-portrayals of, 12, 44; single mothers as, 51, 79–80; threatened with deportation, 144–45, 152; through deception, 82–83; violence against, 41, 54–56, 111–12, 115–16, 120, 126–28; women, 75–76, 79–83
organ trade (Egypt): as border security issue, 38; as economic lifeline, 148; as informal economic activity, 5, 39, 131–32; as moral gray zone, 19; as morally acceptable, 31, 44; reliance on live donors, 44; structural vulnerability behind, 153–54; suppression of research on, 150
OSB (Operation Sovereign Borders), Australia, 89
outcome-orientated approaches, 136, 139

paid donation of organs, 32, 136–38
Pakistan, 4, 21, 146
Paoli, Letizia, 42
paperwork rendering transplant legal, 57–58
partial decriminalization, 139, 142–43, 162n2
Patel, Priti, 88
patient-buyers, 48, 131
Patrick (organ seller), 56, 77, 144–45, 147
"people of concern" status, 37, 69, 149
people smuggling: connection with organ trade, 93, 105; versus human trafficking, 15, 88–89; protection money, 99; by sea, 99; for travel outside Egypt, 66. See also *samsara* (people smugglers)
Petros (organ seller), ix–xvii, 1, 104, 135, 144
Philippines, 4, 128, 146, 160n12
police: aiding smuggling, 99; arranging sales of kidneys, 77; Asha's statement to, 124, 149; Atta in protective custody in Italy, 93–94; crackdown on Cairo organ trade, 113–14; decriminalization as aid to, 143–44; deporting refugees, 70; deporting victims, 104, 114; hostility, apathy toward migrants, 76–77, 81; Martha's experience with, 128; monitoring organ networks, 38; not feared by "organ mafia," 118; as perpetrators of violence, 148; public fear of, 56, 62, 81; report on raids by, 151; taking girls as sex servants, x; and UN, xvi, 133
political action, 7, 18, 29
Portugal, 140, 146
Precarious Life (Butler), 142
press restrictions in Egypt, 37, 113
price paid for kidneys, 52–54, 107; to Dawitt, 102–4; negotiated with broker networks, 48, 57, 109, 118; under paid donation system, 136–38; to Petros, xiv; prior to Egyptian ban, 28; by recipients, 20; standardized payment models, 143; at "street markets," 38
private medical insurance, 23
private residences, organ extraction in, 126–29, 144
privilege of nondisclosure, 59
Professional Code of Ethics, 58–59
prohibition, pro and con, 30–37, 44, 48, 112–13, 134–37, 152–54
"protection space" for migrants, refugees, 92
Protocol Against the Smuggling of Migrants by Land, Sea, and Air (UN), 160n5
PSTIC (Psycho-Social Services and Training Institute in Cairo), 149
public healthcare expenditure, 23
"public sphere of debate," 142
purpose element of trafficking, 41

Rashad (smuggler), 82
Red Cross, International, 96
refoulment, 92, 97
refugees, 63; asylum seekers in Cairo, 65–72; avoidance of term, 97; backlog of, 130; blue card (refugee status), 69, 71–72; Convention Relating to the Status of Refugees (UN), 71, 97, 132; deportation of, 70, 147, 149; education for, 69; Egypt as main destination for, 65–66; Egypt's treatment of, 67–72; refugee status, 66–67, 69–70, 83. See also asylum seekers in Egypt; Eritrean refugees in Egypt; Ethiopian refugees in Egypt; Somali refugees in Egypt

refugee status determination (RSD), 66–67, 69, 160n7
Regeni, Giulio, 159n2 (ch3)
regularizing status, 71–72 *(71)*, 83, 102
regulated market approach, 9, 44, 135–40, 154–55
relatives donating organ, 26–27, 35
religious concerns: organs donation and sanctity of human body, 18; souls of brain-dead patients, 24–25
remittance needs as motivation to sell, 14, 51–52
renal disease, 23, 146
repatriation of trafficking victims, 147
resettlement, 70, 129–30, 149
residency permits, Egyptian, 1, 66, 71–72, 83
Reuter, Peter, 113, 129
RSD (refugee status determination), 66–67, 69, 160n7
rumors of kidnap, murder for organs, 114–16
Russian Mafia, 42

Salvini, Mateo, 89
Samir (migrant), 96–97, 147
samsara (people smugglers), 16; abandoning migrants, 100–101; as alternative to UNHCR process, 108; becoming professionalized, 98; as criminal or not, 88, 161n10; demanding more money, 101; Ibrahim, 98–100, 105–7, 130; involvement with organ sales, 87, 126, 129, 135, 144; reliability of, xi, 100–101, 105; role of, 161n10
Sawa military camp, ix–x, *90*
Scheper-Hughes, Nancy, 145
scouts for organ brokers, 50–51
securitization agenda, 66
September 11 attacks, effects of, 89
"service fees" (bribes), 113
"service industry" of organized crime, 131
sex work, sex workers: decriminalization trends, 140–42; exploitation, 6, 159n3 (ch3); included in organ sales deals, 53; no physical, financial security in, 107; selling kidneys, 76, 79–80

Shaker (recruitment broker), 13, 49–50, 55, 58
Shubra neighborhood, 12
single mothers, 51, 79–80
single-purchaser system, 138
Sisi, Abdel Fattah el-, 8, 29–30, 66, 91, 150
6th of October satellite city, xi, 67, 101
smugglers/smuggling, xvi, *90*; cost of, 93; deaths at sea, 86–87; distinguished from trafficking, 15, 89; financed by organ trade, 93–95; lack of migrant protection leading to, 97–98; smuggling of migrants defined, 160–61n5 (ch5); smuggling routes, *90*, 99. See also *samsara*
social controls, 32, 66, 116, 144, 151
social exclusion, 9; competition among excluded, 76; crime controls adding to, 152; enabling exploitation, 15, 64, 108; and organ trade, 18, 34, 105, 147; and structural violence, 162n4
socioeconomic motivations for organ sales, 7, 24, 27, 32
Solomon (translator), ix–xvii, 11–13, 47–48, 123
Somali refugees in Egypt, xvii; deaths en route, 87; Khartoum route for, 101; kidnapped, murdered for organs, 115, 124, 127; and UNHCR, 68; "voluntary" relocation by, 65; Yasmin, 37–38, 51
souls of brain-dead patients, 24–25
Spain decriminalizing cannabis, 140
"special status," 68
"sphere of appearance," 142
squatter communities, 74
The State v. Netcare Kwa-Zulu (Pty) Limited, 39, 60
Steinfatt, Thomas, 41
street markets for organ negotiations, 11, 36, 38–39 *(38)*, 45–46, 49
structural exploitation, 65
structural violence, 162n4
Sudan: displaced persons camp in, x; nationality law in, 103; smuggling routes in, *90*; Wadi El Nil Treaty, 67–68, 159n3 (ch4)
Sudanese in Egypt, 39, 64–65; Anita, 73; "approval of kinship" forms, 102;

blamed for attack on Mubarak, 68; death of general after transplant, 118; denied refugee status, asylum, 64, 83–84; Fatimah, 62–63, 84, 159n1 (ch4); kidnapped for organs, 124, 127–28; lost at sea, 87; Martha, 126–29, 144; murdered for organs, 115; as organ brokers, xvi–xvii, 48; as organ recipients, 114–15; organ recruitment network, 49–52; as organ sellers, 47–48, 52–53; preferred destination, xvi; rights of, 67–68; shifting status of, 67–69, 74; social ties to Egypt, 45
Supreme Council of the Armed Forces (Egypt), 8
surplus demand for organs, 19, 21–22, 28, 44, 46, 143, 154
Swedish sex work example, 141, 143
symbolic reward, 30–32
Syrian refugees, 15, 65, 85, 92, 105, 160n5 (ch4)

Tahrir Square uprising, 8
Talia (potential organ seller), 55–56, 60, 76, 144
Tantawy, Mohamed Sayed, 25
The State v. Netcare Kwa-Zulu (Pty) Limited, 39
threshold of intolerability, 33
tissue typing, 20, 22, 48–50, 52, 54–58, 159n4
Trafficking Protocol (Article 3): action, means, purpose, 41; compared to Egyptian Law, 147; legal definition, 3, 10, 59, 64, 157n3; "smuggling of migrants" defined, 160n5 (ch5)
trafficking/traffickers: coordination of, 93–94; defined, 6, 41; Egyptian Law of Trafficking in Persons (Law 64/2010), 44, 148; elements of, 6, 41; importance of terminology, 5, 30; law enforcement treatment of, 59–60, 154; methods of persuasion used by, 2–3; moral outrage toward, 40–41, 152; organ trade as form of, 134, 152; "service industry" for, 131; and smuggling, 15, 89; UN Trafficking Protocol, 3, 10, 30, 41, 64, 147; US statements on, 7, 15; victimization by, 41, 44; working with organ brokers, 94–95. See also Trafficking Protocol
transnational organized crime, 40–41, 135, 160n5 (ch5), 161nn9, 2
Transplantation of Human Organs and Tissues Act (Egypt Law 5/2010), 8, 28–31, 39, 44, 58, 76, 131, 158n11
transplant centers, clinics, 19; under 2010 law, 44; coercion by, 54–56; controlled access to, 49–50; informal networks supplying, 32; intra-familial donations, 27; organ laundering by, 57–59; and price negotiation, 52
"transplant commercialism," 3–4, 19
transplant practice: as a criminal industry, 134–35; simplistic good/bad views of, 43–44; transplant physicians, 26–27, 48, 51, 59
Transplant Society, 4, 19
transplant tourism, 4, 19–24, 43
Trump, Donald and Trump administration, 6–7, 85, 89, 129–30
Tunisia, 93
Turkey, 92

Under world, Inc., 17
undocumented migrants, 11; as criminal threat, 132; determined by skin color, ethnicity, 83, 159n1 (ch4); as expendable, exploitable, 33–34, 72, 74–75, 108; and NGOs, 149; police violence against, 148; targeted for organs, 10, 44, 135, 154; vulnerability of, 5, 30
undocumented worker analogy, 33
UNHCR: apathy toward abused migrants, 62–63, 67, 78, 105–6, 124–25, 148–49; difficulties navigating, 73, 108; "durable solutions" eligibility, 69; educational programs by, 69–70; handling refugee issues for Egypt, 63, 66, 68–69, 72–73, 83, 126–28; "illegal" interpreters at, 70; incomplete statistics from, 65; Memorandum of Understanding with Egypt, 66; *Projected Resettlement Needs 2019*, 129–30; and PSTIC (Psycho-Social Services and Training Institute in Cairo),

UNHCR (continued)
149; remote location of Cairo HQ, 67; resettlement process, 106, 108, 153; selling refugee cards to Egyptians, 77; as surrogate state, 66; suspending RSD interviews for Sudanese, 160n7; using illegal interpreters, 70; and "voluntary" repatriation, 70–72; Zarif's difficulties with, 114

United Arab Emirates, 21

United Kingdom, 5, 22, 88, 140, 149

United Nations: Convention against Transnational Organized Crime, 40, 160n5 (ch5), 161nn9, 2; Convention Relating to the Status of Refugees (1951), 71, 92, 97, 132; Declaration of Basic Principles of Justice for Victims of Crime and Abuse of Power, 158n10; in Egypt, xi, xvi; help for refugees, escapees, xi; Security Council, 90–91, 161n6; UNICEF, 96; UNODC (United Nations Office on Drugs and Crime), 3, 40–41, 60, 133. *See also* Trafficking Protocol; UNHCR

United Network for Organ Sharing (UNOS), 19, 22

United States: cost of kidney transplant surgery, 23; Medicare, Medicaid, 23; Office of National Drug Control Policy, 108, 140; prevalence of immigration offenses, 108; "Trafficking in Persons Report," 15, 160n4 (ch5); Trafficking Victims Protection Act (TVPA), 157n4; Trump, Donald and Trump administration, 6–7, 85, 89, 129–30; "war on drugs," 113, 141

UNOS (United Network for Organ Sharing), 19, 22

unregulated market, organ trade as, 8, 45, 73–74, 131

UN Trafficking Protocol, 3, 10, 30, 41, 64, 147, 157n3

U.S. v. Rosenbaum, 39, 60

Valletta Summit, 91

"vessel," defined, 160n1

"victims of crime," defined, 158n10

voluntary organ donation, 102, 132–33, 145

"voluntary" repatriation, 69–70, 72, 95

"vulnerable" versus "illegal" people, 132, 133

Wadi El Nil Treaty, 67–68, 159n3 (ch4)

wage labor without bargaining power, 74–75

waiting lists, 23, 29, 138

"war on drugs" (U.S.), effect of, 113, 141

Weitzer, Ronald, 41

WHA (World Health Assembly), 3–4

WHO (World Health Organization), 3–4, 17, 19, 22, 29

women. *See* female migrants

Working Group on Incentives for Living Donation, 138

work permits, 34, 70, 75, 153

World Food Program Cairo statistics, 27

Yakuza (Japanese), 42

Yasmin (NGO worker), 37–38, 53

yellow card (Egyptian asylum), xv, 67, 69, 81

Yemen, xvii, 39, 85, 88

Yusef (organ recipient), 20–21, 26

Zarif (organ seller), 82, 114–15

zero-tolerance policies, 43, 111

Zia (asylum seeker), 50

Lightning Source UK Ltd.
Milton Keynes UK
UKHW011104280922
409568UK00002B/231